MERCHANTS OF MEN

Loretta Napoleoni is the author of international best-sellers, *The Islamist Phoenix: The Islamic State (ISIS) and the Redrawing of the Middle East*, *Rogue Economics: Capitalism's New Reality*, and *Terror Incorporated: Tracing the Money Behind Global Terrorism*. As chairperson of the counter-terrorism financing group for the Club de Madrid, Napoleoni brought heads of state from around the world together to create a new strategy for combating the financing of terror networks. She lives in London and Montana, USA.

MERCHANTS OF MEN

HOW KIDNAPPING, RANSOM AND TRAFFICKING FUND TERRORISM AND ISIS

LORETTA NAPOLEONI

ATLANTIC BOOKS
London

In memory of Luigi Bernabò

—ᄴᄴ—

First published in 2016 in the United States of America by Seven Stories Press.

First published in hardback and e-book in Great Britain in 2017 by
Atlantic Books, an imprint of Atlantic Books Ltd.

This paperback edition published in Great Britain in 2018 by Atlantic Books.

1 2 3 4 5 6 7 8 9

A CIP catalogue record for this book is available from the British Library.

Paperback ISBN: 9781782399933
E-book ISBN: 9781782399926

Printed in Great Britain by Clays Ltd, St Ives plc
Atlantic Books
An Imprint of Atlantic Books Ltd
Ormond House
26–27 Boswell Street
London
WC1N 3JZ

www.atlantic-books.co.uk

contents

My research into kidnapping and human trafficking started more than a decade ago. Shortly after 9/11, I began meeting, in several cities around the world, with people involved in anti-terrorism and money laundering. They all agreed that the Patriot Act had prompted the Colombian cartel to establish joint ventures with Italian organized crime to launder their drug revenues in Europe and Asia and to find new routes to bring cocaine to the Old Continent. Venezuela, the infamous Gold Coast of West Africa—from where cargoes of slaves had sailed to America—and the Sahel became key transhipment areas.

African smugglers soon tapped into this business, carrying cocaine overland. Gao, in Mali, became their main hub. From Gao, cocaine travelled across the Sahara to the Mediterranean shores of Morocco, Algeria, and Libya. From there, a fleet of small boats took the drugs to Europe.

In 2003 a group of former members of the Algerian Armed Islamic Group (GIA) involved in smuggling in the trans-Saharan regions branched off and kidnapped thirty-two Europeans in Mali and southern Algeria. The hostages were transported along the trans-Sahara contraband routes to camps in northern Mali. The European governments paid rich ransoms to get their citizens back, enough to bankroll a new armed group: al Qaeda in the Islamic Maghreb (AQIM).

Among the people I have met since 9/11 are several hostage negotiators. As brokers between the parties, they have unique insight into the kidnapping business. From our conversations, it emerged that the abduction of the thirty-two Europeans proved that snatching Westerners could be an important profit center for criminal and armed organizations. Hunting season for Western hostages was now open.

By the second half of the aughts, a mere five years after 9/11, the cocaine business accelerated the destabilization of the Sahel. Several failed and semi-failed states appeared, prompting their citizens to become economic migrants seeking passage to Europe. Al Qaeda in the Islamic Maghreb was quick to invest part of the profits of its kidnapping business into trafficking migrants.

Negotiators believe that the governments' failure to publicly denounce the kidnapping crisis in the Sahel prevented any proper intervention in the region. Hence it was easy for the kidnappers to branch off into human trafficking.

As a chronicler of the dark side of the economics of globalization, I discovered that the policy of secrecy on the part of governments sprang from their wish to hide the failings of globalization. The proliferation of failed states and regions where law and order has broken down since the fall of the Berlin Wall provided an opportunity for kidnapping and trafficking to flourish in a way that was historically unprecedented. And the secrecy of the great nations allowed the conflagration to proceed unchecked. It was as if all the firefighters had decided to go on strike during a forest fire.

Leading negotiators and former hostages agree that the supply of valuable prey has been plentiful. For the past twenty-five years a false sense of security about the globalized world has encouraged young, inexperienced members of the First Nations club—I will call them Westerners even though they may be from Tokyo or Santiago as easily as from New York or Copenhagen—to explore and report from every corner of the global village, as well as to bring aid to populations trapped inside war zones or plagued by political anarchy. These journeymen reporters and humanitarian aid workers have become some of the primary targets of modern kidnappers.

Since 9/11 the number of kidnappings has increased exponentially and so too have the sums demanded for ransom. In 2004, $2 million could free a Western hostage in Iraq. Today over $10 million can be paid. A member of the Italian crisis unit joked that freeing Greta Ramelli and Vanessa Marzullo—two young Italians kidnapped in Syria in 2014 and sold to al Nusra—cost Italy close to a percentage point of its GDP, €13 million! Equally, the number of private security companies specializing in abduction has multiplied and the cost of employing them has skyrocketed. A decade ago $1,000 was the going rate per day. Today it is $3,000.

Is the economics of kidnapping immune from the laws of economics? Ten years of exceptionally low inflation coupled with strong competition among kidnappers and private security firms should have pushed prices down but instead, they have gone up. The reason is simple: the number of prospective Western hostages is almost infinite, and governments and private negotiators compete with each other to free their own citizens, driving prices up for fixers, informers, drivers, and others.

Today we know that exporting Western democracy to every corner of the global village has backfired. Since the fall of the Berlin Wall, the world has become a much more dangerous place not only for North Americans and Europeans, but also for Asians, Africans, and Latin Americans, millions of whom have been forced to become migrant laborers and economic refugees. As Middle Easterners share this bleak destiny, the core business of hostage takers in this region is shifting again, the focus now being on trafficking people escaping the miseries and depredations of civil war. Today these merchants of men handle a new variety of human cargo: not hostages but rather migrants. A surreal interdependency, therefore, links the kidnapping of Westerners and the trafficking of migrants.

When, in 2015, the migrant crisis erupted in the Middle East, kidnappers and smugglers easily became traffickers. They already had a sophisticated organizational structure in place, and plenty of money from trading hostages to invest in this new venture. Netting about $100 million per month in the summer of 2015, the merchants of men delivered tens of thousand of people per week to European shores. It is a profitable business because demand far outstrips supply, and the cost of reaching Europe keeps rising. Ten years ago someone could pay a smuggler $7,000 to be brought from West Africa to Italy. In the summer of 2015 that sum was the price to cross the short distance from Syria to Turkey to Greece.

Fifteen years after the destruction of the Twin Towers, most of the Muslim world is on fire. The winners are the merchants of men, and a mix of criminal and jihadist groups who snatch, buy, and sell people for a price. What next?

The migrant crisis could force an entire continent to confront the hypocrisy of its own politicians who kept silent when they should most have spoken out, and the absurdity of the myth that we are moving towards an integrated and egalitarian Europe. But above all, it will expose once again the fragility of our respect for human life and our defence of human dignity. The merchants of men are no different from the slave traders of the eighteenth century, the colonizers of the nineteenth century, or the Nazis of the twentieth century: they have all thought that the lives of others are theirs to dispose of freely.

Due to the nature of their profession I could not mention the names of the negotiators who helped me understand the complex phenomenon that is kidnapping. Their anonymity must be protected for security reasons; these are people who often risk their lives to save someone else's, people who have extensive networks of informers in countries where kidnapping is an everyday occurrence. Instead of creating aliases for them, I have removed their names and indicated in a general way something about their general sphere of influences or origin. And most often, I have simply referred to them as "a negotiator" or "the negotiator."

It is 3 p.m. and outside it is already pitch dark. A carpet of snow covers the suburbs of Umeå, a university town in the north of Sweden. The streets are empty and the few cars we encounter drive with their high beams on. Without these searchlights illuminating the road, the road would be indistinguishable from the front gardens of the houses. As we drive, the combination of darkness and snow-reflected light plays strange optical tricks.

When we reach the hotel, I open the car door and step into what feels like a meat locker. It is cold—so cold that I can measure the capacity of my lungs as the sub-zero air fills them. It is the end of November 2006; technically speaking it should still be autumn, but it surely feels like an arctic winter.

We have come to Umeå for the *Iraqi Equation*, a political art project that is part of an effort by a group of artists and intellectuals to carry on the opposition to the Iraq War well beyond the "preventive strike." After months and months of demonstrations against the military intervention, in Spring 2003 the world went quiet, perhaps shell-shocked by Bush and Blair's defiance, and by their indifference to public opinion. Three years later, our group is still campaigning; it is our duty because we know what is happening in Iraq.

Among the artists are several Iraqis. They fled as soon as the coalition forces landed, targeted by the many armed groups operating within the country. The invasion has unleashed a rage repressed for decades, as criminal, jihadist, newly formed Shia militias, and pro-Saddam groups turned against the civilian population. For those who escaped and now join us in this room, their flight from Iraq is merely physical. Their hearts and minds are still there, linked by an invisible thread to the bloody reality of "liberated" Iraq.

We were told that there would be many Iraqis at the opening of the exhibition, but we did not expect two hundred of them. They outnumber the Swedes. Men, women, and even children, bundled up in warm clothes, have come from near and far, braving the Nordic climate. They silently stream into the exhibition rooms, shake our hands, smile, and begin peeling off layer after layer of clothing. Soon the most spoken language here is Arabic.

Some women extract huge containers of food from their bags, all wrapped in tin foil, and place them next to the cheese and vegetable snacks the organizers of the exhibition have provided. Their food looks so colorful and delicious. The aromas tease our nostrils. As Catherine David, the artistic director of the project, begins her speech, we feel as if we are starting a celebration, perhaps a wedding between a Swede and an Arab. It is a magical and unforgettable feeling. For a moment we all forget that this is the opening of an event to denounce military aggression.

Later in the evening, as people start to say goodbye, a young man approaches me. Quite fair for an Iraqi, he has broad shoulders and is of medium height. He introduces himself as Rashid, a common Iraqi name, but I know that this isn't his real name. Something in his light brown eyes seems uneasy with that name. He also speaks English with a strong French accent, as North Africans do. Rashid says that he has read my books and wants to congratulate me on my work. We begin talking. He wants to know about my contacts in London with former mujahideen. Do I know so-and-so? He mentions several Algerians who have fled to London after the military coup and received asylum.

Rashid is a troubled soul. I realize he wants to talk to me about something dark in his past, but doesn't know how to begin. So I suggest we go back to the hotel and have a hot chocolate. And so we do.

He never tells me his real name, but he reveals his nationality and age: he is from Algeria and has just turned twenty-nine.

His father was one of the founders of the Islamic Salvation Front. Soon after the military coup (backed by the French and other Europeans), Rashid's father was imprisoned together with Rashid's brothers. They all vanished inside the maze that is the Algerian political detention system. "When the police came to arrest my father and brothers, I was fishing," says Rashid. He was the youngest of the family, at the time was only fifteen years old, and wasn't interested in politics. He wanted to become a sailor and a fisherman and travel the world. "But after they took my father and my brothers, I was forced to deal with politics."

Rashid's mother arranged for him to leave Algiers right away. But that same evening, after returning from his fishing trip, he joined a group of men who belonged to his father's party, several of whom had fought in Afghanistan as mujahideen. They went south, to the edge of the Sahara, where they regrouped and began plotting their return.

Rashid spent the next few years in southern Algeria, in the Saharan desert, thousands of miles from his beloved sea. He never joined the GIA, the *Group Islamiste Armé*, the organization born from the ashes of the Islamic Salvation

Front that fought against the military regime for almost a decade, triggering yet another bloody civil war in Algeria. Instead, he became a smuggler, endlessly traversing the trans-Saharan routes.

Then came 9/11. "Everything changed," he says. "For years we had led a monotonous life, smuggling mostly cigarettes from Algeria to Mali and to West Africa. But suddenly new opportunities materialized. The entire region was bursting with rage and pride. We began trading arms, drugs, and then someone had an idea: let's have a go at kidnapping."

From a smuggler, Rashid became a kidnapper, a job he loathed.

When Rashid stops talking, I look outside. It is snowing so heavily that the sky is white. What a contrast this must be with the heat of the Sahara, I think. What a change for people like Rashid, born and raised in a hot climate. "Why are you telling me this story?" I finally ask. Rashid does not answer immediately. For a while he looks straight into my eyes, searching for the right words. "Someone needs to know," he says.

He departs from the hotel on foot, leaving prints in the snow that the storm quickly erases. I know I will never see him again. I do not even know where he lives or what he does. All I know is that some time after his group began trafficking migrants from West Africa to Libya, Rashid managed to get on a boat to Italy by pretending to be an Iraqi refugee. It was 2005 and Europe was welcoming those coming from Iraq. From Sicily, he reached the sanctuary of Sweden. When they asked him where he was from, he said, "I am Iraqi." With a lie that harmed no one, he finally escaped a violent life he had not chosen. Can we blame him?

PART 1

chapter one

Al Qaeda in the Islamic Maghreb Protocol

In late January 2011 Maria Sandra Mariani set out from San Casciano in Val di Pesa, a small town in Tuscany, heading to the southeast corner of the Algerian Sahara. The fifty-three-year-old Italian woman was looking forward to her annual holiday in a breathtakingly beautiful region of the Maghreb. She had booked a group tour of the region's natural features and archaeological ruins—some dating back as far as the Neolithic period—and was planning to spend a few days visiting local villages. Every winter since 2006, Mariani had vacationed in the Sahara desert, partly as a tourist and partly as a "humanitarian aid volunteer" to, in her words, "bring medicine and goods to the local population."[2] As she had done many times before, she booked her tour with Ténéré Voyages, a well-known travel agency specializing in the Sahara. And as in the past, Aziz was going to be her guide. Aziz, a polite Algerian whom Mariani had befriended over the years, had even visited her and her family in Tuscany.

When Mariani landed at the Djanet Airport, approximately one hundred miles from the Algerian-Libyan border, the first person she saw was Aziz. He welcomed her, and seeing how pale she looked, he asked if she had had a rough journey. Mariani admitted that she was not feeling too well. "I must have eaten something bad on the plane and I felt awful," she says, "but we left right away. We were heading for the desert of Tadrart,[3] between Algeria and Libya. A few days later, I was still unwell. Aziz suggested we stop in a small tourist resort, with just a few bungalows, which was also owned by Ténéré Voyages."

Mariani took a couple of days to recover. By February 2, she felt well enough to go on a small excursion. "We had a great day," she recalls. "The light, the air, the scenery, everything was perfect. I was happy, happy to be well again, happy to be in my beloved Sahara."

Mariani and Aziz drove back to the resort at sunset. "I got out of the car and suddenly, while we were walking towards the bungalows, Aziz saw two black SUVs fast approaching. Thinking that they were robbers or smugglers, he told me 'go, go, they should not see you,' and I rushed to the bungalow, but they had already seen me. As I learned later on, they had spotted me with binoculars; they were on the lookout for foreigners. I was not veiled because there was nobody around. We were in the middle of the desert and the hotel was empty, so I did not think to disguise myself. But they saw me and they knew I was a Western tourist," remembers Mariani.

The men quickly surrounded the middle-aged woman, Aziz, and the hotel concierge. "For a long time they kept asking, 'Where are the other tourists? Where is your husband?' They could not believe that I was alone," says Mariani. "They also spoke in English because they thought I was English. Twenty days earlier, in the same resort, there had been a large group of English tourists for the New Year's holidays."

Frustrated, the men, who clearly had expected to find a large number of Westerners, grabbed Mariani and pushed her into the back of one of the SUVs. A couple of them forced the concierge and the guide to follow in Aziz's car. "When they locked me in the SUV, we all understood that they were not robbers or smugglers, but kidnappers. I felt hopeless, my heart sunk and I gasped for air," says Mariani. "Later on, when I asked them 'Who are you?' they looked at me and proudly said, 'We are al Qaeda.'"

As night fell, Mariani found herself alone in the back of a truck being driven across the desert by fourteen members of al Qaeda in the Islamic Maghreb. However, seeing the lights of Aziz's car behind her was comforting. "Aziz was my friend. I was sure that he would protect me," she admitted. But about five hours into the journey, her kidnappers decided to let the guide and the concierge go because their car was not as fast on the desert trails as their SUVs. "They broke the lights of Aziz's car so that he would not be able to travel home until daybreak, and then we left," remembers Mariani.

The kidnappers were professionals. They knew that they had to move away from the site of the abduction as quickly as possible. After all, they were not interested in kidnapping two Algerians. It was foreigners they wanted. As the kidnappers drove into the night leaving Aziz and the concierge stranded in the desert, Maria Sandra Mariani realized that she was totally alone.

Sinking into the back of the truck, listening to the sound of her heart racing, the middle-aged Italian woman did not know that, due to a surreal string of events, her terrifying ordeal was linked to a controversial piece of US legislation enacted by the Bush administration a decade earlier: the Patriot Act.

A JOINT VENTURE IN CRIME

The Patriot Act was introduced in the United States in October 2001, just a month after 9/11. The Act diminished the civil rights of Americans, increased government surveillance, and established a set of new financial and banking rules in order to disrupt the international flow of criminal proceeds and money laundering in US dollars, forcing the Colombian drug cartel to find alternative cocaine smuggling routes to Europe and alternative ways to launder their ill-gotten gains. The chosen route was through West Africa and across the Sahel. Mariani's kidnappers, al Qaeda in the Islamic Maghreb (AQIM), had tapped into this new business early on and branched off first into kidnapping foreigners and later into trafficking migrants. To understand this surreal chain of events that turned jihadists into drug smugglers, kidnappers, and human traffickers, a sort of freak-terronomics, one needs to retrace the money trail to its source: the Colombian cartel in the aftermath of 9/11.

Until the attack on the Twin Towers, the bulk of global drug profits was laundered in the United States in US dollars.[4] Because 80 percent of these revenues were in cash—in the form of US dollars—money had to be transported physically to the US. The main entry point was through offshore facilities and shell banks located in the West Indies. The Patriot Act made this process much more difficult, if not impossible. For example, US banks and US-registered banks could no longer do business with offshore banks, such as those located in the Caribbean. In addition, the new legislation gave US monetary authorities the right to monitor dollar transactions across the world. Hence, it became a criminal offence for US banks and

US-registered foreign banks to not alert the US monetary authorities of suspicious transactions in dollars anywhere in the world.

It is easy to understand why the Patriot Act was a major blow to the Colombian drug cartel. However, the key problem was not so much how to launder the dirty profits produced by the sale of cocaine inside the United States, but how to do it in US dollars anywhere else in the world and how to transfer the profits from one country to another without alerting the US monetary authorities.

The solution to this problem came from an Italian immigrant to Colombia, Salvatore Mancuso. As head of the United Self-Defense Forces of Colombia (AUC), the Colombian paramilitary terrorist organization, Mancuso brokered a deal between the cocaine cartel and the Calabrian organized crime the *N'drangheta*, which turned the newly born euro into the global monetary currency of drug profits. The *N'drangheta* offered a full-service operation: handling the sale of cocaine in Europe and laundering drug profits in the European and Asian markets.

The absence in Europe of legislation analogous to the Patriot Act made it easy for this unusual joint venture in crime to succeed. "Drug profits generated in Spain became real estate investment earnings in Belgium," says a Europol source. "From there they could quickly be transferred in euros to Bogotá without any screening."[5]

After 9/11, Maria Sandra Mariani's Italy became a key European transshipment hub and money laundering hot spot for the cocaine trade. Data from the Italian law enforcement agency Guardia di Finanza, for example, shows that from 2001 to 2004, money laundering in Italy increased by 70 percent.[6] Hence, with the new millennium came the advent of a veritable European Golden Age of money laundering thanks to the Patriot Act and to the *N'drangheta*'s clever strategies to circumvent it. However, shipping cocaine from Colombia directly to Europe proved much more problematic than washing dirty profits clean in the Old Continent, as shown by the success of "Operation Decollo."

FROM THE GOLD COAST TO THE COKE COAST

In the fall of 2003, the Italian Guardia di Finanza made a major breakthrough with a three-year sting operation code-named *Decollo* ("Take-off"). Indeed, its success was due to a stroke of luck in the shape of an informer—a rare occurrence when dealing with the *N'drangheta*. The informer had revealed that a large shipment of cocaine was due to arrive in a cargo of Colombian marble at the Port of Gioia Tauro, Calabria, deep in the territory controlled by the *N'drangheta*.

Hidden inside the blocks of marble the *finanzieri* found 5,500 hermetically sealed bags of cocaine, each weighing one kilogram. From the captain's documentation, it emerged that Miguel Diez, a fake import-export company set up by the Colombian drug cartel, had chartered the ship. The shipping company, the Danish Maersk Line, had no idea of the true nature of the cargo; neither did the crew nor the captain.

What happened that day was exceptional. For each illegal cargo discovered, hundreds, if not thousands, of shipments go unchecked.[7] Without an informer it would have been impossible to locate the cocaine cargo. Nonetheless, the bust exposed the weakness of relying on direct shipment to Europe in a post-9/11 environment. Heightened security measures in Europe after 9/11 and the terrorist attacks in Madrid and London confirmed the need for alternative routes and new transshipment countries to get cocaine from Latin America to Europe. Venezuela and West Africa proved ideal.[8]

Since the mid-1990s, the Colombian drug cartel had worked to establish good relationships with politicians in neighboring Venezuela, showering them with money, an investment that proved very wise. Already after his election in 1998, Hugo Chávez had offered sanctuary to armed and criminal groups engaged in the Colombian cocaine trade. After 2001, he even encouraged them to move their coca plantations across the border.[9] So, when at the end of 2001 the cartel thought to use Venezuela as a key transshipment point to smuggle cocaine to Europe via West Africa, it found strong support and an established infrastructure.

As its African transshipment hub, the cartel choose Guinea-Bissau, part of what used to be known as the Gold Coast, that infamous stretch of West Africa where slaves had been shipped to the New World. Daniel Ruiz, who in 2006, as the UN representative in Guinea-Bissau, denounced the nation's rise in cocaine trafficking, noted that the country's features made illegal shipments especially difficult to detect. "Guinea-Bissau was a good geographical choice for a transshipment point. It is flat, with an archipelago of eighty islands, all covered by a thick jungle and with easy access by sea. It was equipped with twenty-seven airstrips constructed by the Portuguese during their colonial wars, ideal for small planes flying from Venezuela across the Atlantic with their cocaine cargoes. Finally, Guinea-Bissau used to be an important fishing hub. Hence, its ports had huge empty warehouses where the cartel could store the cocaine."[10]

The business model that the cartel put in place was both sophisticated and linear. "There were always two lines of shipment: one small using 'mules'—Africans who swallow small quantities of cocaine and travel by plane—these shipments generated cash for the corrupt local politicians and police. Then there was the big one: shipments of tons of cocaine hidden in containers, in cargoes of commodities all sailing towards Europe," says Ruiz.

However, when the cartel landed in Guinea-Bissau they found another, unexpected avenue to smuggle large quantities of cocaine, which proved very efficient and successful: overland, across the old trans-Sahara smuggling routes, hiding the cocaine inside trucks and SUVs. These were the same sandy trails that, years later, Maria Sandra Mariani's kidnappers would use to reach and abduct her.

"I knew that in the Sahara desert there was a lot of smuggling. Sometimes Aziz would point out to me empty containers in the sand and tell me, 'See this? It is from the smugglers, they must have stopped here.' They smuggled everything: oil, cigarettes, hashish, everything that was in demand," said Mariani. They also smuggled something else that people like Mariani did not know: cocaine.

According to security sources, "The full extent of the growing links between jihadists and Latin American cartels became evident when military officials located a burned Boeing 727 in the middle of the desert in Mali in 2009. The plane had been loaded with cocaine and other contraband in Venezuela, flown across the Atlantic, crash landed in the desert, and burned to eliminate the evidence."[11]

That same year, just two years before Mariani was kidnapped and brought to Mali, the United Nations Office
on Drugs and Crime (UNODC) estimated that every year
between fifty and sixty tons of cocaine reach Europe via
West Africa, smuggled across the trans-Sahara routes,
and account for about 13 percent of the total European
trade. Drugs destined for Europe arrived in West Africa
from Colombia, by far the most important among Latin
American states in this sector, but also from Peru, Bolivia,
Venezuela and Brazil.[12]

Right from the beginning, between 2002 and 2003, it
was easy for the vast network of African smugglers—who
already controlled the trans-Sahara contraband routes
of the Sahel linking West Africa to the Mediterranean
shores—to tap into the new business that the Colombian cartel had brought to West Africa. The smugglers
were predominantly from Algeria, Mauritania, Mali, and
Morocco, and among them there were several groups of
jihadists. They headquartered in Gao, a town that sits on
the Niger River in northeast Mali. Gao soon became one
of the main transit points in the cocaine trade with Europe.
From Gao, the caravan of drugs headed north, across the
Sahara desert, primarily to the Mediterranean shores of
Libya. In February 2011, Maria Sandra Mariani travelled
with her kidnappers in exactly the opposite direction.

The cocaine business was very profitable and further
revived the old smuggling routes, boosting the local economies of the Sahel at a time of great economic difficulty.
Yet while these activities kept local businesses afloat, they
further destabilized a region that, since the fall of the
Berlin Wall, had become politically unmoored. Guinea-Bissau was especially vulnerable. "The third poorest

country in the world, with a 60 percent illiteracy rate and almost no supply of electricity, Guinea-Bissau had become one of the many casualties of the dismantling of the Soviet Bloc. In 1998, after its Marxist government had collapsed, the country was plunged into a civil war. Against this background it was easy for the Colombian cartel to buy the political elite, the police force, and to decide the outcome of the 2005 elections," explained Daniel Ruiz.

The lack of strong state authority and the importance of personal, tribal, and ethnic loyalties also made it easy for the smugglers to carry on their business undisturbed and to develop a web of corrupt officials—a fundamental step to guaranteeing the passage of illegal goods. Finally, the profits they made and spent locally earned them the respect of the local tribes. Like Cornwall in the eighteenth century, in the Sahel, smuggling had been in people's blood for centuries, so it was easy to revive it. "Even before the slave trade took off, West and North Africa shared strong smuggling traditions via the Sahel, which had survived globalization," writes Colin Freeman in the *Daily Telegraph*.[13] After the fall of the Berlin Wall, for example, the economy of Mali became totally dependent upon the contraband of Algerian goods, which were cheaper because they were subsidized by the Algerian military government.[14]

Against this background, drug smuggling in the Sahel not only thrived, but it became virtually the sole economic activity of the region. It was only a matter of time before smugglers added another illicit product: human cargo. This human cargo being foreigners like Mariani, kidnapped for a ransom, and migrants who would pay good money to be trafficked to escape the destabilization of West Africa.

AL QAEDA IN THE ISLAMIC
MAGHREB PROTOCOL

It took a week for Maria Sandra Mariani to reach her final destination: a camp in northern Mali. During this journey she noticed that her kidnappers knew well how to navigate the Sahara. "Along our journey, they had stored food, gas, spare tires in hideouts in the desert. They knew exactly where the supplies were and how to get them out," she remembers. Unbeknownst to Mariani, her kidnappers had had almost a decade to perfect the transporting of hostages across the Sahara desert.

Al Qaeda in the Islamic Maghreb (AQIM) was created partly with the smuggling revenue and partly with the ransom money of the first major abduction of foreigners in the region. Back in 2003 the Salafist Group for Preaching and Combat (GSPC),[15] a breakaway faction of the Algerian GIA, had kidnapped thirty-two Europeans and brought them to northern Mali. Their leader was Mokhtar Belmokhtar, the one-eyed former Algerian mujahideen. When the European countries paid €5.5 million for the release of their hostages, Belmokhtar used part of the ransom money to fund AQIM.[16] After that, a plethora of small criminal and jihadist groups, including the GSPC, joined the new organization.

Because AQIM had no links with al Qaeda's traditional financiers in the Gulf, right from the start it was self-funded via the various illegal activities of its members in West Africa and in the Sahel, predominantly the high-yield smuggling and kidnapping of foreigners. Analysts estimate that AQIM spent around $2 million each month on weapons, vehicles, and payoffs to families whose children joined local *katibas*, or combat units. In 2012 the United Nations reported that families in northern Mali received around $600 per child soldier, followed by monthly payments of $400 if the child remained engaged in active combat.[17] Hence, recruitment costs were high.

Generating vast sums of money through illegal activities and paying the members of his *katiba* well made Belmokhtar immensely popular inside AQIM. Earlier, in the late 1990s, he had successfully developed a very profitable smuggling network between Algeria and Mali that had earned him the name of "Mr. Marlboro," after the contraband cigarettes. According to Jean-Pierre Filiu, professor of Middle Eastern Studies at Sciences Po, Paris School of International Affairs, Belmokhtar's popularity was also due to his decision to nurture his relations with the desert tribes through marriage alliances, avoiding extorting money from the local populations, contrary to what the GSPC did in its Kabylia[18] stronghold, in the Tell Atlas mountains of northern Algeria. Interestingly, almost twenty years later, both in Syria and Iraq, the Islamic State—also known as the Islamic State of Iraq and Syria, or ISIS—will implement a similar strategy to obtain the consensus of the local tribes.

Indeed, to compensate for the revenues lost by not pillaging the local populations, in 2003 Belmokhtar branched off into kidnapping foreigners while he was still involved in the smuggling of drugs and weapons.[19] Prior to 2003, kidnapping of foreigners had never been regarded as a profitable business in the region, especially considering that smuggling cocaine to the North African shores produced good revenues. The success of the first abductions in 2003, however, proved to the criminal and jihadist community that this new business was worth pursuing.[20]

Unlike smuggling cocaine, kidnapping foreigners was a business that AQIM could run entirely alone, without getting involved with foreign entities such as the Colombian cartel. Hence, its revenues soon outstripped the profits it drew from smuggling drugs. According to a *New York Times* investigation, from 2003 until Mariani was kidnapped in 2011, AQIM had collected $165 million in ransoms.[21]

The supply of foreigners in the region was also plentiful. Prior to their capture, none of the hostages had any idea how dangerous the Sahel had become in the space of just a few years, nor did they know that the trans-Saharan routes were busy avenues for smuggling cocaine and trafficking of migrants. They were as ignorant as Maria Sandra Mariani was about the risk involved in traveling to these areas. "A few days before I left for Algeria, I saw a program on France 24 about two French hostages that had been kidnapped in the Sahel six months earlier. Sarkozy was saying that France would not pay any ransom," adds Mariani. "I thought that it was easy for him to say that, but for those hostages the ransom represented the difference between life and death. However, I never considered that something like this could happen to me. I had been traveling to the Algerian desert for five years and had never felt unsafe."

Western governments had succeeded in keeping the growing kidnapping crisis out of the media, reinforcing a false sense of security vis-à-vis the global village in tourists like Mariani as well as in journalists.[22] News of people being kidnapped appeared as isolated exceptions in what was otherwise a peaceful and safe region of Africa. Additionally, it was not public knowledge that the Colombian cartel had established new smuggling routes across the Sahel, and that a new breed of criminal was flourishing there, or that jihadist organizations were getting rich off of both businesses.

Soon the business kidnapping foreigners was so profitable that al Qaeda Central in Afghanistan issued guidelines about how to implement it in other regions, encouraging its affiliated jihadist groups to get into the business of abducting Westerners, emulating AQIM in the Sahel. Thereafter, kidnapping of foreigners became known as the al Qaeda in the Islamic Maghreb protocol, a model that, as we shall see, would be replicated across the jihadist world.[23]

The AQIM protocol centered on kidnapping foreigners in areas without any proper authority: failed or semi-failed states, which, in the Sahel, were indeed plentiful and included Niger, southern Algeria, Mauritania, Mali, and elsewhere. AQIM's access to a secure hideout in northern Mali, a semi-failed region, was also crucial. The ultimate keys to its success, however, were a strict division of labor and equally strict discipline inside the organization.

Mariani and all other hostages were kidnapped by low-skilled, low-ranking members of the organization. Ordinarily, these people received instructions from their bosses and could not make executive decisions on the ground. An even less-skilled group of people looked after the hostages in the camps. These extremely simple men shared everything with their hostages, including food. "Those who looked after me were very, very simple people," said Mariani. "They were afraid even to glance at me when they brought me the food. They were all very religious and they prayed five times a day, on the dot. Apart from praying they did not do much."

As months passed, Mariani's jailers became increasingly nasty to her. They wanted their money, their share of the ransom, and they longed to leave the camp—to go back to their homes and spend the money. Despite their impatience, nastiness, and boredom, no jailer ever harmed her. On the contrary, after she was bitten twice by a scorpion, they got her a camp bed, and after she woke up one night with a snake curled over her head, every night from then on, they made sure the tent was free of snakes.

One of the few tasks of her jailers was to keep Mariani apart from other hostages in the camp. "I knew that there were two other hostages, the two French people I had seen on France 24. I had seen them at a distance, but we could not talk to each other; we were kept at opposite ends of the camp," said Mariani. Indeed, Mariani was imprisoned in the same camp as Marc Féret and Pierre Legrand, who would both be freed in October 2013.

When it came to negotiating the ransom, only top-ranking members of AQIM would be involved. Unlike the simple jailers, these men were sophisticated and very skilled, and often handled several negotiations at the same time. Mariani's negotiator was Abu Alid Saravi. He spoke several languages, had a university degree, and was a Sahrawi,[24] from southwestern Algeria. After her liberation, while being debriefed, Mariani recognized him as the kidnapper of another Italian, Rossella Urru. "I kept saying to the secret service that he was the same guy who had kidnapped Rossella, but they were reluctant to believe me," says Mariani. Urru was abducted on October 23, 2011, together with two Spanish aid workers, Ainhoa Fernández de Rincón and Enric Gonyalons in a Sahrawi refugee camp in Tindouf, in southwestern Algeria. By then Abu Alid had left AQIM for a breakaway group of AQIM composed predominantly of Sahrawi Algerians known as the Move-

ment for Oneness and Jihad in West Africa (MUJAO). The
kidnapping of the three aid workers was MUJAO's first
terrorist action, and Mariani is adamant that Abu Alid masterminded it.

"I did not see Abu Alid for all summer of 2011. When
he came back in early October he had shaven his beard
and looked very different. When I asked him where he
had been he said he had left Africa; he had gone abroad. I
believe that he had disappeared to organize the kidnapping
of Rossella Urru and of the other hostages."

Before October 2011, Abu Alid visited Maria Sandra
Mariani several times, filling her in on the progress of the
negotiations for her release. He was polite and talkative,
mentioning several times that the Italians were not cooperating, possibly because she was just a tourist. He claimed
that he had contacted the Italian government on February
17, 2011 but no one had replied. So in June 2011, he had
approached Mariani's family, who had in turn tried to get
in touch with the Berlusconi government directly.

"At a certain point my sister was given a direct number
for Berlusconi," remembers Mariani. "When they called
that number, a secretary said that the president was busy
with the election and that they should call back after the
vote. When I asked Abu Alid to show me the number, I
realized that it was not a mobile number but a landline
number. They had given my family Berlusconi's secretary's
number! Later on my sister admitted that in the summer of
2011, the foreign office had asked my family to be patient
because they were dealing with nineteen kidnappings all
at once."

As we shall see in the following chapters, governments
do indeed rank hostages in order of importance and attach

to each of them an indication of the ransom they would be willing to pay for their lives. In other words, not only kidnappers but also governments put different prices on different hostages, one life worth more than another.

chapter two

Feeding the Bears

On July 18, 2012, Rossella Urru, Ainhoa Fernández de Rincón, and Enric Gonyalons were freed after nine months in captivity while Maria Sandra Mariani remained a hostage for fourteen months. According to the kidnappers, the Spanish and Italian governments paid €15 million to release the three hostages.[25] Clearly freeing an aid worker was a priority over the liberation of a tourist.

Kidnappers know very well how governments rank hostages. The MUJAO, for example, purposely selected Urru, Fernández de Rincón, and Gonyalons as the victims of their first kidnapping operation to maximize the impact of the abduction. The hostages worked for aid agencies headquartered in different countries: Urru for CISP (*Comitato Internazionale per lo Sviluppo dei Popoli*), Fernández de Rincón for *Asociación de Amigos del Pueblo Saharaui de Extremadura*, and Gonyalons for the Basque NGO *Mundubat*. They were taken inside a Sahrawi refugee camp[26] and, because of that, it was particularly shocking not only to Italian and Spanish public opinion, but also to the international humanitarian aid community. There are five Sahrawi refugee camps all near Tindouf, near the border between Algeria, Morocco, and Mauritania, and local population is mainly dependent on humanitarian assistance for subsistence, as income-generating activities are very scarce. In 2015 it was estimated that there were 165,000 refugees in the camps. By targeting workers in the camp, the MUJAO sent a clear message: the Sahrawi refugee camps—fertile ground for the recruitment of jihadists—would henceforth be off-limits to NGOs.

The aim of the kidnapping was threefold: to rid the Sahrawi camps of Western aid agencies, to free a number of jihadists linked to their organization, and to receive a ransom. Such demands could never have been attached to the freedom of a single tourist like Maria Sandra Mariani.

The three hostages were taken to a different camp from where Mariani was, though also located in northern Mali, it was a camp run by the MUJAO and not by AQIM. On December 10, 2011 a video showing the three aid workers with fully armed masked men in the background began circulating on the Internet. However, negotiations had started earlier, possibly as soon as they were snatched, likely initiated by their aid agencies. "The procedure is standard," explains a European negotiator I interviewed.[27] "Aid agencies have a protocol in place and know what to do." However, only large aid agencies can afford to implement a proper safety protocol. Small NGOs do not have the money or the organizational capacity to do so, and must rely on governments to negotiate the freedom of their employees taken hostage.

CRISIS MANAGEMENT

In the 2010s, the kidnapping crisis prompted donors to demand that NGOs produce safety plans, hire advisers to deal with abductions, and train staff. "This was a very good development," says Liban Holm, a member of the Global Safety team of the Danish Refugee Council (DRC), one of the largest and best-funded NGOs in the world. "It motivated the humanitarian aid community to develop safety plans."[28] For example, the DRC in its planning drew extensively on its experience of two aid workers being kidnapped in 2011, American Jessica Buchanan, and Dane Poul Hagen Thisted, by a group of Somali pirates who had moved inland.

The two aid workers, whose task was to raise awareness on how to avoid land mines, were based in northern Somalia, but the abduction took place while they were on their way back from the more dangerous southern region, where they had gone for training. In her book *Impossible Odds*, Buchanan hints at how security about the trip could have been improved. "My NGO's plan is for me to fly from Hargeisa to North Galkayo where, for safety, the excursion from North to South is to be made in a three-car caravan. The security caravan is our standard mode of travel, and I'm not at all surprised to be using it now. But what my colleagues have neglected to tell me is that there is a kidnapping threat for expats in the area, and that our destination is situated about five hundred meters from a known pirate's den."[29]

The pirates had likely known Buchanan and Thisted were going to conduct the training session and decided to kidnap them. This is a standard procedure among criminal groups in highly destabilized areas.

Since then DRC has worked hard to further improve its crisis management plans, both at the headquarters in Copenhagen and on site, wherever the abduction takes place. These teams can become operational extremely quickly. "We have pre-set teams for crisis management units both in our headquarters and in the countries where we operate," explains Holm. In other words, they act with an intense awareness of how important the first few hours can be after a kidnapping in determining the eventual outcome.

The Danish Refugee Council has made sure that despite good in-house resources the NGO can call upon support from a specialized team. The relationship between the crisis management team and the security company is crucial. Members of the safety team meet regularly with kidnapping experts, often informally over dinner, to discuss political developments and potential risks in the thirty-seven countries where DRC operates.

During the exchange of information, the contribution of aid workers is also essential for the security company, as aid workers can provide useful information about the regions where they are based. This solid relationship is constructed over time in order to prevent situations in which, for example, someone is kidnapped in Somalia and the security company sends an expert in kidnapping from Afghanistan. At any given moment, the crisis management unit of DRC knows exactly who to reach out to in each location.

Back in 2003, when AQIM snatched the thirty-two

Europeans, and even in 2011, when Rossella Urru was kidnapped, no one had yet developed such a complex and efficient safety plan. Nor at that time was the role of the experts and of the families regarded to be as crucial as it is today. The advice of external experts in kidnapping and ransom is fundamental: they have extensive knowledge in the field as they deal with hundreds of kidnappings at any given time, while the aid agency's experience may be limited to only a few cases, if any. Holm also finds that "when the families get involved, the presence of an experienced expert validates what we are doing." In other words, it reinforces the strategy put in place by the aid agency and helps encourage the families to embrace it.

The relationship between NGOs and the governments of the hostages' countries of origin can be difficult. "We always explain our strategy to them and why we would be the best people to deal with the crisis based on a strategy of community outreach," explains Holm. However, some governments find it very difficult to let humanitarian aid agencies do that and want to take over, primarily because the latter do not engage in direct negotiation with the kidnappers. Other governments are on the other hand more than happy not to be directly involved. Hostage negotiation is a very risky business for governments because of the scrutiny of public opinion, plus they lack the extensive knowledge of the area and the local population as compared with NGOs. So overall, when dealing with kidnapping, governments tend to stall. This can be—and often is—disastrous. The "wait and see" approach is often exactly what they should not do.

Countries that "officially" do not pay ransom are less intrusive but not necessarily less active. In the case of Buchanan and Thisted the Americans had a plan for the rescuing of the hostages. DRC, however, was not informed that the US Navy Seals were launching a rescue operation. When Buchanan got very sick it was not a surprise that the rescue mission happened. Luckily, the rescue mission was successful. Overall these operations do not have a high success rate. About one in three fails and causes the death of the hostages or of the rescuers. Hence, their limited use.

Naturally, DRC, a humanitarian aid organization, would never have facilitated an armed military rescue operation. Its approach to kidnapping and negotiations is very, very different from the one employed by governments. For a start, they never pay ransom. "If you accept to pay a ransom, you automatically put a price on a human life," explains Holm. It follows that DRC does not rank hostages either; every life is equally important.

Because for the kidnappers the hostages are an investment that incurs daily costs from the moment of the abduction, negotiations can be done on the basis of these variable costs: transportation, food, labor costs, and such. Would this approach have saved Buchanan and Thisted? Would this approach have brought home Rossella Urru, Ainhoa Fernández de Rincón, and Enric Gonyalons without spending €15 million of taxpayers' money? It is impossible to say, but for sure if governments pay such ransoms it becomes increasing difficult for NGOs to pursue alternative strategies. "If you keep feeding the bears, the bears will keep coming into the camp," wrote Amanda

Lindhout in her book *A House in the Sky*,[30] which recounts her kidnapping in Somalia.

Soon after the abduction of Buchanan and Thisted, the DRC staff mobilized the local population. They reached out to the elderly, bringing together rival clans. The message was that these types of actions were not good for anybody, especially for the local population that badly needs the help provided by humanitarian programs, which are often forced to shut down their operations in the wake of an abduction. In the ultimate analysis, the kidnapping of an aid worker is an issue in which the local leaders must be involved to seek a solution. So the approach of DRC is to involve the local population. In the case of Buchanan and Thisted, for example, the crisis management team had learned that the kidnappers were moving the hostages often, which was thought to be a sign of their limited support in the area. They were pirates with relatives in the area who had moved inland because business had been bad at sea. It was thus they came to know of the presence of foreign aid workers. DRC obtained this information through their close relationships with the local authorities and population. Government secret services would never have access to such leads.

The DRC approach, which could be defined as "soft" vis-à-vis governments' protocol for kidnapping, rests on a few main principles: a human life has no price; armed rescue missions should be avoided; and a peaceful solution to a kidnapping can often be found by engaging the local population in the negotiations. Hence, abduction should be handled as much as possible as a localized phenomenon.

Overall, governments' approach to the kidnapping of their own citizens is not as well structured as that of the top humanitarian organizations when their aid workers are snatched. When the hostages are from a country that pays ransom, such as Italy or Spain, governments always handle the negotiation and pay the ransom, bypassing the NGOs. Small aid agencies have no problem delegating this task to government officials, especially when their safety protocol is faulty, as proven by the kidnappings of Simona Torretta and Simona Pari in 2004.

THE TWO SIMONAS

On September 7, 2004, an armed commando unit burst into the Baghdad offices of the Italian NGO *Un ponte per . . .* and seized two twenty-nine-year-olds, Simona Torretta and Simona Pari. The two hostages became known as the Two Simonas. Along with the two Italians, the kidnappers also took two Iraqi colleagues, Raed Ali Abdul Aziz and Mahnaz Bassam, who worked for another Italian humanitarian aid organization, INTERSOS.[31] The following day, on the website Islamic-Minbar.com, the group Ansar al Zawahiri (partisans of al Zawahiri) claimed responsibility for the kidnapping.

"It was not a political abduction," says Karin Weber, a retired aid worker and former colleague of the Two Simonas. "In Iraq there were two types of kidnappings: political and financial. The kidnappers of Simona Torretta and Simona Pari were common criminals. They wanted money, nothing else. Hence, they treated them very well; the girls were valuable merchandise." But this is not how the Italian government and the media portrayed the abduction. According to government officials and the press, the Two Simonas were victims of Iraqi jihadists. So powerful was this propaganda that Jama'at al Tawhid wal Jihad, the group led by al Zarqawi, even issued a statement denying responsibility for the kidnapping.

In 2003 Weber was working as an administrator at *Un ponte per . . .* in Basra. After the capture of Saddam Hussein, she wrote a memorandum explaining in detail that in the fast degenerating Iraqi political climate, the security of its aid workers was at risk because their safety plan was faulty. From the Rome headquarter of *Un Ponte per . . .* , Weber received a reply dismissing her fears. Iraq was safe. But Weber had been right. Soon after the invasion of Iraq, in March 2003, kidnapping became a source of financing for various criminal and insurgent groups.

"What we saw, especially in the South where I was based at the time," says Maiolini, a former Italian ambassador in Iraq, "was an increasing number of abductions of wealthy and professional Iraqis at the hands of various groups." By the end of 2003, when most of these people had left the country, foreigners became the most sought-after prey. A decade later this pattern would be replicated in Syria during the civil war.

"When I told the Two Simonas that I was resigning because of the lack of proper security, one of them accused me of being a coward," remembers Weber. "It did not bother me. She was young and very inexperienced. I was a middle-aged woman, with a solid professional background in humanitarian aid. I was not afraid. I knew how dangerous it had become to remain in Iraq without proper protection." The Two Simonas were abducted just two months after Karin Weber left Iraq.

"I also explained to them that the lack of proper security could end up harming our humanitarian mission. When a humanitarian aid worker is kidnapped in war zones, and in 2004 Iraq was a war zone, that means that the NGOs have been targeted. So for security reasons everybody is evacuated, leaving behind only the non-critical staff, such as local aid workers. One of the cardinal principles of the UN and of all NGOs is *do no harm*. When you want to help people, you need to make sure that you do not damage them," explains Weber, echoing Holm's sentiments about rescue missions as harmful to humanitarian missions.

As Weber had predicted, "the kidnapping of the Two Simonas prompted the evacuation of all NGOs from Iraq, leaving the population in the hands of the militias and the jihadists who were fighting a bloody war against coalition forces.

"The problem with *Un ponte per . . .* was that it was a very small NGO, with no more than seven people in Rome working for them, and with only one contract: the one that the Two Simonas supervised in Iraq. They had no money to provide proper security, so their only option was evacuation. But this would have meant shutting down the entire operation, losing the donors, having to dismiss all the aid workers, including the Two Simonas. Leaving Iraq for them was to lose their dream job. So they stayed, pretending that it was safe and ignoring the consequences that their abduction would produce for the entire international humanitarian aid mission in Iraq."

The Two Simonas remained in Iraq even after the Italian diplomatic staff was evacuated. "After the tragedy of Nasiriyah[32] we left Iraq, so when the Two Simonas were kidnapped, we were not there. This is why I was not involved in the negotiation for their release," says Ambassador Maiolini. This may explain why the Italian Red Cross got involved in the negotiations.

"The Italian secret service and the Red Cross negotiated the ransom. I think the Red Cross contributed $1 million," explains Weber. "I do not know how much the Italian taxpayers paid. All I know is that they paid the ransom." On September 28 Al Jazeera showed the Two Simonas being welcomed by the extraordinary commissioner of the Italian Red Cross, Maurizio Scelli, who took them back home to Italy. "Imagine how many things we could have done with the ransom money. We could have built schools, hospitals. . . . Instead the humanitarian aid community had to pack their bags and leave Iraq and the money that should have gone to those in need ended up in the pockets of a gang of Iraqi criminals." says Weber.

Governments' approach to kidnapping, i.e., paying a negotiated ransom with the kidnappers, purposely ignores that this money funds terrorist or criminal activities, encouraging more people to snatch foreigners. Humanitarian aid organizations only reimburse the costs of the kidnapping, hence they do not fund future activities. At the same time, by engaging the leaders of local community to put an end to this crime they attempt to find a long term solution to kidnapping in certain areas of the world. However, kidnapping often becomes a political issue for governments, to be easily manipulated for propaganda purposes.

When they got back home, the Two Simonas were regarded as the heroines of the coalition forces' mission in Iraq to free the Iraqis from a heinous dictator. They were the two doves of peace snatched by the evil jihadists. They even appeared on the cover of *Time* magazine.[33] The Italian government and the media wove their abduction into the fictional narrative of the preventive strike in Iraq to prove that, indeed, the invasion had been badly needed and that the presence of troops in Iraq was essential to bring peace to the country.

JAPAN'S CONTRADICTIONS

A completely different reception awaited three Japanese hostages kidnapped in southern Iraq in 2004 by the Saraya al Mujahideen (Mujahideen Brigade). The hostages were eighteen-year-old Noriaki Imai, a member of the Campaign to Abolish Depleted Uranium who arrived in Iraq on April 1 with plans to study the impact of depleted uranium on children in Iraq's poorest areas; Nahoko Takato, a thirty-four-year-old aid worker and peace activist who was on her third trip to Iraq to help homeless children in Baghdad; and Soichiro Koriyama, a thirty-two-year-old former soldier who had gone to Iraq as a freelance photojournalist to provide material for the Japanese magazine *Asahi Weekly*.

Rather than regarded as heroic humanitarians, they were accused of having brought shame on Japan, causing their own ordeal by defying the government's advice not to travel to Iraq. Each hostage, on being freed, was also presented with a bill of $6,000 for their air ticket home, though not for the ransom paid for their freedom.

The kidnappers had initially demanded the withdrawal of Japanese troops from Iraq, but eventually settled for a ransom through the negotiation of the Islamic Clerics Association, a group of Sunni religious scholars. In December 2003 the Japanese government had sent six hundred troops to the southern city of Samawah. Though Japan's involvement in Iraq was to remain confined solely to peacekeeping, any participation in Bush and Blair's War on Terror was regarded as extremely controversial, and the majority of the Japanese population remained opposed to the war on Iraq. For that matter, judging by the anger shown to the freed hostages, Japanese public opinion was opposed to any involvement with Iraq, even when the purpose of such involvement was to uncover facts that could prove useful in opposing the war in Iraq.[34] This somewhat contradictory position, betraying a deep sense of uneasiness regarding any war of non-self-defense, will be further discussed in Chapter Thirteen.

In 2004 the homecoming of another Japanese hostage, Junpei Yasuda, produced similar outrage among the Japanese population. Yasuda had quit his position as a staff reporter at a regional newspaper to travel to Iraq as a freelancer in order to report on the role of Japanese troops. His motivation sprang from the poor coverage in the Japanese media about the war in Iraq, a phenomenon notably common in most of the countries that participated in Bush's coalition.

The harsh criticism of Junpei Yasuda when he got back home did not prevent him from continuing his quest for the truth. In July 2015 he was kidnapped once again as soon as he secretly crossed into Syria from Turkey. He had defied once more his government's advice not to travel to Syria to report on the war and on key issues concerning his own country, such as the execution of Kenji Goto, a freelance journalist beheaded by the Islamic State and a friend of Yasuda.

Although the response of Italy and Japan to the kidnappings of their own people was completely different, offering opposite narratives to justify involvement in Iraq and the payment of ransoms, both countries negotiated and accepted conditions to free their own citizens. Hence, the kidnapping of the Two Simonas, the first high-profile abduction of foreigners in a country sliding into political anarchy at the hands of criminal and jihadist groups, as well as the abduction of the Japanese hostages, proved to the insurgency that the kidnapping of foreigners, especially aid workers and members of the international humanitarian community, was a profitable business, one that could bankroll its violent insurgency. It reinforced the belief that most Western governments would pay millions of dollars to bring their citizens home, an idea that less than a year before, the payment of the ransom for the thirty-two foreigners kidnapped by AQIM had introduced. Western governments were feeding the bears and the bears would keep coming into the campground for more and more.

Between 2003 and 2004 the hunting season for foreigners began in earnest and it migrated from country to country, year after year, and will continue to do so for as long as the ransoms keep coming. Aid workers and UN employees have been the prize catch, but it didn't take long before anyone carrying a Western passport was considered valuable prey.

Chapter Three

Trafficking Migrants

In April 2009 the oasis was buzzing with new life. It was springtime in the Sahara and the winter had been unusually wet. The acacias and shrubs were especially verdant and fragrant. Spring in the desert smells of new life, say the Tuareg. But Robert Fowler and Louis Guay, the two UN special envoys in Niger whom al Qaeda in the Islamic Maghreb had snatched four months earlier, could not smell a thing. After 126 days in captivity in one of Mokhtar Belmokhtar's Malian prison camps, their senses were dull and they no longer paid them any heed.

This oasis was the hand-off point of the hostages. Locked inside the pick-up truck that had brought them here, Fowler and Guay watched as swarms of AQIM fighters greeted the men holding Fowler and Guay captive. With Kalashnikovs in hand, some of the fighters periodically cried "Allahu Akbar." Others lifted their weapons to the sky as if to show the power of automatic firearms to their maker. To an outside observer, the gathering might have appeared both surreal and celebratory, as the army of ragged, heavily armed men jumped up and down, hugging each other like kids after scoring the winning goal in a soccer match. But to Fowler and Guay, their captors' glee signaled an all-too-real danger.

Soon another convoy of pick-up trucks arrived. It carried two female hostages: Marianne Petzold, a retired teacher of French from a town near Hamburg in Germany in her seventies, and Gabriella Greiner, a Swiss national in her fifties. In January 2009 they had been abducted near the Algeria-Mali border together with other European tourists, including Greiner's husband, Werner. But their kidnappers did not belong to the *katiba* of Belmokhtar. They were members of a group led by his rival, the other emir of AQIM in the Sahara region, Abdelhamid Abou Zeid.[35]

According to Fowler,[36] on that spring day Belmokhtar looked inside one of the trucks that had just arrived and was shocked at the physical condition of the two women. They were indeed in very bad shape. One had been bitten by a scorpion and her arm had swollen, turning black. Both suffered from advanced dysentery, and although during the negotiations their governments had sent medicines, Abou Zeid had refused to let them take them.

Belmokhtar asked Fowler for his dysentery tablets and gave them to the women. He then had an argument with Abou Zeid concerning their release. Apparently, Abou Zeid had changed his mind and did not want to let the women go as originally planned. Watching this unfold, Fowler was struck by what he took to be Belmokhtar's empathy for the sick and elderly hostages.

For a while and with trepidation, the hostages watched the two emirs argue through the tinted windows of the pick-up truck. Like two Saharan scorpions, they shook their tails in front of their *katibas*. But the jihadists were not interested in their fight; they were too happy catching up with old friends. All they wanted was to enjoy this short break from the hard life they lived as criminal jihadists.

FROM JIHAD TO CRIME

Criminal jihadism is a relatively new activity in the field of terrorism. To describe it requires a prior understanding of what terrorism is—no easy task considering that there is no single definition accepted internationally. Professor Paul Gilbert produced the best short definition of terrorism: "a crime with war aims."[37] The motivation can be national-istic, as was the case with the Basque organization Euskadi Ta Askatasuna (ETA) and the Irish Republican Army (IRA), or it can be purely political, as it was for the Italian para-military group, the Red Brigades. However, sometimes the criminal activities and the profits that these illicit actions generate corrupt the members of armed organizations, leading them to stray from their political goals. As the boundaries between the war aims and the illegal means used to achieve them are blurred, terrorists morph into criminals. This is indeed what has happened to Arafat's Pal-estine Liberation Organization (PLO), which long before his death became riddled with corruption and motivated by pure greed. Other times, the war aim, the political goal, can be weak right from the very beginning, serving as little more than a pretext to legitimize a life of crime. Indeed, that's the case with AQIM.

Right from the outset, as noted in Chapter One, AQIM had a very strong criminal component, relying heavily on illegal activities to fund itself: kidnappings for ransom, human trafficking, and drug smuggling in the largely ungovernable areas of the Sahel. This explains why it never worked with local insurgent groups, which indeed turned against it in Chad in 2004 and in Mali in 2006. On the con-trary, several of its founders maintained strong links with the smuggling networks that stretched from West Africa to North Africa, including small- to medium-sized criminal organizations that operated across the Saharan Sahel.

In early 2000 the Sahel countries offered an ideal breeding ground for criminal jihadism.[38] The region's grinding poverty provided AQIM a steady flow of recruits, whom the organization welcomed no matter how low their jihadist commitment, nor how high their criminal motivations. By no means is this a phenomenon limited to this region. "Criminal groups and some political groups have cross-fertilized over the last twenty years, and they've created these sort of hybrids,"[39] said Vincent Cochetel, who was kidnapped on January 29, 1998, in Vladikavkaz,[40] in the Northern Caucasus near Chechnya while working for the UN High Commissioner for Refugees. As we have seen, criminal jihadism was also present in Iraq after the 2003 invasion.

Interestingly, in the Sahel, jihadism produced little more than low intensity guerrilla activity between criminal gangs and government forces. It never took the shape of a proper insurgency. The jihad was nothing more than an ideological veneer that hid the true criminal nature of most AQIM members. Hence, the evolution of AQIM follows a well-known pattern observed in organized crime in areas prone to political destabilization: as opportunities arise, the organization keeps tapping into new illegal activities seeking to maximize profits. From smuggling cigarettes, it moved to carrying cocaine across the trans-Saharan routes; then it branched into kidnapping foreigners, and eventually got involved in trafficking migrants from West Africa to Europe. The curriculum vitae of Belmokhtar tracks this evolution.

As such, what, in April 2009, Robert Fowler took to be Belmokhtar's humane treatment of his hostages may well have been little more than the manifestation of his business acumen. Belmokhtar was, after all, a merchant of men. He traded people for money, and he knew very well that not honoring agreements reached during the hostage negotiations would undermine his business in the future. He also knew that delivering badly damaged merchandise—and indeed for him what was true of these hostages might also be true of the drugs or cigarettes he smuggled across the Sahara—was bad for future business.

His rival Abou Zeid was different. He represented the jihadist soul of AQIM. For him infidels deserved nothing more than brutality. He was not a merchant of men and despised those who were; he was not interested in the "business of the hostages." For him, foreigners were only enemies, not goods. Drukdal, the emir of the GSPC in Kabylia, had purposely selected Abou Zeid as the other emir of the region to balance the power of Belmokhtar. Abou Zeid's task was to curb and contain the popularity of the Algerian among the members of AQIM. But it was not an easy task. Belmokhtar, a former mujahideen and member of the GIA, had greatly contributed to financing the birth of AQIM, something that had generated great admiration among its members.

Personal rivalry, therefore, was at the heart of the relationship between the two emirs of AQIM, and the kidnapping of Westerners became the ideal contest, as witnessed by Robert Fowler. By now, kidnapping represented AQIM's primary source of income. From 2003 to 2012, ransoms had increased and ranged from $1 million to $4 million per Western hostage. The AQIM model of kidnapping had even become a very successful source of income for other jihadist organizations, such as the Taliban, which had replicated the model in their own territory.

By the end 2009, as Belmokhtar and Abou Zeid grew more and more competitive, their rivalry produced a new wave of kidnappings. "Three Spaniards were caught on the Mauritanian coastal road. An Italian couple was captured in Mauritania near the Malian border. A French national, and longtime humanitarian worker in northern Mali, was kidnapped in the eastern town of Ménaka."[41] Then, in Arlit, Niger, Abou Zeid carried out his boldest operation and seized seven foreign hostages, including four French nationals. Finally in June 2009 Abou Zeid executed Edwin Dyer, a British hostage kidnapped with Marianne Petzold and Gabriella Greiner in Niger in January of the same year, and held hostage in a camp in northern Mali. Dyer was killed when the British government refused to pay a ransom and free Abu Qatada held in Britain pending deportation to his native Jordan. Dyer's execution, however, was also aimed at intimidating other European governments that do pay ransoms. As we shall see, this is a technique that the Islamic State also used in 2013.

The surge in kidnappings ended the profitable tourist industry in Timbuktu, its historical sites becoming no-go areas for international visitors. Tourists also shunned desert-trekking adventures in Mauritania. One of the shortcomings of financing criminal and terrorist activity via kidnapping is that as a business, it has a way of suddenly depleting, its own supply. In Iraq, the kidnapping of the Two Simonas prompted the evacuation of all humanitarian aid personnel (potential hostages). In Mauritania and Mali, the increasing number of tourists being kidnapped put an end to tourism.

With no tourists to target for kidnapping in Mali and Mauritania, the finances of AQIM were soon in trouble. Personal rivalry between Belmokhtar and Abou Zeid risked driving AQIM out of business. To hunt for hostages, AQIM had to travel east to Algeria and Niger. There, the business was still profitable, as proven by the abduction at the beginning of 2011 of Maria Sandra Mariani.

Though the infrastructure that AQIM had built to run the kidnapping business was very efficient, it became increasingly difficult and expensive to handle its logistics in faraway regions, such as Niger or southeastern Algeria. "If you need to travel for thousands and thousands of miles in the Sahara desert to kidnap someone, you need to make sure that sufficient supplies are buried along the route. You also must know whom to bribe and how much money you need to give them," explained a former owner of a second-hand mobile phone shop in Tripoli who stayed until the fall of Gaddafi and then moved to Mali to work in a kidnapping camp there. As Maria Sandra Mariani had noticed, her kidnappers arrived too late to snatch other tourists. Someone must have tipped them off.

From 2003 onwards, across the Sahel, government officials and politicians became important players in the kidnapping business. In his memoir *A Season in Hell*, Robert Fowler recalls that President Tandja of Niger so detested the UN and the mission that Fowler and his colleague had been given to believe that Tandja did not offer them any security.[42] "I believe [. . .] that the government of President Mamadou Tandja arranged, however indirectly, for information relating to our movements to reach AQIM," Fowler writes.[43] It goes without saying that paying for information about the two UN special envoys must have cost AQIM dearly.

Despite the need to go far afield, when the kidnapping ran smoothly, profits continued to be high. In 2010, for example, AQIM freed Pierre Camatte, who had spent just ninety days in captivity. It was a quick turnover for the organization. Negotiations had gone according to plan. France had convinced the government of Mali to release four jihadists, as requested by al Qaeda in the Islamic Maghreb. According to former US ambassador to Mali, Vicki Huddleston, the ransom for Camatte was part of a $17 million ransom that France paid in 2010 to free four French hostages kidnapped by AQIM.[44]

But speedy negotiation and the fast release of hostages was very much the exception. Indeed, negotiations often took a very long time, especially when governments were involved, partly because bureaucrats typically have no sense of urgency when dealing with kidnapping. Fowler recounts that less than ten days after his abduction, the Canadian government was offered a video of him, possibly for a price, but decided not to receive it or even to engage in negotiations with the intermediaries because it did not trust them. It was only six weeks later that, after seeing press reports from Agence France-Presse detailing what was in the video, the Canadians decided to acquire it.[45]

Against this background, as new business opportunities arose thanks to the ongoing political destabilization of West Africa, people like Belmokhtar flocked to them. At the outset of the new millennium, the trafficking of migrants was fast becoming West Africa's primary resource.

TRADING LIVES

In 2004 the International Organization for Migration (IOM) published shocking statistics for the previous decade: over one million people from West and Central Africa had emigrated clandestinely to Europe over the course of the decade. Human trafficking had become the biggest crime racket in Africa after drugs.[46] Today these figures seem very, very low, especially if compared with the number of refugees currently traveling and seeking asylum in Europe. In 2015 alone, one million migrants successfully entered Germany. In the winter of 2016, three thousand migrants on average reached the Old Continent every day. The discrepancy between these numbers and those of just over a decade ago shows that, unlike kidnapping, trafficking is a long-term business and can be increasingly profitable.

Back in 2004, obtaining a forged passport and entry visa for the European Union cost up to $4,000 in wealthy countries such as the Ivory Coast, while in poorer nations, for example the Central African Republic, the price was much less, about $1,900. In 2004, for those who could not afford an airline ticket from the Ivory Coast or Senegal to Europe, the traffickers offered a journey overland to the shores of Libya and by boat to Italy at a cost of between $1,000 and $2,000.[47] In 2015, before the EU unofficially opened its borders, a Syrian who wanted to enter Europe with a real passport, either from Romania or Bulgaria by plane, could expect to pay between €10,000 and €15,000. A journey overland to Europe from Syria was priced between €2,000 and €4,000. Traffickers have always applied different prices to different people according to which type of journey they could afford.

In 2004 Interpol estimated that those controlling the immigration racket in the Ivory Coast earned between $50 million and $100 million per year, while the middlemen in Senegal pocketed over $100 million. Today these figures are ten times as high for those who traffic migrants from the Middle East and Asia to Europe. In 2015, in Libya alone, this business netted about €300 million. Already in 2004 smuggling of migrants from West Africa to Europe using the trans-Sahara routes was much more profitable than kidnapping foreigners. Equally today, the trafficking of Syrian refugees is an easier and more lucrative business than kidnapping foreigners.

People like Belmokhtar and his criminal jihadist partners, who possessed kidnapping and smuggling infrastructure across the trans-Sahara route, good contacts in Libya, and headquarters in northern Mali, were all well positioned to tap into the trafficking business. Hence, moving into the trafficking of migrants and refugees seemed to be the natural evolution of any kidnapping enterprise.

At the beginning of the millennium, for example, Mali was not only the kidnappers' chosen place to hide hostages, but it also became a key transshipment point for trafficking human cargo. Almost all the caravans of illegal migrants heading for Europe via Libya left from Mali. Some of them were run by *katibas* of AQIM but the migrants could not distinguish between common traffickers and criminal jihadists. Among them was M, an undocumented immigrant who reached Italy in 2009 and who was part of the rebellion at Rosarno, in Calabria.[48]

"I was nineteen years old when I left Conakry, in Guinea. It was 2006. I had moved there to look for a job; Conakry was the biggest town near my village. I did not find any employment so I paid a smuggler to take me to Libya. He asked for $1,000 but I had only $800 and he took it, but he told me that I had to reach Bamako, in Mali, by myself. I spent only one night there. The morning after I was told to get into a truck with many other people. There were many, many trucks. Some, I discovered, had carried cigarettes from Algeria and were traveling back empty, but I later on found out that they had cocaine hidden inside. Others, which looked much older, were used to carry people like me to Libya.

"We crossed the desert in a convoy of three trucks. We entered Libya from Niger. On the road we only stopped to pick up supplies; the drivers knew exactly where the petrol and the water were hidden. The drivers were all from Mali and seemed to know the route very well," recalls M.[49]

In 2007 Fabrizio Gatti, an Italian investigative journalist, published a book *Bilal* in which he recounts his shocking voyage from Senegal to Italy disguised as an illegal migrant. He travelled from Senegal to Bamako, where his journey through the desert began. Gatti, who also reached Libya through Niger, describes the business of trafficking people along the trans-Sahara smuggling routes as a vast industry, the biggest in the entire region, and an industry structured as a pyramid of crime.

At the top there are the merchants of men and the drug traffickers, who hide among the battered trucks crowded around with desperate people, the new trucks being used for the transport of cigarettes and cocaine. At the base there are cab owners who ferry the migrants to the pick-up points in old vehicles; shop keepers, often as miserable as the economic migrants, scattered along the route; and corrupt policemen and military personnel who often rob migrants at checkpoints. Gatti estimated that in 2006 those with the task of controlling the desert routes net between €1 million and €2 million in bribes or theft per month. In short, trafficking migrants kept the economy of the region afloat.

Against this background, at the turn of the twenty-first century, the Sahel was a world plagued by poverty and crime more than it was a fertile terrain for the jihad. Accordingly, the rivalry between Belmokhtar and Abou Zeid could have been much more than personal, resulting from the clash between two opposing views of this part of the world and of the role of organizations such as AQIM. For Abou Zeid, the destabilization of the Sahel was a step towards carrying out AQIM's main task: igniting the jihad to build the Caliphate. Kidnapping Westerners was not a business but a way to weaken the far-away enemy, the West, and to fund the jihad. Trafficking migrants, on the other hand, had nothing to do with the jihad. Hence, Abou Zeid was not interested in participating in it.

For Belmokhtar, AQIM was a tool to make money in a highly destabilized region of the world where business opportunities arose from illegitimate activities. He was not interested in the jihad or in building the Caliphate. A true merchant of men, he did not distinguish between smuggling cigarettes or cocaine, and kidnapping foreigners or trafficking migrants. Each of these businesses of trading valuable cargo made him money.

DIRTY DEALING WITH GADDAFI

In 2008, when Belmokhtar's men abducted Fowler and Guay, his *katiba* was already involved in trafficking migrants to Libya. This was a sort of "side business" that was becoming more profitable than kidnapping. Perhaps this is the reason why Belmokhtar accepted a very modest ransom, about $1 million, for the two UN special envoys. Possibly this is also why that April 2009 morning in the desert of Mali, Abou Zeid was angry with him.

Over the years, the criminal nature of AQIM had been growing steadily, engulfing the political and religious motivation, blurring the boundaries between terrorism and criminality, as proven by the rift between Belmokhtar and the Shura Council of AQIM. In 2013 the Associated Press found a letter in one of al Qaeda's hideouts in Mali.[50] The document stated the Shura's disapproval of the poor ransom paid for Fowler and Guay. The letter also mentions how, in 2010, Belmokhtar's constant insubordination led to his group's break-up with AQIM.[51] According to Malian officials, Mokhtar Belmokhtar was expelled from AQIM for his participation in the drug trade, which is condemned by the jihadist creed. In addition, they claim that he had increasingly gone rogue with his *katiba*, frustrating the leadership of AQIM and its members.[52]

Libya offered the best opportunities to make money trafficking African migrants, as the main hub for those illegally bound for Italy and Europe. Belmokhtar had good connections in Libya, cemented through his tobacco-smuggling business, so it was easy for him and his followers to tap into this market. Indeed, among the criticisms expressed by the Shura about Belmokhtar's insubordination were his frequent and lengthy trips to Libya.

Libya has steadily profited from the trafficking of migrants. In 2003 the Berlusconi government began secret negotiations with the Libyan dictator Gaddafi to reach an agreement about "containing" and "blocking" migrants traveling through Libya. That same year, Italy sent "supplies" to help Tripoli deal with migrants: boats, SUVs, trucks, diving equipment, twelve thousand blankets, one thousand body bags, and a large number of containers, which Gaddafi used to transport African migrants from the coast back inland to detentions camps in the Libyan desert.

"There are two types of containers, one small and one big. I travelled inside both of them," said a former migrant. "They say they have been provided by Italy. They say they were a gift from the Italian government to Gaddafi."[53]

What the Italian media named the *journey of hope*, a migrant's journey to Europe and to a better life, was in fact a deadly and inhuman voyage to hell and back, as described by some African migrants who ended up being traded as merchandise and moved around Libya in containers.[54]

"When we got to Misrata there was a container waiting for us," said one migrant. "It was very long. They forced us inside it. We did not even know what it was. While we were there they brought another hundred people from the prison. They came from different countries; many were from Somalia, Sudan, Eritrea. I was supposed to reach Italy and instead from Misurata, trapped inside the container, I went back south, to Kufra."[55] At the edge of the Libyan Sahara, near the border with Sudan, Kufra was Gaddafi's biggest detention center. Sooner or later, all migrants ended up in Kufra.

"They locked me in a container with another 110 people. During the journey half of them passed out. When we reached the destination the prison was full and could not take us. We were in Ajdabia. So they put us back into the container, without giving us any water and drove us to Kufra. People started to die next to me," remembers another migrant.[56]

To assist Gaddafi "in the migration flows," Italy also provided cash. The financial law of December 2004 granted Libya €25 million for 2005 and €20 million for 2006. In 2007 the Libyan dictator's thank-you letter arrived promptly: Eni, the Italian multinational oil and gas company headquartered in Rome, would participate in the development of Libya's gas supplies in a ten-year deal worth $28 billion. It was a contract written with the blood of the migrants.

The agreement between Italy and Libya was a dirty deal which benefitted traffickers, turned migrants into hostages and slave labor, and diverted large sums of Italian taxpayer money into Gaddafi's pockets, all the while enriching Italian companies linked to the political elite. Berlusconi promised to provide Libya with €200 million over a period of twenty-five years through investments in Libyan infra-structure projects, among which was a radar system built by the Italian security company Finmeccanica to monitor Libya's desert borders.

On December 29, 2007, the center-left Italian gov-ernment of Romano Prodi (former head of the European commission) granted an additional €6 million to Libya and signed an agreement to contain migration from Africa into Italy. In 2008, during the electoral campaign, Berlusconi openly campaigned in favor of a full agreement with Libya on matters of migration, which eventually was signed after his election. To celebrate the signing, Gaddafi came to Rome with his female bodyguards. He planted his tents in the capital's public parks and entertained politicians inside it, as a true Bedouin king.

It was a shocking deal, which legalized Libya's twenty-first-century gulag system.[57] However, the international community welcomed the new friendship between the two nations and paid no attention to the protests of organizations such as Human Rights Watch. "It looks less like friendship and more like a dirty deal to enable Italy to dump migrants and asylum seekers on Libya and evade its obligations," commented Bill Frelick, refugee policy director at Human Rights Watch.[58] Is Angela Merkel trying to achieve the same results with Turkey? Indeed, this seems to be the aim of the €3 to €6 billion deal negotiated by the European Union in 2015 and offered to Turkey in exchange for beating back the migrants from Europe's gates.

INSIDE THE LIBYAN GULAGS

For migrants, the effect of the agreement was disastrous: it led to more failed attempts to reach Europe and greater profits for merchants of men like Belmokhtar, the Libyan traffickers, and the Libyan authorities. Traffickers took migrants to the coast and alerted the police who immediately arrested or kidnapped them. The trafficker in turn received a ransom payment. Trapped inside metal containers, the migrants would then cross the Saharan desert one more time, traveling south toward the Sudanese border ending up in Kufra, a twenty-first-century gulag where they would be imprisoned for a while.

"I was traveling with my sister. I was twenty-five and she was twenty-two-years-old," remembered Salima, a Somali woman who now resides in Canada. "When we got to Kufra they locked us inside a room with 120 other people. It was very hot and we were dying of thirst. There was no water. They gave us a bottle of water per day and you had to use it for everything—drinking, washing. We were all very, very dirty. Almost everybody had scabies; some women had scars, which bled all the time. There were so many of us in the room that at night it was hard to lie down. Next door they kept the men. They had it much rougher than us; the guards regularly beat them up. We could hear their screams but there was nothing we could do, so some women just cried and cried and cried. I thought I had reached hell. All I wanted was to die."[59]

After a few weeks, or even months, the jailers would pretend to release those who had survived. "They would tell you that you were going to be expelled to Sudan," one migrant explained. "Two land cruisers of the police, vehicles that they say the Italian government had provided, came to pick you up from the prison, but, instead of taking you to the border they took you to the local traffickers, who were waiting outside the prison, ready to buy you. Some of them were from Sudan and paid thirty dinar for each migrant. It is not a lot. But they then made much more money selling you to the Libyan traffickers, who would take you back to Tripoli, charging you up to $400 [for your freedom]."

Migrants were sold over and over to a series of intermediaries. Each time they would be instructed to call home and ask for a ransom for their release. "My family sent the money to Mesfin, [a place] in Sudan. Even if you pay, they stop you on the way. I was stopped at Ajdabia [in Libya] and asked for more money. If you do not pay they tie you up like an animal or they hand you over to the police who will take you back to Kufra and the ordeal starts all over again."[60]

In a sadistic *Groundhog Day*–type ritual, migrants were

captured and recaptured, ferried across the desert in containers, and kidnapped over and over again. They could be trapped inside the Libyan Sahara for months, sometimes years. "I thought that the journey would be from Sudan to Kufra, from Kufra to Tripoli and then to Italy," remembered another migrant. "Instead, before reaching Italy, I went back and forth from the Libyan coast to Kufra, being bought and sold five times and kidnapped seven times."[61]

Did the Italian government know how Gaddafi kept the migrants at bay? In 2005 an Italian delegation arrived in Kufra. "The guards locked up all the common criminals and those who came from Nigeria, Chad, Senegal, and Darfur, who were with us," remembers a migrant who at the time was imprisoned in Kufra. "The Italians came with new, shining cars with the Italian flag. A young man from Eritrea began talking with them in Italian, so the guards would not understand what he was saying. They asked if we liked the place, if there was enough to eat, if we had access to showers, soap, etc. And the young man said that the place was a gulag. We were regularly beaten, sold to intermediaries, and kidnapped by the police. When they left they said that we were under the protection of the UN and that things would improve from then on. But nothing changed."

Did the EU know about what was happening in Libya thanks to strategic agreements to contain migration to Europe? In 2007 a delegation from Frontex, the agency of the European Union established in 2004 to manage the cooperation between national border guards, organized a mission to Libya and visited Kufra. When, a few years later, a former detainee at Kufra asked the president of Frontex if he knew about the condition of migrants at Kufra, he said that he was not familiar with it, but had heard that "there was room from improvement."

Frontex tasks include detecting and stopping illegal immigration, human trafficking, and terrorist infiltration; however, from its 2007 report it is clear that it did not discover nor did it denounce the Libyan gulags. Instead the Frontex delegation wrote about Kufra: "During the visit to the Southern region of Libya, the members of the delegation had the opportunity to appreciate the size and variety of the desert; no European region can be compared to it." They, of course, did not travel across the Sahara desert inside a container.

chapter four

The Economics of Piracy

On the tenth anniversary of 9/11, Judith and David Tebbutt, a middle-aged British couple, arrived at the Kiwayu Safari Village, a beach resort north of the coastal city of Lamu, in the northern part of Kenya's coastline. The couple's lodging was a bungalow on a white sand beach, just steps from the ocean. That evening the Tebbutts had dinner at the resort restaurant, followed by drinks with the owner. They were the resort's only guests.

In retrospect, Judith Tebbutt admitted to being slightly worried that there were no other guests at Kiwayu Safari Village and that their bungalow was far from the reception area and the restaurant.[62] She also did not like the fact that there were no doors or windows that could be locked, and that their bedroom was completely open. They were told the Kiwayu Safari Village was so secure that locks weren't necessary. The management did advise the Tebbutts to put their jewelry in a box to protect it against the mischief of monkeys though. Clearly the resort was safe, or so the Tebbutts thought.

The couple fell asleep to the gentle sound of the Indian Ocean's waves lapping against the sandy beach just outside their bedroom. It was to be a dream holiday, but it was the last time Judith Tebbutt would lie next to her husband. When she awoke in the middle of the night, her husband was on his feet shouting at an armed man as another man pointed a weapon at her head. In the space of a few seconds, Judith saw her husband fall to the floor while two men began dragging her out of bed and toward the beach. She thought David had been hit and fainted. Barefoot, in her pajamas, Judith soon realized that she was being abducted. Two men threw her into a boat waiting just a few feet from the porch of her bungalow, where a few hours before she had smiled for her husband's camera while lying in the hammock.

The boat took off at high speed, heading towards the Somali coast, which was a mere twenty-five miles away.

GLOBALIZING CRIMINAL LABOR

Judith Tebbutt was the first hostage to be taken by Somali kidnappers onshore in Kenya. Until September 11, 2011, the world had heard only of Somali pirates, swarms of people on small boats hijacking large cargo ships in the Gulf of Aden. Tebbutt's kidnapping, however, was the first of a series of similar abductions in Kenya. In the following weeks, a disabled French woman, Marie Dedieu, was taken from another beach in northern Kenya; next, two Spanish aid workers were kidnapped from a refugee camp. Clearly, Kenya, a country Westerners regarded as a holiday resort, was not safe.

Judith Tebbutt was held hostage for more than six months. The kidnappers moved her often, sometimes to camps deep in the mangrove swamps of the southern coast of Somalia. While in captivity, during her first phone call to her son, she learned that her husband had not survived the attack.

Her ordeal was similar to that of many other foreign hostages: she was fed just enough to be kept alive; the kidnappers tried to dehumanize her; she fell sick from poor food, dirty drinking water, the harsh conditions of her captivity, and the lack of proper hygiene. Like Maria Sandra Mariani, Judith had time to observe the interactions among her kidnappers and came to the conclusion that her jailers were very simple people and that the group functioned according to a well-defined hierarchy, a power structure respected by all its members.[63]

Mariani and Tebbutt sensed that discipline was maintained through punishment; however, they did not know that it was applied predominantly through monetary fines, which would be deducted from the share of the ransom owed to the kidnappers. This indeed was a general rule that all kidnappers followed, regardless of where they operated. In Somalia, for example, pirates who mistreated the crew or fell asleep at one's post had to pay a $5,000 fine and twice as much if someone refused to follow an order.[64] Theft, on the other hand, was an offense punishable by death. The Danish sailor Søren Lyngbjørn, who was kidnapped in 2011 by Somali pirates, said that when some of the kidnappers tried to steal a car full of *khat*,[65] the drug that pirates chew all day, they were caught and shot on the spot.[66]

In Somalia, as in Mali and across the Sahel, at the base of the kidnapping and hijacking labor pyramid one finds uneducated, unskilled youth who turned to crime to survive. In 2011 the supply of these people in Somalia was more than plentiful. From 1950 to 2010, this country had experienced an unprecedented demographic boom: its population had grown from two million to eight million, even as those decades saw an exodus of more than two million Somalis. Paradoxically, this exceptional growth in the population occurred at the same time as the economy and the state progressively vanished.

SOMALIA: CASUALTY OF THE COLD WAR

It is commonly believed that Somalia's serious troubles started in 1992, when the United Nations and the United States launched Operation Restore Hope. After the fall of dictator Mohamed Siad Barre at the hands of local rebel militias, the UN sent some thirty thousand international peacekeepers into Somalia to restore law and order and protect the civilian population. When on October 3, 1993, however, two US UH-60 Black Hawk helicopters were shot down in Mogadishu and rebels dragged an American corpse through the streets of the Somali capital like a grotesque war-trophy,[67] US and UN troops were pulled out of Somalia and the country was quickly declared a failed state.

Despite the appeal of this well-worn story of Somalia's decline, the true genesis of the country's troubles occurred decades earlier, specifically in the late 1960s, when Somalia was drawn into a Cold War-era proxy war. In 1969 General Siad Barre had overthrown Somalia's fragile democracy and declared the country a socialist state. Under the umbrella of the Soviet Union, he began receiving arms and foreign aid. When in the late 1970s Moscow decided to back Ethiopia in the contest for control of the Ogaden region, however, Siad Barre turned to Washington, which welcomed him. More arms and aid were soon dispatched to Mogadishu. This militarization and Cold War client relationship damaged the economy and left it highly weaponized, setting the stage for later troubles.

Frank Crigler, US ambassador to Somalia from 1987 to 1990, claims that the US armed Barre for strategic reasons: "It was valuable to have back-up access to military facilities if they became needed."[68] But Barre had never been interested in fighting for the superpowers. Using his deep knowledge of the Somali clans, he distributed arms to those loyal to him, located mostly in the South, and encouraged them to attack the clans of the North, who opposed his regime. Hence, for two decades, Soviet and American arms fueled a violent civil war that the dictator instigated and bankrolled to maintain his own power.

With the end of the Cold War, the US ceased supporting Barre, who was soon after overthrown by rebel factions. His removal, however, did not restore peace. At the beginning of the 1990s, Somalia was a country brutalized by war and awash in weapons. The North declared independence under the name Somaliland, while the South was plunged into civil war. No wonder Operation Restore Hope failed. It was launched in 1992 when the damage had already been done. Sadly, a few decades later, the civil war in Syria, which has morphed into a war by proxy, is reenacting the same dystopian scenario.

As a failed state, Somalia was soon targeted by globalized criminality. For example, without a navy it could no longer patrol its coast, so illegal fishing became rampant. At the beginning of 2000, it is estimated that seven hundred foreign-owned vessels were fully engaged in unlicensed fishing in Somali waters, exploiting high value species such as tuna, shark, lobster, and deep-water shrimp. Within a few years, illegal fishing destroyed Somalia's rich fishing industry, pushing a large section of its population into poverty. Somalia's coastal waters also became a global dumping ground for electronic waste and radioactive junk. In 2009 the cost of dumping toxic waste offshore in Somalian waters was approximately 1 percent of the cost of disposal in Europe.[69]

It was only a matter of time before Somali criminals began exploiting the vast, unpatrolled coast of their country, an area of thousands of square miles stretching from the Mozambique Channel to the Red Sea. "The length of its coast and its geographic position at the entry of the Red Sea makes Somalia strategically unique," explained Giacomo Madia, an Italian insurer. Somalia is also very close to Europe's main energy supply, the oil fields of Saudi Arabia and of the Gulf, so oil tanks sail regularly along its shores.

In retrospect, letting Somalia become a failed state was indeed an enormous mistake: winning the Cold War did not change the geography of the planet. On the contrary, Somalia's strategic position became paramount because globalization boosted international trade and an increasingly large share of it ended up in transit off the coast of Somalia and the Horn of Africa. This unpoliced trade route created a rich new resource ready to be exploited by Somali pirates through hijacking and kidnapping.

NEGOTIATING WITH PIRATES

On April 6, 2009, Somali pirates hijacked the *Malaspina Castle* and kidnapped its crew in the Gulf of Aden, off the coast of Somalia. Though the owner of the ship was Italian, the *Malaspina Castle* was sailing under a British flag company. This was an important factor, as Italian law prevents the payment of ransoms for kidnapping by freezing the wealth of those who are targeted. Had the ship been registered in Italy, the owner would not have been able to negotiate a ransom.[70]

The *Malaspina Castle* had sailed a few days earlier from Novorossiysk and was heading for China. It was the last ship in a convoy sailing from the Suez Canal towards the Indian Ocean, so for the pirates it was the easiest target in the group. It carried a delicate cargo—DRI, Direct Reduced Iron, a ferrous product that at high temperatures can explode—so it was imperative that this material was kept in the right conditions during the hijacking. And indeed it was.

"Right from the beginning we realized that we were dealing with professionals," remembered Giacomo Madia, who acted as coordinator for the owner in the negotiation of the *Malaspina Castle*.[71] "We put immediately in force a crisis team where a marine lawyer, our hull claim director Mr. Nunzio Natale, a marine engineer, and the fleet manager, were always attending and monitoring any emergency. They (the hijackers) immediately established a good relationship with us, clearly to avoid tensions and any type of problems during the negotiations. Indeed, the only impasse we encountered was when it was refused their initial offer—they were asking for more than $3 million. At that time the going rate was $1.5 to $2.5 million. Then, of course, in 2010 and 2011, the ransoms went up, reaching even $5 or $6 million. But in 2009 demanding $3 million was too much."

A professional team of negotiators, ArmorGroup, was immediately appointed and talks with hijackers started from the very day after the taking of the vessel at sea via a dedicated telephone line and then every two days after that. "They were very skilled negotiators," Madia remembered. "They even tried to put pressure on us using the crew. They allowed the members to talk to their families. Relatives would then call the owner and press [him] to accept the conditions of the ransom . . . . The master, as well, was permitted to talk with the fleet manager and keep him informed on the crew's condition and on the humidity and temperature levels that might eventually affect the vulnerability of the ship because of the special type of cargo, DRI, carried on board. At a certain point, after our repeated refusal to pay, they even threatened to take ten members of the crew onshore and kill them. I asked the negotiator from ArmorGroup (the British company we employed not only to guide us in the negotiation, but also to comply with all remaining activity) if they were serious and he said that they were bluffing. It was a psychological tactic to make us accept a higher offer. In fact after twenty-four hours we resumed the negotiations and in less than one month we received an offer of about 1.8 million . . . which was then accepted."

The kidnappers of the *Malaspina Castle* were also very well organized when it came to the delivery of the ransom. Madia was told in great detail what the ship-owning company should do: the ransom had to be delivered where the ship was laying up. So, once the sum was available in Djibouti, the money had to be withdrawn in cash and put in suitcases, which in turn had to be sealed in plastic. Finally, ArmorGroup chartered a PiperJet and parachuted the suitcases onto the ship. "They were very meticulous in telling us how to drop the money right on the ship. This was a risky operation because all the instructions were given via radio message and anyone could listen in." If the drop was too far away from the boat, other pirate groups, tipped off by the instructions given over the radio, might reach the suitcases first. "If that had happened we would have been in big trouble because we were not covered for that kind of risk," Madia explained. "We had successfully obtained the full cooperation of our London under-writers that I visited immediately after the Malaspina hijacking, throughout the negotiations and managed to use our insurance for risk of war to pay for the ransom." Risk of war included the risk of piracy, under the General Average clause, and Giacomo Madia managed to get the approval of the insurers of the *Malaspina Castle* to pay not only the ransom, but also all the ancillary expenses the ship-owner had to front, including the rental of the PiperJet, to bring the ransom by plane, and those that arose on a daily basis, among which was the expense of employing ArmorGroup at a cost of £1,750 per day.

THE PIRACY INDUSTRY

Kidnapping and hijacking present fixed and variable costs for the pirates as well. The longer the negotiations, the lower the profits. This principle applies to any type of kidnapping. In the business model that the pirates had developed in Somalia, kidnapping and hijacking were treated as natural resources and negotiation classified as part of the cost of their exploitation.

The Somali piracy model evolved along the same lines as the kidnapping business model of AQIM in the Sahel. Almost mirroring the dystopian nature of the failed state in which they lived, both the criminal jihadists of AQIM and the Somali pirates replaced the classical nineteenth- and twentieth-century centralized Mafia system with a form of decentralized and destructured criminality, aimed primarily at foreigners and foreign interests. As later detailed in Chapter Fourteen, this is also the model that the migrant traffickers currently embrace.

The Somali pirates, however, turned out to be more sophisticated than the criminal jihadists of AQIM. For a start, piracy targeted one of the businesses that most benefitted from globalization: international trade. Secondly, pirates not only kidnapped crews, but also hijacked ships and cargoes, so negotiations involved more just than the release of hostages.

Piracy entailed higher initial investments than kidnapping and required financiers. Often, a large mother ship was involved in the hijacking. The cost of investment, therefore, was high; financiers could spend as much as $30,000 on a crew in the Indian Ocean and more than $10,000 in the Gulf of Aden. In addition, to make sure rival clans did not steal the hostages or the ransom, pirates hired local militias for as much as $10,000 per month. Money was also needed to buy electronic gadgets to intercept the ships and to coordinate the attacks.

Finally, piracy demanded a larger number of better-equipped, skilled people than kidnapping of foreigners in the Saharan desert did. Pirates needed sailors. This in part explains why recruitment initially took place among former fishermen, people who knew the sea and had seen their livelihood disappear due to overfishing.

Unlike the AQIM kidnapping model, which did not require large initial investments, piracy mimicked the classic investment model of early capitalism, hence, the return on capital was much higher than the cost of labor thanks to a plentiful supply of cheap labor. Investors could pocket up to 75 percent of the profits with as little as a 25 percent share to the pirates. However, in a country where per capita GDP was estimated at around $600 per annum, a single pirate could easily earn $10,000 or even more after a successful hijacking, such as the *Malaspina Castle*. From these large sums pirates had to deduct their expenses and fees, which often were very high.

PIRACY'S TRICKLE-DOWN ECONOMICS

According to former pirates, when a captured ship was brought onshore in Somalia, a complete economy came to life to support it. Cooks provided catering services for the crew and the pirates. *Khat* was brought onshore, and many other products and services, including alcohol and prostitution, were on offer. All these people, including the entrepreneurs involved in piracy, were paid once the ransom was collected. Each expense would be recorded and the receipts safely kept until payday.

Ironically, borrowing and the trickle-down effect, both so dear to the Western neo-liberal doctrine, were fundamental to the success of the piracy model in Somalia. Investors covered the initial cost of the hijacking, and during the negotiations, pirates funded themselves by incurring debt. In other words, investors dealt with fixed costs while current costs were met by borrowing from local businesses. Naturally, until the ransom is collected, the debt increases with interest, which can be as high as 100 percent. For instance, if a pirate requests ten dollars of airtime for his cell phone, and promises to pay once he receives the money from an upcoming ransom, he will have to pay back twenty dollars to the shopkeeper who provided him with the service.[72]

When a ransom is received, it is payday for everyone. Local elders and clan leaders command between 5 and 10 percent of the ransom for anchoring rights. A further 10 percent is distributed to the security squad, including ex-militiamen and interpreters. The pirates, their commander, the crew of the mother ship, and the attack squads share about another 30 percent of the ransom, from which they repay their personal debts. "A bookkeeper gets to each guy owing money and collects the money once [the ransom] is paid," explained a former pirate.[73] Sometimes, part is spent to pay warlords who offer protection to the pirates from their own clans to keep their identities concealed, so the pirates do not have to share the money with their tribe. Finally, a percentage also goes to the negotiators.

In her memoir *A Long Walk Home*, Judith Tebbutt describes the trickle-down effect produced by the payment of the ransom. "The sum paid in ransom for me had to be divided many ways: it's quite likely that the first cut went to settle a loan with interest that the pirates took out to finance the operation in the first place. Keeping me captive was a pricey business: if I was cheaply fed, I was expensively guarded, and those guards had to be kept in cooked food and *khat* and wages. When those bills were all accounted for, the rest of the proceeds will have been divided up from the top down."[74]

The trickle-down effect goes on at the local level. Low-level pirates, for example, spend their money very, very quickly in the local economy. In an interview conducted with members of the Youth Organization Against Piracy in Garowe (the capital of the Puntland region in Somalia), one of the former pirates told how he had participated in a hijacking that had produced a $2.5 million ransom. His investor received about $800,000, and his share was about $40,000. He bought a car for $10,000, he loaned $20,000 to a friend who wanted to reinvest in another operation that ultimately failed, and then he spent the remaining $10,000 on "leisure activities" in Garowe, such as alcohol and prostitutes.[75]

The business model of piracy is deliberately structured in a way that forces foot soldiers back to sea. It has also turned piracy into a national industry, funding a large number of ancillary businesses in Somalia. The UN estimates that from April 2005 to December 2012 piracy generated between $350 and $420 million in the Horn of Africa. During this period the number of hijackings and kidnappings rose exponentially. In 2006, 188 people were taken hostage, in 2009 the number reached to 1,050, and by 2010 it was 1,181. In parallel, ransom payments increased from hundreds of thousands of dollars in 2006 to an average of $5 million in 2011. In 2011 piracy was the second largest source of income in Somalia, bringing in over $200 million annually, second only to remittances of the diaspora, estimated at around $1 billion per year.

Unsurprisingly, Somali pirates regarded their activities as fully justified, referring to themselves as *badaadinta badah*, or "saviors of the sea," which is often translated as "coastguard," as opposed to *burcad badeed*, which is the Somali word for "pirate."

FOREIGNERS: THE INDIAN OCEAN'S RICHEST PREY

Long before Judith Tebbutt was abducted and her husband killed, just forty kilometers from Somalia, Somali civil society had vanished. By the time the Tebbutts reached the sandy beaches of Lamu, most of the population had regressed into an almost primeval tribalism. Trapped inside increasingly violent clans, and struggling to make ends meet, people had lost their moral compass.

In a BBC interview, Judith Tebbutt recalled that one day the English-speaking Somali kidnapper who acted as her translator told her that his brother wanted to ask her a question. He wanted to know if she thought that they were bad people because of what they were doing to her. She tried to explain why what they were doing was wrong, but the young Somali brothers seemed unable to grasp the meaning of her words. Mariani had similar experiences with her youngest captors in Mali.

In 1998, while working for the UN High Commissioner for Refugees, Vincent Cochetel came to the same conclusion after he was captured and held hostage for 317 days in Chechnya.[76] Locked in an underground cellar in total darkness for twenty-three hours and forty-five minutes of every day, he was given a candle that would burn for only fifteen minutes, together with a big piece of bread and a bowl of soup. One day, a new jailer approached him. In a very soft voice he said, "'I'd like to thank you for the assistance your organization provided my family when we were displaced in nearby Dagestan.' What could I possibly reply?" says Cochetel. "It was so painful. It was like a blade in the belly. It took me weeks of internal thinking to try to reconcile the good reasons we had to assist that family and the soldier of fortune he became. He was young. He was shy. I never saw his face. He probably meant well. But in those fifteen seconds, he made me question everything we did, all the sacrifices."[77]

In Somalia, as in Chechnya, against an increasingly dystopian political scenario, good and evil vanished and foreigners fell prey to predators, who themselves were victims of the failed state. Hunting for foreigners took place everywhere, at sea, on shore, and in neighboring countries.

Everyone seems to be involved in the hunt, including, as Jessica Buchanan recounts about her ordeal in Somalia, children. "It gets dark and we've changed vehicles a couple of times. More people have come. They're screaming. And I hear from behind me a higher pitched voice going on and on in Somali. And I think, 'My god, they have a woman involved in this.' And I turn around, and I see a small child in the back of the land cruiser with an AK-47 draped in ammunition. And I think of the irony of why I came to Africa in the first place."[78] This child soldier was, in Buchanan's words, "learning the trade." Globalization has a frighteningly dark side. It has turned several areas of the world into modern jungles where criminals seek youth apprentices to learn how to prey upon foreigners and tourists. Governments continue to be reluctant to admit this, and yet, it is the reality.

Soon after Judith Tebbutt's abduction, the Kenyan authorities launched an investigation. The official explanation was that two Somalis and six Kenyans had forced a resort guard at gunpoint to reveal which bungalow was occupied. According to the police, they were common criminals tipped off by a worker at the Kiwayu Safari Village.

Though the kidnappers were never found, the Kenyan authorities convicted Ali Babitu Kololo, a woodcutter from a nearby village who, the police believed, had taken the attackers to the Kiwayu Safari Village. No further investigation was carried out.

In October 2015, however, Al Jazeera revealed the contents of a leaked MI6 briefing note that was produced just two days after Judith Tebbutt's abduction. According to the document, the Kenyan resort where the British couple was staying had been under surveillance from al Shabaab (the Somali jihadist organization founded in late 2006) for several years before the attack. The report cited Kenyan intelligence as saying that in September 2008 four men thought to belong to al Shabaab had been arrested near the Kiwayu Safari Village while apparently conducting reconnaissance on its security. In February 2010 the Kenyan security services managed to prevent an al Shabaab kidnapping attempt of Westerners at the same resort.

Were the criminals working together with the jihadists? Or, more likely, was al Shabaab in Kenya following the suggestion of al Qaeda's leadership to venture into the kidnapping business following the success of the AQIM model? The final ransom for Judith Tebbutt was $1.1 million, not a bad profit for six months work. Indeed, the report also stated that two months before Judith Tebbutt was kidnapped, Kahale Famau Khale, an al Shabaab commander, had discussed the possibility of abducting Western tourists from the island of Lamu, and even talked of obtaining a boat to move them north to the Somali coast. A few days before the attack at the Kiwayu Safari Village, Khale was seen in Ras Kamboni, a nearby border town.

In her book *A Long Walk Home*, Tebbutt states that her kidnappers were pirates and "they had to have precise understanding of the local tides and of the challenging coral reefs around the shore that could otherwise make navigation highly hazardous."[79] However, it would not be unfeasible for al Shabaab to have expert sailors among its followers or to pretend to be someone else. As we shall see, kidnappers often disguise the organization they belong to. More relevant is the policy of the British government not to get involved in any dealing or negotiations with terrorist organizations such as al Shabaab. So Judith Tebbutt was lucky that the authorities were convinced that her kidnappers were pirates and not terrorists, though the distinction may have been merely semantic.

The leaked MI6 document, in fact, suggested that al Shabaab was also dabbling in the Somali piracy trade, and hijacking large ships. However, as we have seen, piracy was a sophisticated national industry. It is highly unlikely that al Shabaab had the investors, the structure, and the expertise to hijack cargo ships. Nor did it have the backing of the local population. Indeed, there is no evidence that Islamist Somali piracy vis-à-vis commercial ships ever existed. As a powerful presence in some parts of the country, however, al Shabaab did indirectly benefit from this type of piracy. In Haradhere, for example, a port north of Mogadishu, pirates paid a "development tax" of 20 percent to al Shabaab, which controlled the region.[80]

Al Shabaab's venture into the business of kidnapping foreigners, both in Somali and in the neighboring countries, however, was not as successful as AQIM's was in the Sahel. Though it did successfully hijack and kidnap several foreigners sailing in private boats, al Shabaab came to this business too late, just a few years before foreigners realized the danger of traveling to those countries or sailing along the Somali coast.

People like the Tebbutts did not know that the total destabilization of Somalia and of the Horn of Africa had progressed so far as to affect Kenya and other neighboring countries and turn their dream destination into a no-go zone. They probably did not even remember that in 1998 al Qaeda had bombed the US embassies in Kenya and Tanzania, Osama bin Laden's first transnational attacks. It was a sort of dress rehearsal for 9/11, proof of the presence of jihadism in those countries well before groups such as al Shabaab emerged in Somalia.[81]

In 2011 the British still thought of Kenya as a friendly country, a former colony where one might go on an exotic holiday. But this was one of the many fantasies that Europeans had constructed around Africa post-9/11. Kenya was very much part of a region—the epicenter of which is Somalia—that had become one of the many casualties of the new world disorder, a process set in motion by the fall of the Berlin Wall and by the advent of globalization. The kidnapping of foreigners and hijacking of ships were just a few of its symptoms. Criminal jihadism was another.

Judith and David Tebutt were not only victims of their kidnappers but also of the false sense of security instilled by Western governments who were well aware of the real dangers.

chapter five

The Somali Diaspora's Gulf Connection

On January 12, 2011, Somali pirates hijacked the *Leopard*, a Danish ship carrying a cargo of explosives destined for the mines of the eastern regions of Malaysia. For the mother ship, the pirates used a Chinese fishing vessel, the *Shiuh Fu No. 1*, which they had hijacked in the Indian Ocean and whose crew of twenty-eight they forced to help hijack the *Leopard*.

The attack came off the coast of Oman, the day after the *Leopard*'s escort had left. The *Leopard* had picked up the escort at the southern end of the Suez Canal and used it as protection to sail along the Red Sea and across the Gulf of Aden, in what were considered pirate-infested waters. The ship was still wrapped in barbed wire to prevent pirates from climbing on the deck with ladders. But after the escort departed, the hijackers managed to board the *Leopard* through a tiny section that had been cleared of the wire. The pirates violently pushed some buttons damaging the gearing system, hence they could not bring it to mainland Somalia and use it as a negotiating chip with the owner.[82]

Before the pirates boarded the ship, Lopez also managed to send a distress message by radio, which was picked up by a Japanese naval patrol aircraft. A NATO warship,

250 nautical miles away, was immediately contacted. But when, two days later, the *Leopard* was finally found adrift in the Indian Ocean, it was empty. The crew and the pirates had disappeared.[83]

THE VANISHED CREW

The crew had been taken hostage. When the pirates understood that the ship had been disabled, they kidnapped the six members of the crew: two Danish men—Chilean-born Captain Lopez and Søren Lyngbjørn—and four Filipino crewmembers. They took them onshore, south of Hobyo, in Somalia. Soon, ransom demands began to reach the owner of the *Leopard*, the Danish company Shipcraft.

Right from the beginning, the hijacking of the *Leopard* was unique: the attack came far from Somalia, possibly while the pirates were on their way back from hijacking the fishing vessel. According to Søren Lyngbjørn, the Chinese boat was hijacked near Madagascar in December 2010; they had to abandon the *Leopard* and its cargo, which the owner retrieved undamaged after a few days. Finally, after keeping the crew for six months on the ship *Polar* off the coast of Somalia, the pirates decided to take it inland. That is, the hijacking of the *Leopard* had turned into a kidnapping. The initial negotiations took a very long time, likely because of all these peculiar factors.

"For a year and an half the owner carried on the negotiations with the pirates in total secrecy," recounts historian Karsten Hermansen, who wrote a book on the ordeal of the *Leopard*.[84] "Apart from the families of the hostages and the government, nobody in Denmark knew what had happened. During this time, the pirates kept moving the crew to different hideouts, clearly fearing to be discovered. Finally, in July 2012, the Danish negotiators were told that within ten days the hostages would be free. They had reached an agreement." Then, suddenly and unexpectedly, one of the Danish tabloids, the *Ekstra Bladet*, reported the kidnapping and launched a media campaign to "free the hostages." "Apparently, they had got hold of the story from someone who lived in the same village as Søren Lyngbjørn, one of the Danish hostages, someone who falsely claimed to be his best friend," concludes Hermansen.

The *Ekstra Bladet* ran several articles about the hijacking on the front page and put posters everywhere publicizing their coverage of the story. The Danish public soon demanded that the hostages be freed. The media campaign was also a turning point for the kidnappers. Just a few days after the *Ekstra Bladet* printed the news of the hijacking, the Danish negotiators were told that the original deal was off. They had to start all over again. "Clearly the pirates were well aware of the media campaign in Denmark. They had contacts among the Somali diaspora," Hermansen suggested.[85] Indeed, it is highly unlikely that Somali pirates could read Danish and had access to Danish tabloid media.

THE SOMALI DIASPORA

According to the United Nations and the World Bank, Somali pirates have been entwined with the diaspora right from the beginning of this hijacking phenomenon. In the course of an investigation, the United Nations Monitoring Group on Somalia and Eritrea identified many "financial transfers between Somali pirates and individuals in the Somali diaspora, linked to a number of hijacking cases."[86]

Banks in North America, Africa, Asia, and Europe have all been implicated in holding funds "related to cases of maritime piracy and kidnapping for ransom off the coast of Somalia,"[87] reads a World Bank report on piracy.

The pirates of the *Leopard* cleverly exploited the media exposure that the kidnapped crew received in Denmark and used the Somali diaspora to invite the media to interview the hostages. A Norwegian-Somali freelance journalist conducted several interviews with the hostages at a camp where they were being held, documenting his visit with photos and videos. "He then sold the story to the Danish media. Everybody in Denmark could see their conditions. They were appalling," recalls Hermansen.

When freed, Captain Eddy Lopez revealed that prior to the interviews the kidnappers had seriously beaten him and Lyngbjørn to make them appear more scared and vulnerable.[88] As in the case of the *Malaspina Castle*, the pirates wanted to exert psychological pressure on the negotiators by exaggerating the appalling conditions the hostages faced in order to mobilize Danish public opinion in favor of paying a large ransom.

Captain Lopez began a proceeding against the media for exploitation of his condition as a hostage. In May 2016, Søren Lyngbjørn and Eddy Lopez won the case against *Ekstra Bladet*. Copenhagen Municipal Court decided that *Ekstra Bladet*'s actions were wrong. *Ekstra Bladet* was convicted to compensate Søren Lyngbjørn and Eddy Lopez with 300,000 kronor (approximately €40,000) each. The two sailors were happy and said they would give half the money to the four Filipino members of the crew. *Ekstra Bladet* decided not to appeal.

"Of course the journalists were not pirates," admits Hermansen. "However, they were somehow connected with the kidnappers, through the Somali diaspora in Denmark or in Norway. Otherwise, people like [the journalist] Abdi Fitah Gelle would never have gained access to the hostages."[89] Interestingly, while the kidnappers of the crew of the *Leopard* moved the hostages from one camp to another many times for fear of being discovered, and, possibly, to prevent raids by rival kidnappers, they let journalists visit the hostages while in captivity. Clearly they trusted them and the intermediaries from the Somali diaspora who had arranged such visits.

Between the business structure of Somali piracy, which requires investors, and the belief, widely held among the local population, that piracy is not a crime but a necessity for survival, members of the diaspora had few reservations about becoming part of the industry of piracy. Working directly and indirectly, they provided funds for families and friend involved in this business; they helped launder the profits of the ransoms; and, in the case of the Danish hostages of the *Leopard*, they likely acted as a go-between for the media and the pirates to make sure the highest ransom would be paid.

Hence, piracy has been a good business also for some Somalis abroad. As a UN investigation revealed, "pirate stakeholders include financiers/investors, pirates, the diaspora community as well as the local community. The profiles of investors vary from international businessmen to local private investors such as Sahra Ibrahim, a twenty-two-year-old divorcée, who contributed a rocket-propelled grenade received from her ex-husband in alimony for the operation involving an attack on a Spanish tuna-fishing vessel. Her financial reward for her investment of the rocket-propelled grenade was $75,000 in 38 days."[90]

According to Hermansen, the Somali population, both in Somalia and in Denmark, was complicit in the ordeal of the hostages of the *Leopard*. "In Somalia, of course, because the ransom money is mostly spent locally, piracy became a source of income for the population. As such, piracy is accepted. There is no alternative. Its profits are part of the national economy. While this is not the case in Denmark or in any of the Nordic countries, the Somali diaspora in these nations largely shows the same indifference towards the ordeal of the MV *Leopard* hostages as do their desperate relatives in Somalia."[91]

After *Ekstra Bladet* and the Danish media began talking about the hijacking of the *Leopard* and the kidnapping of the crew, Somalis residing in Denmark did launch several initiatives condemning the hijacking. Some leaders of the communities even spoke openly against the kidnapping. However, many people in Denmark shared Hermansen's view that this criticism was not enough.

The kidnapping of Captain Lopez and Søren Lyngbjørn, coupled with the media campaign, damaged relationships between the Danish people and the Somali community. Many Danes began looking at the Somali diaspora with suspicion. In effect, the media campaign not only increased the ransom for the release of the crew, it also fuelled racial discrimination and fractured society. Those who gained from it were the pirates, who pocketed a higher ransom than initially negotiated; their sponsors, wherever they were; and, of course, the media itself.

"The media campaign was very vicious and played into the hands of the negotiators of the pirates," notes Hermansen. "For example, at a certain point it revealed that the owner of the *Leopard*, who is from Sweden but resides in Denmark, was buying a house in Spain for nearly $20 million. Danish people were outraged. They thought 'How can he do that?' But surely the pirates were happy to know that he had so much disposable cash." Likely, this information about the owner's liquidity was used during the negotiations.

Finally, in April 2013, after 839 days, an agreement was reached. The ransom was set at $6.8 million. That was a lot of money at the time, well above the average Somali ransom.

As with the *Malaspina Castle*, the money was dropped from a chartered jet in a designated location chosen by the pirates. There were two drops: the first one was $1.5 million and it was for Fadhi, the leader of the pirates. The second one, $5.3 million, was for the rest of the hijackers and kidnappers. The captain of the ship accompanied the pirates to retrieve the ransom and counted the money, to confirm that the correct ransom was delivered.

LAUNDERING PIRACY'S PROFITS

While the pirates spent their take in Somalia in cash, investors, especially those living abroad and belonging to the diaspora, did not. Hence, it had been imperative for them to launder the cash. As reported by the UN Monitoring Group on Somalia and Eritrea, the best and most convenient location to do so was in the Gulf. Following the case of the Belgian ship *Pompei*, for example, hijacked on April 18, 2012, the Belgian authorities located bank accounts and identification numbers in Dubai linked to that ship's pirate negotiator.[92] "In addition, Belgian authorities estimate that, following the ransom drop, the money was taken to Djibouti where it was sent via Money or Value Transfer Services to Dubai."[93]

From 2006 to 2012, in the heyday of Somali piracy, Djibouti and Dubai acted as the main transit points for ransom monies. To launder their dirty profits and send them abroad to the investors, pirates disguised the ransom monies as the sale of Somali livestock to Dubai or to the United Arab Emirates. Funds from such businesses regularly transited between Djibouti and Dubai via Letters of Credits. Invoices were easily manipulated to incorporate ransom money. Many Somali exporters living abroad had opened offices in Dubai and moved money back and forth without any problem.

In a sort of geographic triangulation, the Somali diaspora invested in piracy from wherever it was located, from North America or northern Europe, and then washed the profits clean via its Somali contacts in the Gulf. It was a very profitable business, which saw large sums of money being returned to investors in places like Seattle or Vancouver, as well as to Somalis living in the Nordic countries.

Intercepting these funds was very, very difficult. Most of the money sent or repatriated to the West moved through the *hawala* system, the ancient Islamic money transfer method. In the Gulf, pirates' profits circulated through the Islamic banking system, disguised as payments for commodity trading. Hence, it is impossible to quantify how much money Somali piracy has generated for those living abroad.

Piracy, however—just like kidnapping of foreigners in the Sahel—was short lived. In response to hijackings, international trading companies and insurance firms decided to hire armed guards onboard ships during the entire voyage and often paid for escorts by armed vessels.

Hence, by the end of 2012, Somali piracy was in trouble. The shipping industry and the international community had successfully begun to fight back. Somali pirates and their investors soon realized that piracy had only a few more years to run, so they looked for other business opportunities, complementary to hijacking and kidnapping, such as trafficking migrants to Yemen. Like their counterparts in the Sahel, ironically, Somali pirates and jihadists would soon become merchants of men profiting from the tragedy of the Somali and East African diaspora.

FROM PIRATES TO TRAFFICKERS

Since 2009 Somali pirates were already involved in trafficking migrants, mostly as a side business to piracy. In the hijacking of the *Pramoni*, a Singaporean chemical tanker with a crew of twenty-four people onboard, for example, the pirates' vessel was returning to the Puntland coast of Somalia from Yemen, where it had dropped illegal migrants. On January 1, 2010, during the crossing, the pirates encountered the *Pramoni*, and decided to attack it. The hijacking was successful and the crew and the ship were released on February 26.[94] Convicted pirates have also acknowledged smuggling migrants from Puntland to Yemen while sailing there to pick up cargoes of weapons for Somalia.

Trafficking migrants turned out to be an easier business to run than piracy. Former fishermen or even simple pirate foot soldiers—all stripes of cheap Somali labor—could handle it alone, without needing investors, or involving militia. Profits were not bad when considering that a single journey from Bosaso, in the Puntland region in Somalia, to Yemen took only a day and netted $10,000. Of course, this was only one-third of what a single pirate could earn after a successful hijacking, but to collect these large sums one often had to wait for months. So the appeal of trafficking migrants has always been strong for pirate foot soldiers looking to make money quickly.

As hijacking armed ships and kidnapping crews became increasingly difficult, trafficking migrants grew from a side business into Somali pirates' main activity. "From 2012 onwards, the number of hijackings at the hands of the Somali pirates went drastically down, as proven by the reduction of insurance premiums for K&R insurances," explains Giacomo Madia.

As AQIM kidnappers had morphed into traffickers of West African migrants seeking a better life in Europe, Somali pirates turned into traffickers of East African migrants seeking a better life in Saudi Arabia and in the rich Gulf states.

DESPERATE CHOICES

In 2012 the Danish Refugee Council published the result of an investigation conducted in Yemen from May to June 2012 about the trafficking of Ethiopian migrants. Entitled *Desperate Choices*, the research included interviews with 130 individuals who had been victims of traffickers. The conclusions were shocking. "Kidnap, torture, sexual violence, abduction and extortion are becoming widespread and frequent hazards, sometimes lethal, for migrants in transit to the Gulf States," reads the executive summary.

Though the crossing from Djibouti or Bosaso to Yemen takes only a day and costs between $80 and $150, many of those who have these funds will lose their freedom during the crossing, exactly as what happened to migrants across the Libyan desert. "In a small boat, we were around seventy migrants; some were young girls. Four Yemeni smugglers were on board. They raped the girls on the boat in front of us. We were not able to move or to speak, and those girls had already been sold to Yemeni traffickers," remembers an Ethiopian boy about his crossing in 2011.[95] Once on shore, the traffickers sold women for various activities, such as to be "slave" domestic workers to Saudi Arabian families.

Criminal gangs, often in collusion with smugglers and traffickers, frequently intercepted migrants near the Yemeni coast as described by an Ethiopian boy interviewed in Haradh by the Danish Refugee Council. "When we could see the Yemeni coast the boat stopped. One of the two boatmen was calling somebody in Yemeni. We thought that he got lost. Later, we realized that he was waiting for the smugglers to arrive before he let us reach the beach."[96] When two trucks with armed men appeared, the traffickers released the migrants, who were forced to swim to the shore where the kidnappers were waiting for them. The migrants were loaded onto trucks and transported to a house in the desert where they were held until their family or friends paid ransoms for their release.

Sometimes, instead of turning them over to kidnappers, traffickers abduct the migrants themselves. As in Libya, so too in Yemen, traffickers subject migrants to physical abuse to force their families to pay ransom. "They kept us prisoner until we got some money from our friends or relatives in Ethiopia," explained a male Ethiopian migrant. "If money was sent from our friends or relatives, we would be released and be free. If not, they would beat us to death. Our group was thirty-five at first but three of our friends died due to the beating."[97] In 2012 the ransom ranged from $100 to 300.

Those who have no one to help them are considered disposable merchandise. "I had nobody who could send me money for my release so I was beaten severely and my hand nailed to the ground," remembered a twenty-two-year-old Ethiopian man. "After two months of suffering I was thrown to the desert when they realized I had no money."[98]

Those who manage to survive often end up on the streets. Reports from the town of Haradh, in northwest Yemen, in 2012 suggest that as many as "twelve thousand predominantly Ethiopian migrants, many in a desperate state, were sleeping . . . in the streets and surviving by begging and foraging through dustbins."[99] Every day the International Organization for Migration in Haradh treats migrants who have escaped or survived kidnapping, rape, or torture. Many are unaccompanied minors or elderly.

Despite the horrifying ordeal that these migrants suffer, trafficking continues with impunity and remains less risky than piracy for Somali criminals, as no major international initiative, similar to those to prevent pirates from hijacking commercial ships, has been put in place to save the victims of trafficking. As *Daily Telegraph* correspondent Colin Freeman, who was himself was kidnapped in Somalia, put it, in contrast to its robust anti-piracy operation named Atalanta, the European Union is relatively indifferent to pirates when they wear the trafficker's hat.[100] "Given that the same gangs are often controlling both trades, you might have expected people trafficking to be just as high priority for the foreign navy patrols as piracy," said Freeman.

"Yet, when [in 2009] HMS Cornwall came across a skiff just outside Bosaso that was loaded to the gunnels with people, we did nothing. Cornwall's commanders then explained that it was not their policy to stop traffickers—

firstly because they had no space to put refugees, and secondly because the gangs had a nasty habit of throwing their passengers overboard if they got chased. Cornwall would have been obliged to rescue those thrown overboard before anything else, allowing the smugglers to flee."[101] Freeman concludes that the EU's anti-piracy operations are "spectacularly useless against human traffickers."

This international enforcement loophole also allows international cooperation between traffickers and their international investors, including many in the Somali diaspora. Just as joint ventures traded human cargo from East Africa to Europe and from West Africa to the Gulf, a similar phenomenon is taking place in Syria following the outbreak of the civil war. As discussed further below, kidnapping profits springing from the payment of ransoms always becomes seed money for the trafficking of desperate people. The most recent chapter in this appalling saga is the exodus from Syria and Iraq to the Old Continent. Despite the fact that the interdependency between kidnapping and trafficking has been well established, these facts haven't fully come to light. Paying ransoms is the best kept secret of Western governments.

chapter six

Smoke and Mirrors
of the Syrian Civil War

In Syria, Bashar al Assad's bloody response to the Arab Spring in 2011 opened the Pandora's box of political violence. Crime and the sponsors of the proxy war fueled the proliferation of armed and criminal groups disguised as insurgents. Soon criminal jihadism also became rampant in this corner of the world, and from the outset, kidnapping was one of its main illicit activities.

Ransoms turned out to be one of the main sources of funding for the Assad regime, especially in the North, in areas where the rebels and the jihadists fought door to door against the forces loyal to Damascus. The main target was the Syrian population.

"I owned an ice cream factory in northern Syria, near Aleppo," explains Mohammed, who declined to give his full name. I met him in Milan, near the main station, on a sunny autumn day in 2015. He looked different from the other refugees, exuding an aura of elegance even in his cheap clothes. Mohammed's movements betrayed that he had been a very wealthy man. His father, who still lives in Damascus, owns twenty apartments in the capital, properties worth nothing today, he told me. By the time I met him, Mohammed was penniless, his wealth spent first to send his family to Turkey, then to survive on his own in Syria for two years, and then finally to reach Europe as a refugee.

As Mohammed recalls, "One morning I drove to work and I was stopped by the police on the street where my factory was. They told me that the rebels now controlled the street. They did not say who they were, the Free Syrian Army or some jihadist group. All the police said was that I could not go through. It was the beginning of 2012. A year later I arranged to send my wife and my daughter to Istanbul, where they still live. I stayed and waited until the end of 2013 when finally the government forces re-conquered the area and I was allowed to go back to my factory. There was nothing left. They had looted everything. I decided to go to the police station and ask what I should do, if there was a way to be compensated. They threw me in jail, accusing me of being a supporter of the rebels.

"There were many people like me in the same cell, businessmen who had lost everything because of the civil war and now the regime was accusing them of being part of the insurgency. They beat us regularly, often just to pass the time. It was a nightmare. Then my family managed to pay for my release. Ten thousand dollars was my ransom. As soon as I got out I left for Europe."[102]

Right from the beginning of the civil war, kidnapping of wealthy Syrians proved to be a quick and profitable way to bankroll the conflict. Assad's police and military officers-turned-kidnappers became vicious hostage keepers. They used the regime's jails to imprison Syrian hostages in appalling conditions; they tortured them, pretending they were rebels or rebel sympathizers, and arranged for the families to pay a ransom for their freedom.

"My brother and I owned a clothing factory in Aleppo," remembers Mohammad Jamil Hassan, a Syrian refugee seeking asylum in Denmark. "We employed eighty-five people. It was a very good business. One day, in June 2013, the Free Syrian Army came and confiscated the factory— they said that they needed to use it as their hospital. The building had only one floor and was very large, with big windows all around. They came all fully armed and kicked us out. My brother was not there that day. I tried to pro-test, but they pushed me out, pointing a gun at my head. So I left. At the end of the road I was stopped by the police. They asked me what was going on. I told them that the Free Syrian Army had taken my factory at gunpoint. They said that I was lying. They handcuffed me and took me to jail accusing me of being part of the rebels, to have will-ingly given my factory to the Free Syrian Army. I spent a month in jail. There were so many people in the room, the conditions were appalling: we had to drink dirty water, eat leftovers, we were never allowed to wash, people got sick all the time, some people died. I was beaten regularly until my uncle managed to pay the ransom, $12,000, to the local police."[103]

Sometimes both the regime and the insurgency made money from the abduction of wealthy Syrians. "A policeman came and took me to the courtyard of the prison. He unlocked the main door and then went to smoke a cigarette on the opposite side. I slowly walked to the entrance and slipped away," continues Hassan. "Out-side there was my uncle, waiting in the car. I got in and he drove north, towards the border with Turkey. I did not even say good-bye to my wife. A few kilometers from the border he handed me over to two thugs from Aleppo. I knew them; they were petty criminals but recently they had joined one of the Jihadist armed groups. They were driving a big pick-up truck—one of those you see on TV in the parades of the Islamic State. It was brand new and still had a Saudi number plate. They took me across the border to Turkey. My uncle paid them $2,000. Before leaving he handed me a small bag full of cash, 'for the journey to Europe,' he said. I never saw my uncle again."[104]

As the Syrian civilian conflict progressed, it became apparent that the opposing forces tended to target different people to be kidnapped. While the regime of Assad concentrated on abducting rich and middle-class Syrians, the jihadists and the rebels focused on foreigners, who were worth millions of dollars. Both prey were easy to catch. The regime worked on the quantity of abductions, the insurgency on the quality of the ransom. Sometimes, however, Western journalists ended up in the hands of Assad, and Syrians were abducted by the insurgency.

"I had spent two weeks in Qamishli, in the northeast of Syria, before being kidnapped by the secret service of the Assad regime on the 15th of February 2015," remembers Joakim Medin, a Swedish investigative journalist. "At the time Qamishli was a divided city: one part was controlled by the regime of Assad and another by the Kurdish rebels. I was embedded with the rebels. That morning my translator, Sabri Omar, was taking me to interview the Kurdish traffic police and we were walking on a street that was shared by both sides. I was walking with my translator when we were stopped by a regime patrol. They forced us into a car, put a hood over Sabri's head, and drove us to the section controlled by them. They locked me in an isolation cell, in total darkness, and my translator in a cell with twenty-five sympathizers of the Islamic State. Through a small opening I could see an office where they tortured people. I saw a fourteen-year-old kid being tortured during interrogation. He was sitting on the floor and they kept beating him."

After three and a half days, Joakim Medin and his translator were taken to Damascus. They flew on a scheduled flight, with civilians on board. People looked at them, handcuffed, beaten, and dirty, but did not do anything. In Damascus they were jailed in Unit 300, the prison for spies and espionage.

"Nobody knew who had kidnapped me," said Medin. "They did not contact my family or the Swedish government. I could have spent the rest of my days being moved from one prison to another, being interrogated by the various secret services. I could have vanished inside the hellish prison system of the [Assad] regime . . . . But luckily the Kurds knew they had me, so they conducted secret negotiation to free me. Eventually they swapped us for two high ranking Syrian officers they had captured."[105]

Joakim Medin was lucky, others, less so.

SLEEPING WITH THE ENEMY

In April 2013 Italian journalist Domenico Quirico and Belgian professor Pierre Piccinin da Prata entered Syria from Lebanon. They entrusted their safety to one of the many groups of the Syrian insurgency. But it was a mistake. Near the city of al Qusayr, the Abu Omar Brigade, a group linked to the Farouk Brigade, kidnapped them and demanded a ransom of $10 million.[106] Born in the summer of 2011, the Farouk Brigade was a branch of the Free

Syrian Army, at the time the largest anti-Assad insurgen group. Quirico and Piccinin's kidnappers belonged to th nebula of "moderate" insurgent groups that the West ha been backing since the outbreak of the Syrian civil war.

Both men were by no means the first Western reporter or academics to be betrayed and taken hostage by an insur gent group inside the territory under its control. Just few months before, a similar abduction had taken place i northern Syria.

A decade after the appearance of the criminal jihadisr of Al Qaeda in the Islamic Maghreb across the Sahel an a few years after the birth of its maritime version off th coats of Somalia, criminal jihadism erupted in Syria. Onl this time the variation on the basic cocktail of crime an jihad was the presence of secular armed groups belongin to the anti-Assad insurgency, part of what have wrongl become known as the Syrian "moderate" forces, whom th West regarded as the "good guys."

The folly of these designations was exposed even befor Quirico and Piccinin's kidnapping, when in December 201 armed gunmen abducted Richard Engel, a US war corre spondent, along with five other members of an NBC New team. They were traveling under the escort of a commande from the Free Syrian Army by the name of Abdelrazaq. A few miles into Syria, after crossing the famous Bab al Haw border, they encountered a checkpoint controlled by wha they thought was the *shabiha*, the shadow men, a Shia militi trained by Iran, which in the old days ran drugs and wome for the Syrian regime's elite. Since the outbreak of the civi war, however, they had become a sort of torture/death squad for Assad. Bound and blindfolded, the hostages spent fiv days at a location called the farm.[107]

From the start, Engels's kidnappers were not very professional. While searching inside the hostages' belongings, without realizing it they had set off the emergency GPS, which immediately sent a distress signal. NBC was able to find out where the farm was and within a couple of days this news had reached the kidnappers. They panicked and thought to kill the hostages, but the main field commander of the area, Abu Ayman, stopped them. Engel later learned the reason: Abu Ayman was negotiating with the Americans for arms and did not want any US journalist killed on his turf.[108]

While holding the hostages, the kidnappers made sure that Engel and his colleagues thought that they belonged to the Assad regime: they spoke with a strong Alawiti accent, drank, and smoke cigarettes. On the fifth day the hostages were put inside a van and told that they would be driven to Foua, a stronghold of Hezbollah. En route they were stopped at a checkpoint. After an exchange of gunfire, a group that claimed to be part of the Free Syrian Army rescued them. Engel wrote a long and moving article about his kidnapping and rescue in *Vanity Fair*, describing the brutality of his Shia captors. It was only in 2015 that, after a lengthy investigation, Engel and his crew discovered that their abduction and rescue had been staged.[109]

In reality, the kidnappers were Sunni, belonging to a criminal gang with shifting alliances, as were the people who pretended to rescue Engel and his crew. Abu Ayman was aware of the plan, and publicly cooperated with the leader of the group who controlled the farm where Engel was taken, Ezzo Qussab, a Sunni with a reputation for being a thug. Multiple local sources say that while he called himself a rebel leader, "Qussab was more of a criminal boss."[110]

Far from the romanticized army of freedom fighters born from the Syrian Arab Spring, the Syrian insurgency was infested with jihadists, thugs, warlords, criminals, and terrorists constantly seeking money and arms.

Given the gang's lack of resources and expertise, it is likely Qussab had planned to sell the hostages to a bigger group, as was done with the two Japanese hostages kidnapped in 2014 and sold to the Islamic State. It is widely understood that only organizations such as al Nusra or the Islamic State have the resources and facilities to buy and hold prisoners for months, sometimes for years, while negotiating the ransom.

Four months after Engel was taken, Piccinin and Quirico were kidnapped by captors of the same criminal description. "The leader of the group holding us was a self-appointed 'emir' who liked to be addressed as Abu Omar, a nickname," writes Quirico. "He had formed his brigade by taking people from the area, mostly bandits rather than Islamists or revolutionaries. Abu Omar gave an Islamic gloss to the criminal activities of his band and had links with al Farouk, the group that then took control of us. Al Farouk is a well-known brigade in the Syrian revolution, part of the Syrian National Council, and its representatives have held meetings with European governments."[111] As Quirico realized too late, his captors, though trusted by the West, were a group of "Somali-style bandits who use an Islamic veneer and the context of the revolution to control pieces of territory, extort money from the population, kidnap people, and generally fill their coffers."[112]

What happened to Quirico and Piccinin, and Engels and his crew before them, had been happening for at least a year. As early as 2012, several segments of the Syrian insurgency began to see journalists and aid workers as easy prey to make a quick buck. However, few foreigners appreciated this danger because "the commonly accepted narrative was very simplistic: the Assad regime is evil and everybody who fights against it must be good," explained Joanie de Rijke, a Dutch investigative journalist. Amidst the smoke and mirrors of the Syrian civil war, Western media were convinced that only the forces loyal to the Assad regime kidnapped Western journalists. This was a naïve belief that the staged abduction of Richard Engel reinforced and which remains hard to eradicate. At the end of 2013, while imprisoned in Aleppo by the Islamic State, Federico Motka heard James Foley, whom he knew, reciting the Koran from a nearby cell. He told Marc Marginedas and the other Western hostages that James Foley was being held in the same prison. Marginedas was shocked because he believed, as did everybody else, that Foley had been kidnapped by the Assad regime, not by the rebels.[113]

Instead, foolishly, journalists trusted "insurgent" groups with their lives, even after colleagues were kidnapped under their protection. "Unlike Iraq, where the media coverage that accompanied these events made us realize immediately that there was enormous risk of being kidnapped, in Syria this option still seemed fuzzy in the summer of 2013. It did not seem a real danger," writes Javier Espinosa in *El Mundo*.[114] Espinosa was kidnapped together with the photographer Ricardo García Vilanova by the Islamic State in September 2013 in the province of Raqqa, while they were on their way back to Turkey. At the time, they were traveling under the protection of the Free Syrian Army. Ironically, just before leaving, their interpreter had warned them that the jihadists paid as much as $100,000 for foreign journalists.

"In Syria the media *de facto* took a side. It broke the cardinal rule of our profession and this is why there have been no reports about Syrians who backed the Assad regime," writes de Rijke. Those who attempted to do so were shunned. For example, in Italy Monica Maggioni, a journalist who now is the president of the Italian broadcasting television station Rai, was widely criticized for interviewing Assad in 2013 and 2015.[115]

Indeed, taking sides also prevented the media from reporting about the Islamic State and its role within the insurgency from 2012 to 2014. The narrative was always the same: the Free Syrian Army, a secular force, wants to liberate Syria from the dictatorial regime of Assad. Listening to the stories of journalists and photographers who have been kidnapped by groups linked to their escorts, fixers, or drivers, one has the feeling that they all fell victim to a sort of Hemingway syndrome: war correspondents supporting the insurgency trust the rebels and place their lives in their hands because they are in league with them. This, of course, was pure fantasy. The Syrian Civil War has little in common with the Spanish Civil War. The insurgency is just a variation of criminal jihadism, a modern phenomenon that has only one loyalty: *money*.

A year after his release, Piccinin managed to track down and interview one of his captors in Lebanon. When asked why he demanded money to release Quirico and himself, whom he knew to be "friends of the revolution," the former kidnapper replied that sympathetic journalists were useless. The insurgency needed "money to buy food and weapons,"[116] and multi-million dollar ransoms paid for these necessities.

The insurgency showed no sympathy for Western journalists, who were often regarded as ignorant and unprepared to deal with the complexity of the civil war. Piccinin's kidnapper described Quirico as someone who "doesn't know anything about Syria. He refused to learn Arabic to speak with us. . . . He didn't know anything about our culture, our groups, and our goals."[117] Unlike Ernest Hemingway during the Spanish Civil War, journalists reporting about Syria were not respected. They were merely merchandise to be exchanged for rich ransoms.

FUNDING CRIME AND TERRORISM WITH RANSOMS

In sharp contrast with the media's Manichaean and simplistic characterization of the Syrian Civil War, the genealogical tree of the so called "moderate" armed organizations in Syria—those that since August 2014 President Obama's grand coalition has openly been backing, either through the bombing campaign, military training, shipment of weapons, and even financial means—is very intricate. More than a tree, it appears to be an incestuous web of alliances, personal relationships, deceit, *ad hoc* criminal partnerships, and joint-ventures among small- to medium-sized armed groups, all operating in a political vacuum. For these gangs, the proxy war in Syria became a cover-up to make money, either through the funding of the sponsors or through criminal activities such as kidnapping, all at the expense of the local population or of the foreigners like Quirico, Piccinin, and Engel. Alliances were forged and broken based upon these goals, leaving Western media and governments little time to catch up.

As one former Spanish fighter pilot, Luis Munar, recounts, "In 2012 I decided to go to Syria and help the rebels against the regime of Assad."[118] Munar recalled that he closed his security company and joined the rebels "because they clearly did not know how to fight." "Among others, I trained the Farouk Brigade, part of the Free Syrian Army, which in 2012 had more than twelve thousand fighters. The insurgency was composed of many groups who, in 2011 and 2012, were bankrolled by the Gulf States. I saw people from Saudi Arabia and Qatar distribute large sums of cash, either in dollars or in Turkish lira, to the various groups, including the Farouk Brigade. The money was handed over to the captain who then distributed it to the various fighters. It was their income."

Sometimes the sponsors came with journalists and TV crews from their countries to show the progress of their involvement in the Syrian Civil War. "I saw the fighters stage fake battles for the Qatari TV, so the TV crew could film the battle without any risks. I witnessed one of these fake conflicts at night. It was staged by the Farouk Brigade while I was training them. They were shooting in the dark, but there was no enemy on the other side," remembers Munar.

The sponsors fueled a propaganda machine at home and abroad that confused everyone, including the West. Watching staged battles and fake victories, viewers believed that the insurgency was winning, while in reality it was sinking into the quicksand of criminal jihadism. The West and the media were basically conned by their Gulf allies and by the insurgency.

Money, though initially plentiful, was never enough for the various insurgent groups. As the Islamic State got stronger, "the sponsors decided to invest in it and stopped funding the other groups, including the Farouk Brigade. Between the spring and winter of 2013, the cash dried up," remembered Munar. At that point getting into the business of kidnapping became a necessity.

It was at this time that the Farouk Brigade branched into kidnapping foreign journalists. As confirmed by Piccinin's kidnapper, when asked later on what he had done with the ransom money: "It is very simple: we have no support from outside Syria—I mean, from other countries. Even from the Gulf; they stopped helping us. So, we needed this money, to buy weapons, food, medicine, and so on. We have no choice, if we want to survive and continue to fight."[119]

Kidnapping Quirico and Piccinin was a good move for the Farouk Brigade and its accomplices. According to Motaz Shaklab, a member of the opposition Syrian National Council who acted as negotiator for the Italian government with the kidnappers, the Italian authorities paid $4 million for the two hostages. The Belgian government refused to get involved, so the Italians negotiated and paid for both hostages.[120] It was a good deal for *la Farnesina*, the Italian foreign office, considering that initially the ransom was set at $10 million.

For the secular insurgency too, joining the jihadists was another way to funds its operations, even if it meant becoming religious. "To make ends meet the fighters of the Farouk Brigade formed the Farouk Islamic Group, that became part of the Islamic Front, which still had money coming from various sponsors," continued Munar. "Naturally, the Farouk Brigade was never a religious group. It was secular, even if there were people in it who were religious. However, fighters moved freely from one group to another, motivated by salaries. Eventually all the members of the Farouk Brigade merged into other Islamic groups. Some went to al Nusra; others joined the Islamic State. These were the organizations with money."

SYRIA'S MERCHANTS OF MEN

Despite the special circumstances presented by the insurgency, Syria's merchants of men share many features with their counterparts in Western and Northern Africa. While in Syria potential Western hostages were journalists and aid workers, not tourists as in the Sahel, in Syria, as in the Sahel, a network of criminal groups specializing in the abduction of foreigners and composed of former rebels and jihadists soon emerged. They snatched people, often to resell them right away.

As a Syrian negotiator whom I met in Paris explained, "The network stretched into Turkey, the media-gate into Syria." Former Syrian rebels or simple criminals "pretended to be refugees and established themselves in the towns where journalists sought fixers and drivers to get into Syria." As the negotiator described, these rebels in disguise offered help to their selected targets. "Sometimes they promised them unique stories about the civil war." Engel, for example, was told that he could film four Iranian and two Lebanese fighters that the Free Syrian Army had captured as proof that the Iranian government and Lebanese armed groups were directly supporting President Bashar al Assad and his death squads. Finding these leads irresistible, journalists fell into abductors' waiting traps.

The best targets, however, were the less experienced, the freelance journalists, mostly kids traveling alone with a camera and a tape recorder. However, professional journalists like Quirico, Piccinin, Engel's NBC crew, and many others, including veteran French war correspondent Didier François, a fifty-three-year-old reporter for the French radio station Europe 1, were hardly immune from abduction. François for his part ended up in the prisons of the Islamic State together with other foreign hostages, including James Foley and two other French journalists, Nicolas Hénin and Pierre Torres, kidnapped near Raqqa in June 2013.

According to a Syrian journalist working for the BBC, Omar al Muqdad, the driver who took Didier François and twenty-three-year-old photographer Edouard Elias into Syria in June 2013 was the same person who would drive both Japanese hostages into Syria a year later when they were kidnapped in two separate incidents.[121] This can hardly be a coincidence.

The two French journalists were kidnapped at a checkpoint north of Aleppo, shortly after they crossed the border. Heavily armed men stopped the car, handcuffed them, and told them in English not to worry—they needed to check their identity. The driver claims he was told to leave, which he did, and never looked back.[122]

PART 2

chapter seven

The Negotiator

"I am a private kidnapping negotiator. I have no problem in saying that I do what I do for money, and my services are not cheap. I am not a charity. I am a professional.

"Do I care for the hostages? Do I empathize with them? Hell yes, I do. But I never let my feelings cloud my judgment.

"I look at each case with calculated detachment. I could not do my job otherwise. If you let your personal feelings into this business, you put your life and the lives of the hostages at risk. Though in every case there is a life at risk, each case is different. In this job there are no golden rules, no easy solutions. If you want to stay a step ahead of the kidnappers, you need to be ready to think outside the box, to reinvent your strategy each step of the way.

"It is a risky business, no doubt about that. You are never safe, you never know if you will succeed, and you are constantly on edge, waiting for your opponent's next move. I hardly sleep. It is a luxury I do not know.

"Some people vilify my profession. Others see me as a mercenary, someone you pay to free your loved ones held hostage. When governments prevent families from negotiating with terrorists, as was the case of James Foley and many other hostages, my services have even been considered to be illegal. I do not care; I am not interested in foreign policy. I believe that attempting to save your loved one's life is a human right. It goes against our nature not to do so.

"This is a job that never ends. I guess when you finally sit on a plane, at thirty-three thousand feet, with a drink in your hand and the person sitting next to you is the former hostage, then yes, you could say that the job has been done. And yet, you know that when you land there will be other urgent requests; that you will need to start all over again. For each individual you take safely home there are many others, too many, who remain captive.

"I have been a negotiator for thirty years. I worked with governments, private security companies, insurance companies, families, and even international nongovernmental organizations, but never before have I seen such an increase in the number of abductions as during the last decade. We are facing a kidnapping crisis of global proportions. You might think that this would be good for people like me, but you would be mistaken. This type of exponential growth makes my job more difficult; it increases the risks and reduces the rate of success. The kidnapping business is like a cancer that has metastasized: Western hostages are traded and stolen constantly because they are very valuable. Profiteers, crooks, corrupt fixers and politicians, local mediators, any kind of dodgy people who want to make a quick buck on the back of an abduction fuel a global ancillary industry, muddying the waters for people like myself. It becomes harder and harder to know who to trust, or which is the correct avenue to follow when negotiating with the kidnappers.

"The end of the Cold War and globalization are responsible for this crisis. Kidnapping has been booming in two main regions of the world: where the state is breaking down and where there is exceptionally strong economic growth, for example, in China. You can say that what feeds the kidnapping industry is both political anarchy and economic prosperity and, of course, greed, the main characteristics of the new world disorder.

"When the state fails and law and order break down, kidnapping becomes a way of survival. This is what has happened in Afghanistan, Somalia, Mali, and many other countries. Initially, local people are abducted to fund insurgent groups, as happened in Syria right after the Arab Spring. Professionals, businessmen, industrialists, even shopkeepers, were kidnapped and released after the families paid ransoms. But as the country was plunged into a civil war, rich people moved abroad, so foreigners became the primary source of revenue for everybody with any power: warlords, jihadists, criminal groups, and local businessmen.

"The easiest prey are always Western kids who travel to war zones, failed states, or any other dangerous areas in the world; young and inexperienced kids who want to see the world, report its atrocities and fix it, dreaming of becoming freelance journalists or humanitarian aid workers. Sometimes they behave as if they are about to have an adventure in the wilderness, going camping or backpacking. They have no idea of the risk they run. They are naïve and a danger to themselves and to those whom they interact with. They are often also misguided: how can you master difficult professions such as war correspondent or humanitarian aid worker by simply showing up in the middle of a conflict area?

"Of course they are easy to abduct, easy to scare, easy to sell on the 'kidnapping secondary market', easy to exchange for a ransom. Ninety percent of the time their families or their government pays. Of course, we are not talking about millions of dollars. To get seven figures you need to kidnap someone really valuable—a top executive of an oil multinational, a relative of a politician—but these people are hard to catch because they are professional and are protected by professionals.

"Generally, journalists are worth very little, a few hundred thousand dollars. Nobody really cares about them, unless, of course, they have an Italian, French, German, or some other European passport belonging to a country that pays the ransom and they end up in the hands of professional terrorist groups like al Qaeda in the Islamic Maghreb, al Nusra, or ISIS. These reporters are generally good catches because their governments are afraid of public opinion, so they pay, sometimes also huge figures—enough money to make a difference to the local economy. In northern Mali, after the payment of several million euros for a group of Italian and Spanish aid workers, the euro became the most common currency of exchange in the local economy.

"Nobody has a full, clear picture of what kidnapping really is, not even Western governments or the negotiators, because nobody has all the information, all the pieces of the puzzle. We do not know what happens when the hostages are in captivity, nor do we know what goes through the minds of the kidnappers, the fixers, the local petty criminals who get involved in the business, the corrupted politicians, and so on. We never know the truth. Of course we can guess, but you cannot ever be sure. Certainty is a word we never use because it generally gets you killed.

"So you can look at this phenomenon from many angles. The human angle, this is what the former hostages generally do, they come home, write their memoirs, talk to the media, revealing their struggle to survive what often are inhuman conditions. But this is only a tiny aspect of the business of kidnapping. Then there are people like myself that negotiate their freedom. We work in darkness, away from the media, and very rarely disclose what we know.

"The kidnappers, for their part, have a distorted view of the whole phenomenon. In many regions of the world, for example, kidnapping is perceived as a mechanism that redistributes wealth from the rich West to the poorest areas of the planet. The rules of the game are very similar to those applied on Wall Street. Hostages become the financial instrument that kick-starts a complex investment scheme, a profitable operation where the return on capital is much higher than the return on labor. In Somalia, local investors who financially back gangs of pirates pocket the bulk of the ransom, leaving a small share to the actual kidnappers. Even the way the negotiations are handled are not so different from the frenzy of the stock market because hostages are merchandise, the value of which changes according to certain factors, such as their nationality and profession and time. As market operators evaluate stocks in their portfolio, the kidnappers do their homework before formulating the amount of the ransom. The ransom for the *Sirius Star*, the oil tanker worth $150 million and carrying a cargo of $100 million worth of Saudi oil, was $3 million. So in proportion it was reasonable and the negotiations were concluded in two months. This was a very good business also for the Somali investors because, as in any business, time is money, and keeping hostages is expensive.

"Negotiations can last months or even years when there is no government or insurance money available and it is left to families and friends to meet the demands of the kidnappers, as happened with the family of Daniel Rye Ottosen. These are the most complicated cases. Investors get nervous, kidnappers become restless, hostages get abused, and someone always tries to steal the business, either by physically kidnapping the hostages or by squeezing into the negotiation.

"Often the cost of conducting the negotiations exceeds the ransom. People like me have to travel to high-risk areas and require security and money to buy information and make contacts. Ironically, these funds are spent in the local economy, in the areas where the hostages are kept, feeding the ancillary industry generated by the kidnapping, from the drivers and fixers to the shopkeeper who sells phone cards. This is an injection of hard cash into these economies, which makes the locals regard abduction as a good business.

"Do you want to hear a surreal twist on what I have just said? If there are several hostages from countries that pay, then the ransom rises due to the competition among officials from the different countries to get their guys out before the others. Kidnappers know this and play negotiators off one another.

"This is a survival game, do not think for a moment that there is cooperation. And it is a male-dominated industry, full of testosterone. Everybody competes to get his hostages out and everybody works to achieve this goal, no matter the consequences. So we compete for drivers, fixers, security, informers . . . and, of course, governments have deeper pockets than families, so to get what they want they pay higher prices. This is what happened with the negotiations of the twenty-five hostages held by the

Islamic State from the end of 2012 until the summer of 2014. The first ones to be released belonged to countries that pay the highest ransoms.

"So you see, this is predominantly a business of smoke and mirrors. The United States and the United Kingdom claim that paying the ransom fuels the kidnapping business of terrorist groups. For example, they say that with the Islamic State, that the ransom is an important source of revenue for the Caliphate. Of the twenty-five hostages held by the Islamic State, however, 67 percent were released on ransom for a total of €60 to €80 million. Well, this is not a lot of money for a group that has morphed into a state and that daily levies taxes on a population of eight million people. But the money collected by the ancillary industry from people like me, acting on behalf of the families, and from governments that pay while carrying on the negotiations, represents a strong incentive for the locals to support the kidnapping industry. And the more we compete and the longer the negotiations go on, the more profitable this business becomes. For example, to employ the best fixers, informers, and drivers, one has to pay more money. The law of supply and demand still holds when the commodity that is in play is human lives.

"In the ultimate analysis, no matter what you do, in this business you never win because you have given a monetary value to a human life."

chapter eight

The Ransom

While large humanitarian aid organizations refuse to put a price on human lives, everybody else does it: families, companies, governments, and, of course, the hostage takers themselves. Among the countries that notoriously pay ransom and insist on handling the negotiations and the payment themselves, a group of European nations, including Italy, Germany, France, and Spain, have dealt with a plethora of abduction cases since the outbreak of the kidnapping crisis in 2003. Italy pays the highest ransoms by far, and this may explain why a large number of Italians have been abducted in the last fifteen years. All European governments have established special units, "crisis units," to deal with kidnapping. Generally, they fall under the jurisdiction of the foreign ministry, but they are composed of people from the secret services who liaise with the interior ministry.

"The Italian crisis unit was already in place in 2003 when I went to Iraq," explains Ambassador Maiolini. "Its task was to handle any emergency situations including natural calamities, not only kidnapping." Often, crisis units are multitasking, but they always have a section that deals exclusively with kidnapping. All crisis units rank hostages according to certain criteria, including the impact of their abduction on public opinion. When negotiating the ransom, ranking makes it easier to attach a price to each hostage. As detailed in Chapter Two, kidnappers try to predict the ranking that each government will give to its hostage citizen and negotiate accordingly. In 2011 the MUJAO knew that the Italian government would value the freedom of Rossella Urru, an aid worker, more than the freedom of Maria Sandra Mariani, a single tourist. This is exactly why humanitarian aid organizations like the Danish Refugee Council want to avoid putting a price on a human life, to value one life more than another.

While the DRC is in the minority with its approach, governments and those who easily attach price tags to hostages do not publicize that there is a ranking system. Secrecy surrounds governments' negotiations. Families and former hostages are instructed not to talk about their loved ones' ordeals. "Overall, governments do not want families and friends to talk about kidnapping. The general rule is do not discuss anything with the media, do not talk to friends and even family members, ever!" explains one negotiator. Indeed, this is what the family of Maria Sandra Mariani was told over and over again during the long months of her abduction.

Governments' silencing the families of hostages without involving them in the negotiations illustrates their wrongheaded approach to kidnapping. Even when secrecy is maintained, information circulates among kidnappers. Excluding the family from the negotiations builds resentment, and often, in one way or another, these feelings become public, especially after the hostage has been released or dies. For example, Robert Fowler in his memoir, *A Season in Hell*, is very critical of how the Canadian government handled the negotiations for his release.

"What we learned from the Buchanan and Thisted abduction is how fundamental the role of the family is in the management of the kidnapping crisis," says Liban Holm of the Danish Refugee Council. After the kidnapping of Buchanan and Thisted, DRC put together a family-liaison training program to ensure that staff appointed as the family contact also had the proper training and knew what they were agreeing to. "We knew that the liaison officer should not be part of the crisis management team," explains Holm. The crisis management team represents the inner circle. It sees and knows everything, even rumors and hearsay. The family liaison officer, on the other hand, belongs to a second layer and only sees part of the operation, the known facts. This separation springs from the fact that liaising with families is emotionally and psychologically very draining. It is part of human nature to want to give the family hope and unfounded rumors can, by mistake, be told by the family liaison officer to the family. It requires phenomenal mental strength, training, and a positive outlook to be the best possible support for the family.

Government crisis units are not structured according to this scheme, nor do they have the same sensitivity to the trauma of the families. Generally families are informed sporadically, not when something important happens but when the crisis team decides that it is safe to let them know or when they have no choice but to, as was the case in the negotiations for the release of Robert Fowler.

While her husband was still held hostage by AQIM, Fowler's wife had lunch in London with Canada's High Commissioner to the United Kingdom, James Wright, who was a friend of her husband. Over lunch Wright casually told her, "You must have been pleased to hear of the

new video message, and to know that Bob is still alive."[123]
Seeing the shock that this statement produced in Mrs.
Fowler, Wright excused himself and returned after a few
minutes. Soon after, Fowler's wife received a call from the
Royal Canadian Mounted Police (RCMP)[124] disclosing
the receipt of a second video. Due to "security reasons,"
however, Mrs. Fowler was not permitted to receive
the video electronically in the UK, because it could
contaminate the evidence. To see her husband's proof of
life, she had to return to Canada.

Government officials often feed lies or legal absurdities
to the families to keep them in the dark about the negotiations. This should come as no surprise, as those in charge
are generally members of the secret services, the foreign
office, or bureaucrats for whom the hostages are political
merchandise.

The Italian government did not establish a trusting
relationship with Mariani's family, and the media was not
interested in her ordeal because she was only a tourist. The
same cannot be said for Rossella Urru, Ainhoa Fernández
de Rincón, and Enric Gonyalons, kidnapped in the Sahrawi refugee camp. The media got hold of the story and
would not let it go, just as their kidnappers had hoped.

Right from the beginning, the kidnapping of the three
aid workers was high profile. In November 2011 the UN
secretary general, Ban Ki-moon, publicly requested their
release.[125] In June 2012 during a human rights conference in Florence, the president of the Democratic Arab
Republic of Sahrawi, Mohamed Abdelaziz, declared that
the hostages were alive and negotiations to free them were
still ongoing.[126] The kidnapping of Rossella Urru also
mobilized celebrities via social media. Fiorello,[127] one of

the most popular Italian showmen, asked his followers on Twitter to substitute their photo with the picture of Rossella Urru for a week. During the Sanremo Music Festival, viewed by millions of people in Italy, Geppi Cucciari, a comedian from Sardinia, the region where Urru was born, publicly demanded her freedom.[128]

Although this type of involvement is aimed at helping to free the hostages, "publicity and media attention always guarantees that kidnappers get a better deal, both in terms of the amount of the ransom and the number of prisoners that will be exchanged for the lives of the hostages," said one negotiator. Indeed, this is what happened with the kidnapping of the two Danish sailors from the *Leopard* and, possibly, the three aid workers snatched from the Sahrawi refugee camp. Their ransom was €5 million per hostage when the going rate at the time in the Sahel was €3 million.

Dealing with kidnapping in secrecy keeps the ransom down, but it must be done in the right way, involving the families of the hostages. Keeping them at bay only shields governments from scrutiny for handling hostages like human cargo, trading them for political reasons and pricing them accordingly, dead or alive.

THE COST OF A CORPSE

At the beginning of 2015 US authorities received a ransom request for the bodies of two hostages, Warren Weinstein, a seventy-three-year-old American contractor, and Giovanni Lo Porto, a thirty-nine-year-old Italian aid worker. In January 2015 a CIA drone had opened fire on an al Qaeda compound near the Pakistani border with Afghanistan. When the two men were killed by the American drone, the

CIA claimed that it had had no prior knowledge of their presence inside the compound. The request to sell their bodies did not come from al Qaeda, which led many to believe that they had been sold to some other group. Images from US military drones confirmed that the two bodies had been moved to a different location.[129]

Warren Weinstein had come to Pakistan for J.E. Austin Associates, a private consultancy company working on modernization projects in developing economies on a contract with the US Agency for International Development (USAID). When he was abducted in August 2011, he was preparing to return home from Lahore after a stint as director of the company's international operations.

When word of the ransom demand was released, the US refused to pay, as, officially, it does not negotiate with terrorists. According to the *Wall Street Journal*, however, "In 2012, the Federal Bureau of Investigation helped facilitate a $250,000 ransom payment from the Weinstein family to al Qaeda in a failed bid to secure his release."[130] *The Wall Street Journal* also reported that after raising the funds privately, the family delivered the ransom to a Pakistani middleman whom the FBI had vetted. In June 2012 the ransom was handed over but Weinstein was never released.[131]

At the time Weinstein was captured, President Obama had not yet repealed the legislation that allowed families who pay ransoms to be prosecuted for financing of terrorism. Indeed, for this reason, US authorities had warned off James Foley's family from attempting to raise the ransom themselves after he was captured. Weinstein, however, was another story. "There are ways to circumvent these restrictions, especially for people who work closely with intelligence services," an American negotiator I spoke with explained. Something went wrong with Weinstein's release, despite the fact that after soldiers and intelligence officers aid workers have the highest ranking among hostages.

The story of Giovanni Lo Porto, another high value hostage, is even darker. On January 19, 2012, while working for a German NGO, Lo Porto and his German colleague Bernd Muehlenbeck were kidnapped in Multan about two hundred fifty miles southwest of the Pakistani capital.

Lo Porto was killed in captivity unbeknownst to his family and to the Italian government by a CIA drone attack on the compound where he was kept prisoner by his kidnappers. Nearly a month after Lo Porto's death, the new president of the Italian republic, Sergio Mattarella, expressed his optimism about Lo Porto's liberation in his inaugural speech.[132] Clearly Mattarella was unaware that the Italian aid worker had perished at the hands of one of Italy's key allies, the US. The news of the two hostages' tragic deaths hit the wires months later. Ironically, the news came soon after the Italian prime minister, Matteo Renzi, made an official visit to the White House.

Both Lo Porto and Muehlenbeck had gone to Pakistan on an EU project to assist the local population after two major natural disasters: an earthquake and a flood. According to Margherita Romanelli, a close friend of Lo Porto, when Muehlenbeck was released in October 2014 he revealed that they had been separated after a year in captivity, a sign that possibly one of the two had been sold or handed over to another group or organization. "If not before, from that moment onward, it is likely that the negotiations with the two governments were handled separately," said the negotiator I interviewed. Two months after Muehlenbeck's release, Lo Porto was dead.

Muehlenbeck's revelation directly contradicted the Italian government's earlier assurances to the Lo Porto family. "The foreign office assured them that they were working closely with the Germans," explained Romanelli.[133] Unlike the DRC, the NGO that employed Lo Porto did not provide a liaison officer to the family, so the family was left to rely predominantly on the Italian crisis unit and Lo Porto's colleagues who "unofficially" passed on information.

"Silence was the rule. Nobody talked; nobody said anything. We were totally in the dark," confirms Romanelli. Even today it is hard to piece together the puzzle of his abduction. No video of Lo Porto was ever released. The first and only video confirming the kidnapping of the two men shows only Muehlenbeck. Nobody knows if proof of life was ever produced for Lo Porto. Equally, no information has been produced about how the Italians handled his kidnapping at the local level.

"The first thing that professionals do in these circumstances is search the neighborhood door to door and talk to the local population," explained the European negotiator I interviewed. This is what the DRC did in Somalia with the kidnapping of Buchanan and Thisted. "When Muehlenbeck was freed, he revealed that after the kidnapping they had been held for a week in a house just around the corner from where they were abducted," said Romanelli. It would have been easy to find them had a proper search of the neighborhood been done. But the Italians, who had no military intelligence presence in that region, relied upon the Pakistani forces to track the kidnappers.

Contrary to what many believe, Western governments do not have proper intelligence in most of the areas where their citizens are easy prey for kidnappers, and authorities often reach out to journalists working in these regions to help them. "When in July 2015 [the three journalists] Antonio Pampliega, José Manuel López, and Ángel Sastre, [. . .] were kidnapped in northern Syria, near the town of Azaz, I was in the Ukraine. I knew them and I had an idea of what had happened, so I contacted the Spanish authorities, who asked me to pass on any contact[s] I have because they had no intelligence on the ground," remembers Francesca Borri.[134]

Uncharacteristically for Italy, the case of Lo Porto dragged on for years, producing nagging criticism among the aid worker's friends. "The Italian government has abandoned Giancarlo [Lo Porto] from the early days of his kidnapping," said one of his friends, Filippo Occhipinti. "For three years the Foreign Ministry has ridiculed the family by imposing a strict silence. I ask why, but unfortunately I will never get an answer. Giancarlo was killed first and foremost by the state that abandoned him."[135]

The Italian government did not bring Giovanni Lo Porto home alive but it repatriated his corpse. "When the body arrived in Italy the DNA examination was conducted by the government, not by the family," says Romanelli. "The body arrived by ship at the port of Palermo and the family was not there because they had not been told at what time the ship was due to arrive. The family was advised not to look at the body, not to open the coffin, which was sealed and kept closed during the civil funeral." The following day the cremation took place.

"Although no politician was present at the funeral, two agents from the secret service showed up at the cremation to verify that everything, including the clothes, were burned in the cremation."

Did the body for which the Italians paid a ransom belong to Lo Porto or to someone else? Only the Italian government knows the answer. All the evidence has been turned into ashes. With the repatriation of a corpse, however, the Italian government found closure, away from the media, to a very controversial kidnapping case. The family received a death certificate, necessary to claim life insurance. And so, silently, the Lo Porto affair ended.

THE SILENT CRIME

While dealing with kidnapping in secret is presented as a tactic to prevent kidnappers from raising ransoms to the upper limit, governments' real aim is to minimize their own accountability about the negotiations. For example, when it comes down to the payment of ransoms, every government denies that it pays them. However, kidnappers know very well who pays, and who pays the most.

"This is a business of lies, spies, and cover-up," declares the Al Jazeera documentary *The Hostage Business*[136] about the murky world of kidnapping. The government lies, the kidnappers lie, the intermediaries lie, and families are left alone to fend for themselves with little, if any, information.

In 2011, among the nineteen hostages the Italian government had to deal with, there was Bruno Pelizzari, a South African resident with dual South African and Italian nationality who was kidnapped by Somali pirates on October 26, 2010, while sailing with companion Debbie Calitz. "Initially they asked for $20 million," said Vera Hecht,[137] Pelizzari's sister. When the South African government refused to pay and even to get involved in the negotiations, Hecht reached out for help to a charity in Somalia called Gift of the Givers. Negotiations went on for eighteen months, with constant threats that the hostages would be killed. Then, Hecht received a message through Facebook from someone called Marco saying that he could help. Marco instructed her to obtain proof of life once more and to make a deal. Secret documents obtained by Al Jazeera showed that the Italian government, frustrated by how the South Africans were handling the kidnapping, decided to intervene and to pay a ransom of about $525,000. Pelizzari's Italian passport saved his and Debbie Calitz's life. Naturally, Hecht was told never to disclose that the Italians had actually paid the ransom.

Marco, an Italian intelligence officer, guided Hecht in the negotiations. They used the same Gmail account so they never sent each other a message, but rather talked via that account through unsent e-mails. Three months later, the hostages were released after the payment of the ransom. In June 2012, Hecht, accompanied by Italian intelligence officers, finally saw her brother again. Pelizzari and Calitz, who is not even an Italian national, were freed.

"It is likely that the Italians knew that they could get Pelizzari and Calitz relatively quickly and for much less than Mariani. AQIM ransoms at the time were around €3 million, and they proved to be very tough negotiators. So the Italians probably opted to work with Pelizzari's sister to quickly tick one name off the list of Italian hostages. At the end of the year, what matters for the secret services is how many people you brought home," said one of the European negotiators I interviewed.

The Italian government also arranged for a cover-up

story.[138] When Pelizzari and Calitz returned home to South Africa, the media were told that they had been freed by the Western-backed Somali security forces. Pelizzari and Calitz were debriefed and told not to reveal that the Italian government had paid the ransom.[139]

Amanda Lindhout, a Canadian freelance journalist, was less lucky. On August 23, 2008, two days after having arrived in Mogadishu, she was kidnapped with Nigel Brennan, a thirty-seven-year-old Australian freelance photojournalist. Both the Canadian and Australian governments refused to pay the ransom but "guided" the families through the negotiations. Lindhout's mother was told time and time again that nothing would happen to her daughter because her kidnappers were religious and they would not sexually assault her. Lindhout was reputedly raped by one of her jailers, and, after she attempted to escape, she was gang raped.

Initially, the kidnappers asked for $2.5 million. Eventually, they settled for less than $1 million. According to Lindhout's memoir, *A House in the Sky*, the Canadian government did not have any sense of urgency during the negotiations. All it did was coach her mother to negotiate a lower ransom. At a certain point her mother was told not to answer any more calls, as the government had decided to carry on the negotiations directly. This suggestion defies logic considering that the family, not the government, was going to pay the ransom. According to Lindhout, the kidnappers had repeatedly refused to accept $250,000, a sum that both the Canadian and Australian governments had put together as "expenses," to hide their involvement in the ransom.

Finally, pressured by Nigel Brennan's family, Amanda Lindhout's mother agreed to employ a private negotiator,

John Chase, from the British company AKE. Chase guided Lindhout's mother in the negotiations, as Marco had done with Pelizzari's sister. AKE arranged for a member of the Somali Parliament to receive the ransom of $600,000—a sum very close to what the Italians paid for Pelizzari and Calitz—which was transferred to a Nairobi bank and from there to a kiosk in Mogadishu. The member of Parliament then handed over the money to a group of tribal elders who released the ransom to the kidnappers only when Lindhout and Brennan were set free. On November 25, 2009, 460 days after their abduction, the two were released.[140]

chapter nine

The Golden Hour—
Anatomy of a Kidnapping

When the hunting season on foreign hostages began in Syria in 2012, none of the many criminal and jihadist groups involved in this business had the structure or the expertise to carry out proper kidnapping negotiations. Many could not even speak a foreign language, so they reached out to distinguished and well-connected Syrians to help them. The kidnappers sent them information about the hostages, often using these people as negotiators or translators and as their *de facto* go-between with families and governments. The aim was to get a quick turnover, within a few weeks at the longest. In these cases, if the response was fast enough, hostages could be freed within days for as little as a few thousand dollars. But if this did not happen, then the hostages were traded or exchanged, ending up in the hands of bigger groups who could handle long-term imprisonment and negotiations for large sums of money.

In the late summer of 2014, Samir Aita, a member of the Syrian Democratic Forum who lives in Paris, got a call about a problem that had come up in the negotiations for the release of two Italian aid workers, Greta Ramelli and Vanessa Marzullo, kidnapped in July 2014 in Aleppo. "They wanted me to negotiate with the Italian government," explained Aita. "I immediately asked them for proof of life, but they did not, so I told them that I could not get involved."[141] According to Francesca Borri, Samir Aita contacted her, asking her to alert the Italian authorities about what was happening and the information she had received about the two women, which she did.[142] "The kidnappers were sure that the two girls worked for the secret services. They did not believe that they were just two simpletons who had traveled to Syria to bring useless medical kits," continues Borri. "Their story was so absurd, it was not believable!"

The response of the Italian crisis unit was slow and half-hearted. So Ramelli and Marzullo remained in captivity until January 2015. Their kidnappers, a small criminal group, had traded or sold them to al Nusra, which handled the negotiations with the Italian government. "Eventually, we paid €13 million for their release," said a member of the Italian Senate. "It was one of the highest ransoms ever paid."[143]

The Italian taxpayers will never know if Ramelli and Marzullo could have been freed for a few thousand dollars had the crisis unit of the Foreign Ministry acted right away, within what is known as the "golden hour," had the crisis unit known that they had travelled to Syria. "It took weeks to verify the kidnapping of Greta and Vanessa," says an Italian senator. "They had not even alerted the foreign office about their trip to Syria." When governments are involved in hostage negotiations everything always moves at a snail's pace.

In every high profile conference on kidnapping—and there are many in the world run by the security industry—it is common to have a section dedicated to these first hours and days immediately following an abduction, when the trail of the kidnappers is still warm, and lives can be saved and the ransom brought down significantly. But hardly anyone will admit that to act swiftly, one needs to bypass the authorities, ignore their advice, and even force their hand, as this is what happened in the kidnapping of Joanie de Rijke.

A veteran Dutch war correspondent, de Rijke was kidnapped at the beginning of November 2008 in Afghanistan by a small commando unit of the Taliban while working for the former Belgian weekly *P-Magazine*. She had arranged for an exclusive interview with a Taliban commander, Ghazi, whose group had ambushed and killed ten French soldiers just a few months before. Right from the beginning, it was clear that Ghazi and his followers were acting alone and that de Rijke had been abducted to raise money for the group and its community. As happened to many *katibas* of AQIM, Ghazi's Taliban group had been seduced by criminal jihadism.

Though part of the Taliban community, "Joanie's kidnappers were simple criminals, people who used the ransom money to feed their families, their tribe, not to wage jihad against the West," explained Michaël Lescroart, former editor of the Belgian weekly and the man who, together with a Scottish friend of de Rijke who wishes to be known only as "Dave," negotiated her ransom. "Of course, this does not justify what they have done to her, but it shows how kidnapping in highly destabilized countries, such as Afghanistan, has turned into an industry for a large segment of the population, who otherwise would not know how to survive."[144]

In her book, *In the Hands of Taliban*, de Rijke concurs

with this analysis. "We were driving along the still terrible road, not far from Ghazi's village. I could hear him sighing. 'We need money. To build a good road, so that we can later send our children to school in Surobi if they want to study. Write this down as well. And we want to build a new school in our valley.'

"'For girls as well?' I could not resist asking.

"The reply was as decided as the one I had heard in Kandahar months earlier: 'No! Girls should not go to school. Only boys.'"[145]

After her abduction, de Rijke was forced to trek across Afghan mountains until she reached the camp where she and her captors would spend the night. At that point Ghazi handed her a mobile phone and she called Lescroart.

"I got the call in the evening. It must have been 7 p.m. because I was watching *The Simpsons* with my son," recalled Lescroart. "It was Joanie. She had been kidnapped. I told her not to say where she was but to spell out the location in Dutch and she did it. So I knew more or less where they had taken her. As soon as we hung up I called the Belgian minister of defense. Joanie had travelled with him to Afghanistan a few days earlier, but she had stayed longer to interview Ghazi. He was very helpful and said, 'If we have to pay, we will pay.' These were his exact words. Then, of course, a day later, when he realized that she was Dutch, that she did not have a Belgian passport, he changed his attitude completely and told me that it was the responsibility of the Dutch government to handle her kidnapping."

That same evening Lescroart also called the Belgian foreign minister, who again instructed him to wait—it would take a very long time to sort out the situation. When he contacted the Dutch authorities the next day he heard the same thing. However, right from the beginning the Dutch told him that they "would not negotiate with the terrorists; they would not pay any ransom. If I wanted to do it, however, they would not stop me." Lescroart had the impression that both the Belgian and Dutch authorities were stalling, costing two precious days' time, and "that there was no protocol in place and that they simply improvise."

When the Dutch authorities wanted to take over the negotiation for Joanie, Lescroart resisted. "Joanie, in one of her calls, had told me to trust Dave, a Scottish friend she had stayed with in Kabul while waiting for the OK to interview Ghazi. Initially, I had been hesitant to trust him," Lescroart recalled. "I did not know him and I thought that he was a sort of mercenary. But she was right: Dave knew what to do."

The same evening he received the news of de Rijke's kidnapping, Lescroart had contacted Dave and told him that Joanie had been abducted and that the kidnappers had asked for $2 million. Dave right away had activated his connections in Afghanistan to reach out to her kidnappers and started negotiating the ransom down.

"Joanie's kidnappers were a small group of Taliban, who thought they could get some money from her abduction. They were not professional kidnappers, even when it comes to crime in Afghanistan, everybody is simultaneously an amateur and a professional. But we knew that they were not in it for the long haul and would agree to a fraction of the amount demanded if we paid the ransom quickly. How did we know that? Because a few days before, the same commander, Ghazi, had given an interview to two French journalists and he had not kidnapped them. It was clear to me that handling three hostages was going to be more difficult, if not impossible, than abducting one, even if she was a woman. They did not have the infrastructure to deal with three hostages. They were not professional kidnappers."[146] Likely, Ghazi was unaware that the French government would have paid much more money than *P-Magazine* for its citizens.

Another reason why Joanie's kidnappers wanted a quick agreement is that they knew that they could not have kept the kidnapping of a Western journalist secret for a long time. "I was confident that Joanie's kidnappers wanted a quick deal also to avoid someone stealing the hostage," concluded Lescroart.

As her negotiator in Afghanistan, Dave was lucky because de Rijke was allowed to stay in touch regularly with her editor, so they both knew that she was alive. But the rumors of her kidnapping spread quickly among the media community in Kabul, and Dave and Lescroart had to make sure that the Belgian and Dutch authorities did not alert the Afghani authorities. "At a certain point the Dutch wanted to contact the Afghani police about the handling of the ransom money," remembered Lescroart. "Luckily, the Dutch ambassador in Kabul explained to them that if word would come out that someone had that kind of money in Kabul, not even he himself would be safe. He would not even be able to leave his hotel room. The police would rob the ransom."

Lescroart and Dave worked in tandem, around the clock, ignoring the suggestions of the Belgian and Dutch governments. While Dave brought the price of de Rijke's freedom down to $130,000, Lescroart navigated the political bureaucracy in Belgium and in Holland to send the ransom in cash to Dave as fast as possible. That was a very difficult task.

"It took two days to get the OK to move the money. I had to go to The Hague with a picture of Joanie and tell them that she would soon be a trophy if they did not act quickly. In the end, they agreed. Luckily, the magazine could pay the ransom. So *P-Magazine* transferred €100,000 from its account to the account of the Dutch embassy in Belgium and then within two hours the Dutch embassy in Kabul released the money in cash and in dollars," explained Lescroart.

A week after her kidnapping, de Rijke was on her way to freedom, just in time. Word of her abduction had reached the Taliban leadership, which, in the last hours of her captivity, had attempted to prevent her release and the payment of the ransom to Ghazi's group. But her kidnappers honored the deal and managed to send her back to Kabul. During her journey, she changed cars several times, until she reached the outskirts of Kabul where she was due to be handed over to the negotiator, Dave.

"There were two cars, one arranged by us, which would have taken her to Dave's house in Kabul, and another sent by the Dutch embassy, with a Western woman inside. We had no knowledge of this second car but Joanie got into it," recalled Lescroart. "When she did not show up at Dave's, he called me and said 'I have lost her.' At that point we did not know what to do. We just waited for her to contact us, hoping that she had not been kidnapped again."

De Rijke had no idea that she had boarded the wrong car. "I got into the car and the woman started to talk to me in English. After a few minutes she realized I was Dutch, so she switched to Dutch. She did not even know that I was Dutch,"[147] remembered de Rijke. The woman, who worked for a prestigious think tank in Afghanistan, had been chosen to bring de Rijke to the Dutch compound, where she was debriefed and told that it would be best not to talk to anybody about what had happened. The following day she was put on a regular flight to Amsterdam, without clearing customs or showing her passport.

"The Dutch government knew where the final exchange was going to take place. Perhaps they tapped my phone," said Lescroart, "or Dave's or they followed him, I do not know. However, they sent the car to make sure that Joanie was in safe hands and that the Afghani police would not get hold of her. They wanted her out of the country as soon as possible."

For the Dutch bureaucracy, de Rijke was little more than merchandise to be shipped back home as soon as possible. "Nobody told me anything in Kabul. I learned how I had been freed from Michaël only when I got back to Amsterdam," said de Rijke. "The Dutch authorities would have liked me not to talk about my kidnapping, to go back home and forget those memories. Not only did they do very little to free me, they wanted to erase the entire story. They wanted my ordeal in Afghanistan and their very poor handling of it to be a silent crime." Defying her government, de Rijke was freed because her editor and a local negotiator acted decisively within the golden hour. Kayla Mueller, the young American aid worker kidnapped in Aleppo, was not so fortunate.

A LOVE STORY AT THE TIME OF THE CALIPHATE

"I could have saved Kayla Mueller." The negotiator, who recently brought home other Western hostages held in

Syria, stared into my eyes and watched my reaction. I know he is saying the truth because he has been involved in the negotiation of more than one hostage held by the Islamic State. However, I asked him if he was sure about what he had just said. He nodded. "When the reach-out call arrived, just a few days after she had been abducted, I was in Antakya and I happened to be with the guy who received it. The kidnappers had gone through Kayla's Skype calls and recognized his name. He immediately asked if I could help, but I explained to him that I couldn't take a case unless the family wanted me to. I did not even know Mueller—I had never met her. I did tell him, though, to get proof of life."[148] Though the negotiator declined to get involved in Mueller's case, he was adamant that she could have been freed for a small ransom. "I am positive that, if we had acted immediately, I could have bargained her out for a small sum of money."

The negotiator went silent for a moment, lit a cigarette, and shook his head. "In hindsight, yes, perhaps I should have reached out to her family, but I am not an ambulance chaser. I do not call families directly saying 'I heard your loved one has been kidnapped, do you want my help?' You would like to think that in these situations, when there is a life at stake, that there is a system in place and all you need to do is to press an alarm button to get it in motion. This is not how things work."[149]

According to the negotiator, Mueller got mired in bureaucracy, stuck between the jurisdiction of the State Department and the FBI, and consultation with the CIA and the White House. "It must have taken many, many meetings before they finally got their act together and by then, it was too late."

Though Kayla Mueller ended up in the hands of the Islamic State after some time, no one knows for sure who originally kidnapped her—a small jihadist or criminal group or someone from the Free Syrian Army or from any of the other rebel groups looking for a quick buck. "In 2013 the market for Western hostages in northern Syria was very well developed. Foreigners were traded according to their nationality and profession," concludes a negotiator.

Most likely, Kayla Mueller was sold or traded to an enemy group for weapons or for prisoners, as this is what happened with Joakim Medin. Many of these transactions take place on the Syrian secondary hostage market, explained the negotiator. Journalist Jean-René Augé-Napoli is adamant that the Islamic State did not know that Kayla Mueller was a woman when they bought her. "Generally, hostages are traded without any specification of their sex, so it is likely that ISIS was offered a generic US aid worker. Nobody wants women. It complicates matters for many reasons. Women are a big distraction. Jihadists, in particular, live in a highly segregated male environment and logistically, handling male hostages is much easier and cheaper than handling both sexes."

The negotiator added that he was unsure if the guy who received the original reach-out call, ever spoke with Kayla's family. "A few months after the reach-out call I met him again. He told me that he had been very, very frustrated with the way that the authorities had handled the kidnapping. It is a shame because he could have been the perfect negotiator to deal with the original kidnappers if they had moved quickly." Stalling—exactly the opposite of what is needed—is precisely what governments do when handling the kidnapping of their own citizens.

I first met this negotiator in a bar overlooking the Baltic Sea. It was a bright, warm October morning; the light was exceptionally strong and the water, crystal clear. As we drank cold beverages that mid-October day, we could have been sitting in a bar on the shores of the Mediterranean, in Turkey or Syria. While he spoke of the community of journalists, aid workers, fixers, drivers, mercenaries, refugees, and aspiring jihadists living in the Turkish towns close to the Syrian border, pictures that Kayla Mueller and her boyfriend Omar Alkhani had posted on their Facebook profiles while living among these people, came to my mind. They show two people in love in a warm climate, a Syrian man and a young American woman smiling, showing their happiness while the sun shines in the sky. There is no trace of the war in Syria that is, literally, right next door. The blitheness of the image is almost absurd when compared with the political reality. Indeed, the story of Kayla and Omar is surreal, a love story at the time of the Caliphate, the rising of the Islamist phoenix.

Kayla and Omar met briefly in 2010, in Egypt. For two years they stayed in touch. Then in 2012 they met again in Beirut, and soon after that they decided to move together to Istanbul. Kayla wanted to become an aid worker, Omar a freelance photojournalist and documentarian. They both had big professional dreams and believed that the Syrian conflict offered them a shortcut to their dreams' realization. This is probably why from Istanbul they moved to a small town near the Turkish-Syrian border. Neither of them was a trained professional. Kayla was a volunteer. She helped whoever would accept her offer of assistance. She had no salary, no insurance, and nobody to call if things soured, as this is what happened in early August 2013 when she was kidnapped in Aleppo. Omar was not employed by a newspaper. He worked as a freelancer and supported himself by fixing computers.

However, in the spring of 2013, Kayla and Omar were happy. They were young, in love, and felt that they were witnesses to history in the making. They both blogged on the Syrian conflict. Being only a few kilometers from the front line, they used social media to inform the world of what they saw. Indeed, they believed that this was their task, to observe and report the atrocities of that conflict, and it was only natural for them to do it together.

"I came across a few couples like them in conflict zones," said a European aid worker who asked to remain anonymous. "They want to help. They want to expose to the world what is happening. They are committed to do so and believe that being close to a war will speed up the process to become aid workers or journalists. But they are mistaken. Nobody wants to employ these people because they are not qualified, and frankly, often employing them can even put our work in danger. Being an aid worker is a tough profession. It requires university degrees, years of training and experience. To become one, it is not enough to wake up one morning in the Midwest or in the Middle East and decide to be an aid worker."[150]

Couples like Omar and Kayla end up spending a lot of time together, helping each other in their quest for the "ideal" job to save the world, reinforcing in each other the belief that what they are doing is right, often without understanding the risks involved. In late Spring 2013 Omar took Kayla to a meeting he had arranged in the Turkish border town of Reyhanlı with two American journalists, Nicole Tung, the photographer friend of James

Foley, and Janine di Giovanni. Mueller introduced herself as Omar's fiancée.[151] "Her heart was in the right place," Tung told the *Arizona Republic*. "But, unfortunately, being sort of fresh and new to the conflict zone, especially in a place like Syria, you run into so many different dangers."[152] And so they did, at the beginning of August 2013, when Omar was asked to travel to Aleppo to fix the computer system of Médecins Sans Frontières, Kayla pleaded with him to take her along.

Initially, he refused, but eventually he relented. Though they lived just a few kilometers from the border, Mueller had never been inside Syria; she had never seen Aleppo. Omar thought she needed to witness what was happening, so she could write about it in her blog, *Imbued with Hope*, to help get more help for the refugees. It was perhaps a foolhardy decision, made by two inexperienced individuals who were deeply in love, and believed that they could make a difference through their actions. Humanitarian aid agencies have documented the Syrian tragedy right from the beginning of the civil war. Mueller's visit to the Médecins sans Frontières compound and the account of her trip on her blog did little to ease the plight of the millions of Syrians suffering because of the conflict, but it did cost her her life.

Francesca Borri remembers that "it was Kayla who asked MSF if they could stay the night. Apparently, the couple had not even arranged for a room for themselves. The staff of Médecins Sans Frontières were furious. They had had some problems with kidnapping of local workers, so the last thing they wanted was an American woman staying overnight. But they could not send them out on to the streets, so they let them stay."[153]

The next morning Omar and Kayla took a taxi from the MSF compound to the bus station. As soon as the taxi left, Omar realized that a grey minivan was following them. The van overtook the taxi and forced it to stop. Six masked, armed men with Kalashnikovs and wearing body armor leapt out and surrounded them. They dragged both of them into the minivan and left.

They ended up in the basement of the children's hospital of Aleppo, which had become a makeshift prison. Kayla was locked with the women and Omar was interrogated. He spent two months in captivity being tortured and beaten. Each time they asked him who the woman traveling with him was, he said "my wife." Finally, he was released, alone. Kayla remained in Aleppo.

"I interviewed Omar fifteen, maybe even twenty times," said the negotiator. "Sometimes the details of the story of their kidnapping changed. It is normal; you are under so much stress that memories lapse. I spoke with him because I wanted to know if he had seen some of the hostages whose release I was negotiating with the Islamic State. So I asked him to tell me exactly what had happened while in captivity and I came to the conclusion that he did not sell Kayla off. On the contrary, he was deeply, deeply sorry for having taken her with him."[154]

Indeed, in retrospect, Kayla and Omar's journey to Aleppo shows how little they knew about the perils of the Syrian conflict, their kidnapping being the result of this ignorance. Francesca Borri explains, "Each time I went into Syria I travelled without even a pen. I pretended to be a refugee and did not even carry a telephone. From mid-2013 onwards I tried to go in and out in one day, avoiding spending the night inside Syria."[155]

"When he got out of Syria, Omar contacted Kayla's family. I told him not to tell them that he could solve the case because it was well above his capabilities," remembers the negotiator. Omar told the *Daily Mail* that Kayla's parents had received a thirty second video of their daughter begging for help. The video was accompanied by a message that read: "If you want her alive, it will be twenty million dollars."[156]

Again the negotiator suggested to me that things might have turned out differently if, in the crucial first days, he or someone like him had been empowered to act. However, he believes that the family "followed the instructions of the US authorities, so they could not objectively judge how serious the situation was in Syria. And Omar really believed he could save her; he had a plan, perhaps because he loved her and he felt so guilty for her abduction?" The negotiator paused for a moment, perhaps revisiting those crucial days, then he looked at me and shook his head. "So Omar went back to get her, to save her. He was imprisoned again, this time in Shaykh Najjar, the industrial city north of Aleppo where ISIS had built one of its detention centers. By then Kayla was in the hands of ISIS. He waited for an audience with a judge to explain that she was his wife."

Omar was confident that Kayla would back him. Before leaving for Aleppo, they both had agreed that if they were stopped Kayla would pretend to be his wife, Ayesha. But when the judge asked Kayla in front of Omar if it was true that she was his wife she burst into tears and said that she was his fiancée, not his wife.

"I think she said the truth to save him," says the negotiator. "She wanted to protect him. She was afraid they

would kill him because he was lying. It is likely that sh
was told that if she was honest they would let him go, an
indeed they did." Omar risked his life to save Kayla an
Kayla gave up her chance to be free to save Omar.

In July 2014, almost a year after Kayla's kidnapping, U
Army Delta Force commandos launched an operation i
Raqqa to rescue the foreign hostages held by the Islami
State, including Kayla. But when they arrived the hostage
had already been moved somewhere else. Eighteen month
after her abduction, Kayla Mueller was killed by a Jorda
nian air strike against the Islamic State in Raqqa.

Like all hostages, Kayla became an item in the news, an
the subject of jihadist propaganda. The former used he
to sell newspapers, the latter to proselytize the evil natur
of the Western enemies. Her death did not help the caus
of the Syrian refugees. It did not enhance the knowledg
of their tragedy among Westerners, not did it trigger an
empathy for them. On the contrary, it only added fue
to the hatred among the various factions and sponsor
involved in the Syrian conflict.

Not even the ultimate sacrifice, her death, could mak
Kayla Mueller's dream to improve the world come true.

chapter ten

The Prey—Seeking a New Identity

The negotiator did not save Kayla Mueller, but he did bring home another young and inexperienced man, a Dane named Daniel Rye Ottosen. Ottosen, like Kayla Mueller and her boyfriend Omar Alkhani, saw the conflict in Syria as the shortcut to a new profession, one he desperately wanted to pursue: photojournalism. Like them, he had no idea how dangerous Syria was or how futile his idea was. Citizen journalism almost never leads to professional journalism, but it can get people into serious trouble.

In 2015, after his rescue, Daniel Rye Ottosen was employed as a speaker by the Danish security company Guardian-SRM (security risk management) in one of its excellent survival courses. Indeed, these are essential tools for anybody who wants or needs to travel to dangerous areas, from Afghanistan to Nigeria, courses that neither Ottosen nor Mueller ever took or could have afforded.

Ottosen is a handsome, Nordic-looking young man, tall, very blond, with a glowing white complexion. Before attempting to become a photojournalist, he was a distinguished gymnast.

Ottosen told those who attended the survival course the shocking story of his abduction in northern Syria, how he and the other Western hostages survived their ordeal while in captivity. However, he carefully failed to mention several important details, such as why and how he ended up in northern Syria.

A SHORT CUT TO PHOTOJOURNALISM

"I met Daniel Rye [Ottosen] before he went to Syria, in April 2013," says the negotiator. "He had asked around, among the community of Danish journalists, for someone who could advise him about his trip to Syria. He wanted to report the war in Syria, to become a photojournalist. I had been working on [James] Foley's case since November 2012, so I knew what was going on there, plus I had done a lot of preventive work for journalists traveling to dangerous areas, so several people suggested he talk to me.

"I told him right away that he should not go; it was too dangerous and he was totally inexperienced. He was only in his early twenties and had never been in a war zone. But he would not listen." So the negotiator gave him some tips. "I told him to leave a trail of information inside Syria in case he was kidnapped, clues that someone like me could use as leads. In the kidnapping of James Foley, for example, we could not backtrack his movements prior to the kidnapping. . . . We had no leads."[157]

Daniel Rye Ottosen did go to Syria. He crossed over from Turkey twice. The first time he followed the negotiator's advice and did not spend the night in Syria, but the second time he stayed overnight and the following morning was kidnapped. "There is no doubt that he behaved recklessly," says Carsten Jensen, one of Scandinavia's most distinguished novelists, who attended one of the survival courses of the Guardian Group while researching his most recent novel. "He saw a building that was being used by one of the jihadist groups—I think it was al Nusra—and he wanted to take a picture of it. He was told not to do it, but he did it anyway."[158]

It is unclear if someone noticed him because he was taking photos or if his driver or fixer sold him to his kidnappers. Indeed, after a few days Ottosen's kidnappers released his driver, who soon afterwards vanished, so perhaps the driver did sell him. "Westerners do not understand how dangerous it is to land in Turkey and shop around for fixers and drivers. Some of these people will not think twice to sell you for a few hundred dollars," says Omar al Muqdad, who has produced a documentary for the BBC, *We Left Them Behind*, about Western hostages in Syria.[159]

It is also possible that someone saw a tall, blond, athletic young man with a camera, thought that being a photojournalist was a very good cover for an American spy, and decided to abduct him. It is unclear which group kidnapped him initially, possibly al Nusra. However, as happens with all hostages, as soon as he was taken, someone searched the Internet for his work, his photos. When the search produced nothing, the idea that he was a spy pretending to be a photojournalist was reinforced.

"I would not rule out that he was sold or traded a few times as a spy before he ended up in the hands of the Islamic State," said a Syrian negotiator. "Each time he was traded, his kidnappers tortured him to get him to confess."[160] This explains why initially he was often moved from one location to another. Perhaps he was sold to the Islamic State as a spy. "Daniel was seriously tortured for quite some time because they really thought he was a spy," says Marc Marginedas, a veteran war correspondent from Catalonia who was held hostage by ISIS and who met Ottosen while in captivity. "He was not a journalist. They could not document his work. And he was so fit and athletic that they must have thought that he had been trained by the army and by the secret services. When they finally realized that he was not a spy, they stopped torturing him."[161]

By then he was transformed. Ottosen showed the participants of the Guardian Group survival course the picture that his kidnappers had sent with the ransom demand, after two or three months in captivity. "He had lost 30 kilos and looked like a forty-five-year-old junkie living on the streets," remembers Carsten Jensen.

Although the ransom request came long after Ottosen's abduction, the negotiator says he had been looking for Ottosen almost from the beginning. "I got a call at 2 a.m. from Daniel's father. It was the nineteenth of May. Daniel had been kidnapped on the seventeenth. His girlfriend had gone to the airport to pick him up but Daniel hadn't shown up. Before leaving, Daniel had given his father an envelope to be opened only if he didn't return. Inside was my phone number."[162]

Ottosen made many mistakes: he had gone to Syria, a country he did not know, to document the war and to sell his photos to Danish magazines after he returned; he had gone alone, without an experienced journalist and without being part of a media crew; he had gone as an independent freelancer, without a contract for a story. As in Kayla Mueller's case, with Daniel Rye Ottosen too, these mistakes sprung from his romantic idea of the profession. And similarly, Ottosen would never have imagined that professional journalists and aid workers tended to look down on people like him. However, Ottosen must have learned this hard truth during his captivity.

"He said that at a certain point he was imprisoned in a small cell with twelve other Western hostages," remembers Carsten Jensen. "They all became very intimate. Some of the hostages gave lectures to the others in the subjects they knew best. But Daniel did not have this knowledge." Of course Ottosen's status among these people, some of whom had had long careers in the media as war correspondents, was rather low. He was very young and inexperienced and looked up to them. He admired them. In his talk at the Guardian Group, Ottosen spoke with fondness of the "cinema evenings," when one or another of the hostages recounted a film in detail, a kind of story hour. He used the Danish world *hyggeligt*, which is the quintessential description of coziness.

To raise his status among the hostages, Ottosen realized that he had to offer them something that the others did not know. "He had been a distinguished gymnast, so he organized fitness routines for the group, which raised his status. He also became rather good at cleaning toilets, for which the guards would sometimes give him small rewards that he would in turn offer as prizes for the board games some of the hostages had built using pieces of cardboard,"[163] explains Jensen.

Daniel Rye Ottosen had done some things right: before leaving he had contacted a negotiator and left the negotiator's phone number with his father, and he had purchased insurance (worth around €650,000) so the family could pay the negotiator and raise some money for the ransom. Most likely these precautions saved his life. "When his father called me, I knew immediately who Daniel was: I had met him, I had spoken with him, and advised him. I knew I could help,"[164] says the negotiator.

THE PRICE OF BEING A NOBODY

"Right from the beginning, Daniel Rye [Ottosen]'s kidnapping was one of the most difficult cases I have ever had," recounts the negotiator. "It was complex for many reasons. Daniel being a Dane, that is from a country that does not pay any ransom, and being a nobody, not a famous journalist or an aid worker, he was put right away into the same category as the British and the American hostages. Plus Denmark is the country that produced the cartoons against Mohammed, so killing a Dane can always turn out to be a good propaganda tool in the jihadist world.

"I was also afraid that ISIS would use him to get the other European governments to pay ransom, and to a certain extent its negotiators did. They kept him until the very end while they negotiated with one European government after another: the Spanish first, then the French soon after. All these hostages were freed before Daniel. Yes, we had less resources than those countries had, because we are a private company and they have unlimited resources. But to me the way the kidnappers negotiated one group of people at a time, leaving Daniel to the very end, had not so much to do with the resources these countries had, as much as with the ability that this type of negotiation gave ISIS to expose and profit from the inconsistencies and idiosyncrasies of Western governments when dealing with kidnapping."[165] ISIS knew all too well the governments' shortcomings, especially the competition among different crisis units when dealing with freeing hostages held by the same kidnappers.

Indeed, when dealing with kidnappings, government cooperation is a fantasy. "When I was debriefed after my liberation," remembers Mariani, "I told them that in the same camp where I had been kept prisoner there were two French hostages, and that the young one was very, very ill. I said please let the French government know that they must act quickly because he may not make it. I was told that my message had been passed on to the French but nobody contacted me from the French crisis unit or the embassy. The only foreigners who interviewed me were Americans. Then, when in October 2013 Marc Féret and Pierre Legrand were liberated, I tried to contact them. I called the crisis unit in Paris and explained who I was. They put me through to a woman who told me that they never received any message from the Italian government about the two hostages."

Francesca Borri related a similar experience: "When Joakim Medin was kidnapped, in February 2015, I was supposed to meet him for dinner [that] very evening at Erbil on his way back from Syria. When he did not show up I checked the news and discovered that it was reported that he had been kidnapped in Turkey, but I knew that that was impossible, because he was in Syria; I got a text from him from Syria just a few hours before he vanished. So I called the Italian consul in Erbil and asked him to contact the Swedish authorities and to let them know that Joakim had been kidnapped in Syria. The consul passed the information to the Italian crisis unit, a few hours after the Ministry of Foreign Affairs called me to tell me that, due to a specific protocol, they could not pass on any information about the kidnapping. So I used social media, I put on Twitter an appeal to the Swedish Ministry of Foreign Affairs to contact me about the kidnapping of Joakim Medin. They called me after less than an hour."[166]

By pitting one negotiator against another, ISIS netted a huge amount in ransoms. Ottosen was one of the last hostages to be released, and several sources have confirmed that his ransom far exceeded the €2 million reported by the media. Unofficial sources estimate it at €6 million. In the trade-off between the ransom and the propaganda that his execution would have produced, ISIS opted for several million euros. The timing was also right. After Ottosen's liberation, the Islamic State's attitude towards releasing hostages for ransom changed. As detailed in later chapters, some hostages are a commodity worth more dead than alive.

How did the Ottosen family, people of modest means, raise such a sum? The Guardian Group took Ottosen's case even though the family had no means to pay them. They instructed them how to raise money. Ottosen's sister took charge of soliciting donations among the community of gymnasts, including a campaign on Facebook. She gathered about half of the ransom money. The Guardian Group used its connections among high net-worth individuals and companies to find the balance. The Guardian Group also arranged for the family to meet a lawyer who specialized in this business to control the incoming funds. The Danish government remained in the background. It did not interfere but was kept informed at all times, and eventually it granted permission for the family to release the ransom funds.

It was a remarkable show of solidarity among a security company, a European government, and several segments of the Danish population, including rich ship owners, industrialists, and even bankers. It was a joint effort to save one life, not the life of a celebrity, not the life of a politician or of a famous journalist, but the life of an unknown young Dane. It was a nightmare with a happy ending from the country where even fairy tales didn't tend to end very happily. The same cannot be said of the ordeal of another young European, Jejoen Bontinck.

INTO THE LION'S DEN

In early Spring 2013 journalist Joanie de Rijke and photographer Narciso Contreras accompanied Dimitri Bontinck into Syria to find his son, Jejoen. "Pretending to go to Amsterdam, in February Jejoen had packed his sleeping bag in his backpack and gone to Turkey," remembers de Rijke. "From Turkey he had crossed over to Syria to join some of his friends from Sharia4Belgium, a radical Salafist organization from Antwerp. His father, Dimitri, had recognized him in a propaganda video of ISIS. I saw him being interviewed on the news, saying that he wanted to go to Syria. At that moment we were about to go to Aleppo to bring food and other aid to people stranded there—something separate from journalism. So I called Dimitri and told him that we were planning to go and if he wanted, he could go with us."[167]

Jejoen Bontinck's background is very different from Daniel Rye Ottosen's, as is his story, but somehow he also ended up in Syria trying to find himself. Born to a Nigerian mother, Rose, and a Russian father, Dimitri, Jejoen grew up in a country foreign to both of his parents: Belgium. He was raised Catholic like his devout mother Rose, and attended a prestigious Jesuit school. As it happens to many male teenagers, when he was fifteen, he began having problems at school and with girlfriends and suddenly, he felt lost. There was nobody to reach out to, not a cousin, an uncle, a grandmother. The families of his parents lived thousands of miles away. But there were plenty of other kids like him, children of immigrants who experienced the same emptiness, who felt as lost as Jejoen in the ethnic melting pot of northern Europe.

A Moroccan girlfriend of Jejoen together with a Muslim neighbor, Azeddine, introduced him first to Islam and then to one of its most radical versions, radical Salafism. In November 2011, just three months after first learning about Islam, Jejoen arrived at 117 Dambruggestraat, in Antwerp, the headquarters of Sharia4Belgium, a radical Salafist organization.

"There are thousands of young people like Jejoen, children lost in a complex, scary world. They hit puberty and start seeing how different they are from the others. They all of a sudden feel like misfits everywhere—at school, at home, even among their friends. So when they encounter others who are equally lost, equally scared, they form a very strong bond,"[168] explains a psychologist who works with former jihadists in Europe.

Sharia4Belgium seems to have helped Jejoen, and many other kids like him, to fill their existential emptiness. Radical Salafism became the means to reinvent the world according to their needs. The Caliphate was the Nirvana where they were entitled to a better life as distinguished individuals. Listening to Jejoen's journey to radicalization in Belgium, which took place through lectures about radical Islam delivered by old men, through martial arts exercises, and through bonding with other young men like himself, one cannot avoid noticing how simple and unsophisticated the process actually was. Sharia4Belgium was not a proper recruitment organization whose task was to send fighters to Syria. It had no official ties to ISIS, al Qaeda, or any other groups. It was more like an improvised kindergarten for radical Salafists, inspired by the events happening in Syria, and with the absurd aim of transforming Belgium into a Muslim state, a state run according to sharia law.

Sharia4Belgium was also an arena for low-ranking radical preachers like Fouad Belkacem, a Belgian man born to a family of Moroccan immigrants, to spread outlandish ideas to an audience of immigrants' misfit children too ignorant about the true meaning of Islam to question them. And yet most of the members of Sharia4Belgium, including Jejoen, ended up in Syria fighting for either al Nusra or ISIS.

"The process of radicalization among these kids happens almost by osmosis," explains the psychologist of former jihadists. "Someone goes to Syria, which has been the magnet for quite some time, and starts texting how amazing his life is now that he is fighting for the Caliphate. Pictures are posted on social media. It is a showing off, something that young people do. Naturally, none of these kids understands what war is. They are also too young to have a sense of their own mortality. So the trip to Syria becomes a sort of exotic journey, an adventure to share among friends. When they get there the indoctrination starts. Most of them are brainwashed. In particular it is easy to convince them to trade their own identity with the one of the group, because they do not like themselves in the first place, otherwise, why would have joined groups such as Sharia4Belgium?"[169]

"The bonding of the group is very, very strong and you easily lose yourself as an individual; you just became part of it," confirmed Jean-René Augé-Napoli, who as an embedded journalist spent some time with a jihadist group in northern Syria.

When Jejoen finally reached Syria he joined one of these groups. Its members were enrolled in a training program that took place in a villa in Kafr Hamra, a small town on the outskirts of Aleppo. Less than a month after the arrival of Jejoen, a car stopped in front of the entrance of the villa and Dimitri stepped out.

"We drove to a walled villa in Kafr Hamra, one of the properties taken from the rich Syrian elite," remembers de Rijke. "It was an amazing place, with gardens, orchards. We had no idea what to expect, no idea at all . . . . Dimitri went in with two of our friends from Aleppo and the photographer, the driver and I remained in the car outside. We waited and waited. Then some people came from the villa and ordered us out of the car. They pushed the photographer and the driver against the car while I was standing on the other side and told us that we would be executed. I thought, this is it, I am going to die here, in the shadow of this villa."[170]

De Rijke learned only later what was happening inside while she was threatened with execution. When Dimitri had walked in he was introduced to the commander, who had offered him some tea and asked why he was in Syria. Dimitri answered that he was looking for his son, Jejoen—had the commander heard anything about him, did he have any knowledge of him? His host replied he did not. Then, while Dimitri was taking his leave, two people grabbed him from behind and dragged him into another room where he was stripped, beaten, and interrogated. They wanted to know how had he managed to get to the villa, and who had given him that address.

"Dimitri had contacted an organization, the Free Law-yers of Aleppo, that at the time was helping people locate their loved ones in Syria. They were somehow linked to that commander and had been given his address because they knew that it was a place for training the new recruits," explains a European negotiator I interviewed. But they did not believe Dimitri and continued beating him.

Then "suddenly they stopped," says Joanie de Rijke. "Just like that! The commander had changed his mind. They gave him back his clothes and told him to go. It was a miracle!"[171]

De Rijke admits that none of them knew who the com-mander was. Only later did they learn that Dimitri had stood in front of the highest ranking Syrian commander inside ISIS, Abu Athir, whose real name was Amr al Absi,[172] the Syrian emir in charge of the Mujahideen Shura Council, a group of international jihadists whose goal was to trans-form the northern part of the country into an Islamic state. Abu Athir was very well connected within ISIS, as his *katiba* had provided the first branch of the future Islamic State in Syria. When ISIS leader Abu Bakr al Baghdadi came to Syria from Iraq, Abu Athir had been one of the first jihad-ists to welcome him and to pledge allegiance.[173] He was one of al Baghdadi's right hand men in Syria, an incredibly powerful man.

"His brother was Firas al Absi, originally the emir of Mujahideen Shura Council and the leader of the men who in 2012 had kidnapped John Cantlie and the Dutch photographer Jeroen Oerlemans," explains the negoti-ator I interviewed. After Firas al Absi's death, Abu Athir took over the group, which grew from about one hun-dred eighty foreign fighters to almost a thousand. In the summer of 2013 he was officially charged with managing all the foreign hostages held by ISIS. Most likely he was also the brains behind the ransom negotiations together with ISIS's ruling elite.

"Dimitri was lucky," admits de Rijke. "We were all lucky. We had gone into the lion's den without even knowing that inside there was a feral animal."[174] But according to the European negotiator I interviewed, Dimitri's son, Jejoen, was not so lucky.

When Dimitri met Abu Athir, Jejoen was a few hundreds meters away, in the same villa, which indeed was being used as a major training ground for the new recruits. According to the account of the negotiator, "at the time his father arrived at the villa, Jejoen was in the intermediary stage of training. He was indoctrinated while his loyalty was tested. This involved some tricks; for example, they would show him and the others into a room with a computer and say 'do not touch it,' just to see if they would obey or not. Once they passed this stage, the recruits would be moved to the next level: they would be given small logistical tasks, for example, to do some surveillance. Gradually they would be trusted more and more. Because Dimitri showed up in the villa that day, they thought that Jejoen had contacted him and given the location, so they pulled him out of the training and put him in prison, under surveillance."[175]

This is not the version of events that Jejoen told to Joanie de Rijke and *The New Yorker*. In "Journey to Jihad,"[176] an article that recounts the story of Jejoen and of his rescue, the young man says that he had been imprisoned prior to his father's arrival because he had expressed the desire to go back home. Indeed, this is also the version that Jejoen gave the Belgian police when, after his return home, he was arrested. In the smoke-and-mirrors narrative of kidnapping and jihadism there are often many versions of the truth.

The negotiator's version of the story continues: "After his father pleaded with Abu Athir, Jejoen was taken to a prison in Aleppo where John Cantlie and James Foley were kept, to test his loyalty. The prison was run by Abu Obeida, a Dutch national whom Abu Athir trusted. Abu Obeida had the task of checking out Jejoen to find out how committed he really was. They both could speak Flemish so it was easy to build a relationship. Jejoen was under surveillance for a while, then little by little, he gained more freedom and eventually he was given some tasks, until he was re-inserted into the training program. During this time he kept in touch with his father, who eventually convinced him to come out."[177]

When he finally got back to Belgium, Jejoen was imprisoned and put on trial. He was given a forty month suspended sentence. In jail once again, but this time in Belgium, Jejoen rediscovered his feeling of being a misfit and began looking at his experience in Syria as an adventure he wanted to return to. On his release he again tried to board a plane to Turkey, but was stopped by the police.

After the Arab Spring, the seduction of Arab revolution against tyranny became, for some Westerners, irresistible. Among them was Kevin Dawes, an Asian American from San Diego, California. In June 2011, when he was twenty-nine years old, he travelled to Libya officially as a medical aid worker, but he was particularly attracted to the revolutionary narrative of the anti-Gaddafi insurgency. Dawes soon became an assistant to rebel medics on the Dafniyah-Misrata frontline, and eventually he joined the rebels in Sirte. In an interview with National Public Radio, Dawes explained how he morphed into a fighter: "We actually had an entire ambulance crew dragged out of their ambulance and executed. It was at that point we decided we had no choice. It was either this, or perish here."[178] So Kevin became a counter-sniper, watching windows and taking out people dangerous to his *katiba*.

Kevin Dawes's Libyan experience came to an abrupt end as he decided to leave his *katiba* but not the Jihadist environment.[179] In October of 2012 he travelled to Syria and was kidnapped by supporters of the Assad regime. It is unclear why he went to Syria; he claimed that he wanted to rescue Austin Tice, an American freelance journalist who disappeared in Syria in August 2012 and was previously a US marine, though Dawes also claimed to be a photo-journalist and a doctor on his way to help people in Syria. In addition, people who had met him claim that he was suffering from severe mental health problems including delusions and paranoia.

The story of his liberation in April 2016 is so engulfed in secrecy that some people have even thought that Dawes could have been a US spy. This seems very unlikely. In spring 2012 he unsuccessfully tried to raise money through a Kickstarter campaign called Aerial Battlefield Photojournalism. This project was intended to provide a unique view of the war in Syria via an aerial camera drone.[180] The goal of the project was to raise $28,000. However, Dawes was only able to get thirty dollars pledged. So he decided to go to Syria and report from the front line of the war himself.

In Antakya, Dawes tried to arrange transportation to Aleppo via some Facebook "friends," but when that did not materialize, he crossed into Syria alone and was immediately kidnapped and held hostage in Damascus. The only information released to the public is that John Kerry, President Obama's secretary of state, successfully negotiated his release with the help of the Czech Republic. Kerry, not incidentally, was also a key player in the negotiations to end the sanctions on Iran. It is very likely that Dawes ended up being part of such a deal. Kerry claimed that Tice would likewise soon be freed.[181]

As with the Europeans Jejoen and Ottosen, a distant war in the Middle East was perceived as a cry for freedom and justice, offering the Americans Tice and Dawes the opportunity to reinvent themselves, to acquire a new identity. But far from their intentions of living their dreams, they were all caught in a deadly political game they could not even begin to understand.

Young people have been kidnapped in Syria in body and in mind for years. They have walked into the lion's den without any knowledge of the perils, with the absurd idea that such a journey could offer them deliverance from a life in the West that they do not like or they do not want. They have done it believing that proving themselves in the darkest corner of the global village is not only possible, it is necessary to reinvent themselves.

Photojournalists, aid workers, jihadist warriors—they had all been lured into a phenomenal trap which has stripped them of their freedom, of their own identity, and even deprived them of their lives. They have been manipulated by adults, either in the West or in the Muslim world: by newspaper editors willing to buy their photos and articles for a few dollars; by preachers who utilize the Caliphate to seek fame; and by politicians playing down the political failure of globalization to hide Western policies' mistakes. They have been led to believe that their reckless actions would be valued, making them into better people and the world into a better place. In one way or another, all of these children who have defied their parents, friends, and nations are kids we have lost because we have failed to teach them how infinitely more dangerous the global village is in comparison to the world during the Cold War.

Even those we managed to bring home, like Jejoen, remain misfits, still unsure of where they really belong. They may be physically out of jail, but mentally, they still live very much behind racial and ideological bars.

chapter eleven

The Mythology of Western Hostages

Western governments portray all hostages as heroes, especially if they wear a uniform. Soldiers hold the highest ranking. They are the bravest: abducted while in the pursuit of their duty to protect their country. This is the narrative that justifies the decision to rescue them at any costs, including negotiating with terrorists. No government can ignore this commitment, including the United States.

Perhaps the best account of why, under the right circumstances, every country negotiates with kidnappers, is by President Obama: "The United States of America does not ever leave our men and women in uniform behind."[182] This pronouncement was made on May 31, 2014, in the Rose Garden when Barack Obama announced the liberation of Sergeant Bowe Bergdahl. The then twenty-eight-year-old soldier had been kidnapped by the Taliban in Afghanistan almost five years earlier on June 30, 2009. During the speech the president revealed that to free the hostage the United States had agreed to transfer five detainees from the Guantánamo Bay detention camp to Qatar, the country that had helped broker the deal.[183]

The ceremony held at the Rose Garden was supposed

to be the first of several celebrations to welcome home Sergeant Bergdahl. Instead, almost as soon as he set foot on US soil, things went sour. Several members of his platoon in Afghanistan accused him of being a deserter and someone even hinted that he might be a traitor. Republicans lashed out at President Obama for having secured his release without properly informing Congress, and putting US national security at risk. Some even criticized Bergdahl's father for having spoken a few words in Pashto during the Rose Garden ceremony. As more and more of the details about Sergeant Bergdahl's abduction became known, the polemics linked to his release, abduction, and ransom soared.

THE BOURNE FOOLISHNESS

Bowe Bergdahl was kidnapped on the morning of June 30, 2009, while walking alone in the Afghan desert, a few miles from the tiny outpost known as OP Mest where he was posted. Mest is in the Paktika Province, in eastern Afghanistan, right near the Pakistani border. A few hours earlier, Bergdahl had left his post without permission. Technically speaking, he had deserted his platoon.

Just after sunrise, a Taliban group on motorcycles spotted and approached him, as is customary in any desert region. Because he was not wearing his uniform but Afghan clothes, the Taliban realized that he was not a Pashtun only when they got close to him.

Bergdahl's story begs several questions: What was a twenty-three-year-old soldier doing alone in the middle of the Afghan desert? How did he get there? And why was he unarmed in a region infested by the Taliban?

After his liberation, Bergdahl did not speak to the media, and US authorities did not release any information. Very little was known about the precious hours before his abduction. Privately, however, Bergdahl disclosed the events that led to his captivity to Mark Boal, the screenwriter of *The Hurt Locker* and *Zero Dark Thirty*. Boal approached Bergdahl because he wanted to make a movie of his story. Some of the recorded conversations between them, a total of about twenty-five hours, were used by the popular podcast *Serial* in its second series.[184] The podcast reveals some interesting and disconcerting aspects of Bergdahl's abduction. For example, the kidnapping appears to have been the direct result of a twenty-three-year-old soldier who believed that he could prove to the world and to himself that he was a real-life Jason Bourne, the fictional hero of the Bourne film trilogy based on the Robert Ludlum novels.[185]

For a start, Bowe Bergdahl admitted to Mark Boal that he had staged his own disappearance. His plan was to walk from his base at Mest to the other, much bigger US military post at Sharana. Sharana is about twenty miles southwest of Mest. Bergdahl thought he could reach it in about twenty-four hours, a rather optimistic forecast. The route is long and difficult, especially in the summer heat, traversing the desert. It is also quite risky. The area is under Taliban control and people travel back and forth regularly. Someone was bound to see Bergdahl, approach him, and discover that he was not a Pashtun but an American. But Bergdahl did not consider these likely outcomes. For him, it was sufficient to be physically fit for the trek, and he was confident that wearing civilian clothes would be a perfect disguise.

The key question that Mark Boal asked Bergdahl was, "Why disappear for twenty-four hours?" Bergdahl answered that he wanted to trigger a DUSTWUN, military-speak for "duty status—whereabouts unknown," the army's version of "man overboard," a major military emergency. And indeed this is exactly what happened. When the platoon realized that he had vanished, everyone from the CIA to the Navy, to the Air Force, to the Marines, and all US military contingents present in Afghanistan, were alerted. From there news of his disappearance eventually reached Washington, D.C., the Pentagon, the State Department, and the White House.

It would seem that this young soldier triggered a major military crisis in order to expose another, larger crisis, which he believed was so serious that it required an exceptional event.[186] That is, Bergdahl knew that DUSTWUN would direct widespread attention to him, and that when he reappeared in Sharana he would be debriefed by his superiors. He believed that this was his only chance to sit face to face with high ranking officers, even generals, and be heard. He believed that he could finally voice his serious concerns about the leadership of his platoon, and of the US Army in Afghanistan in general. He had even written to his father about these worries, seeking advice. But the plan was based on delusions of grandeur.

On the night of June 29, 2009, Bergdahl snuck out of the camp and began his trek towards Sharana. Just like Jason Bourne, Bowe Bergdahl acted alone. During the previous days he had sent home most of his possessions to prevent anybody from checking them, and he had withdrawn $300 in cash from his account, money he thought he might need during the trek. He had taken a compass and a knife with him, but he had left behind his night vision goggles, his weapons, and his radio.

When he reached the desert, he suddenly realized what he had done. The magnitude, and perhaps the stupidity, of his plan hit him. Unlike the hero of the Bourne movie series, Bergdahl panicked. Though he wanted to go back, he judged it too risky to do so at nighttime. The sentinels would have shot at him not knowing who he was. But above all, he was concerned about what would happen to him once his superiors realized that he had left his platoon without permission. To the army, he was already a deserter.

Under the Afghan night sky, Bergdahl developed another, even more absurd, plan of action. He decided that if he could return with some valuable intelligence to show, his superiors would be lenient. He remembered hearing that on the road from Mest to Sharana the Taliban sometimes placed IEDs (improvised explosive devices), so he decided to look for people planting them. He would act as a sort of Special Forces soldier and either catch them or follow them to their hideout and then report their location to his superiors. He began to look for flashlights bobbing up and down, and listened for the crackle of radios.

"The idea would have been, if I had seen somebody in the darkness who looked like they were doing something suspicious, I would then slowly, quietly follow them in the night," Bergdahl told Boal. "And then, in the morning, pick up their trail and track them to wherever it is that they're going. Then I'd get that information . . . . [W]hen I got back to [Mest], you know, they could say, you know, well, you left your position. But I could say, well, I also got this information, so, you know, what are you going to do? I have this information of this person who is doing this on this night, and they live here. And so that would be like justifiable, like: He left his post . . . but he collected intel that helped us stop, you know, somebody who was putting an IED in the road. You know, that would've been the bonus point that would have helped me deal with the whole, basically, hurricane of horror—or not hurricane of horror, but hurricane of wrath—that was gonna hit me once I got back to [Mest]."[187]

Listening to Bowe Bergdahl, one cannot help but think how naïve his plan was and how delusional the sergeant was about his "mission." He admitted to Boal that he wanted to prove to himself and to the world that he was a super soldier, someone like Jason Bourne, an imaginary character who singlehandedly could expose a major weakness of the military system. Instead, he behaved stupidly, and was kidnapped and held hostage for almost five years. DUSTWUN triggered a massive search that cost the American taxpayer millions of dollars.

Media reports written soon after Bergdahl was freed claimed that the search for Bergdahl may have even cost the lives of six fellow soldiers, though this claim has since been shown as likely fabricated by members of his battalion. No US soldier's death has ever been directly linked to the DUSTWUN. Nonetheless, at the time, popular attribution of Bergdahl's responsibility for the deaths of six US soldiers compounded public anger over the deal struck by US authorities to bring him home.[188]

As the media spread the story, Bowe Bergdahl's kidnapping and release became more and more political. The White House had agreed to exchange him for five high-ranking members of the Taliban, as part of a reconciliation process between the US and the Taliban first masterminded by Obama and Hillary Clinton in 2009. That reconciliation process ultimately went sour, and Sergeant Bergdahl came to be regarded as just further evidence of its failure.

RECKLESS BEHAVIOR

Most Westerners are kidnapped not because they are heroes but because they fail to comprehend the risk they are taking. Bowe Bergdahl falls into this category. So do many other former hostages, including some of those beheaded by the Islamic State. "The Jim Foley I knew was a real nice guy but he did act exactly as security people who run courses to prevent kidnapping tell you not to behave," said Francesca Borri.

This portrait of Foley partly corresponds to the description of him provided by the European negotiator who tried to bring him home.

"The last time I saw Jimmy was in Aleppo," continues Borri. "We were leaving the Al Shifa Hospital, which was constantly under attack. We stopped to distribute our supplies to the people that stayed behind and to pick up those who were heading for Turkey, like myself, Jim Foley, Narciso Contreras, Antonio Pampliega, Manu Brabo, the boys who later on won the Pulitzer Prize. Everybody had taken off their bulletproof jackets and they were relaxed after a long work day. Suddenly the hospital came under mortar attack. We jumped into the first service van we found and fled. It was a very serious situation: bombs and bullets were flying all over. The driver was so scared that he got lost twice. But Jimmy was laughing!

"I was petrified with fear and Jimmy was laughing. I remember that Narciso Contreras, who was sitting in front, kept looking at me. He had understood very well how scared I was. I was particularly stressed because I had left behind someone I cared about. He had not managed to jump into the van when all hell had broken loose. Jimmy kept laughing at me, telling me that these types of situations are not for women.

"Everybody was hiding behind the doors of the van for fear of being hit by a flying bullet but Jimmy rolled down the window and put his arm out, waving, shouting 'Allahu Akbar, Allahu Akbar!' A gesture that, among other things, shows no respect and sensitivity for the driver who was desperately trying to keep it together and save our lives. This is the last image I have of Jim Foley! Perhaps this reckless behavior was the result of being in a state of shock. Indeed, extreme fear can trigger a sense of immortality," says Borri.

"It's easy to feel invincible, even with death all around," Steven Sotloff, also kidnapped and beheaded by the Islamic State, wrote to the Middle East editor for *Newsweek*. "It's like, 'This is my movie, sucker—I'm not gonna die.'"[189] However, this feeling of invincibility is exactly the behavior that gets one kidnapped and killed.

"Steven Sotloff was my friend," says the Syrian journalist Omar al Muqdad, producer of the BBC documentary *We Left Them Behind*. "Two weeks before leaving for Syria he came to me and said that he needed my help because he wanted to travel to Syria. I told him not to go. It was risky for me. For him it was extremely dangerous, but he did not listen. He mentioned a few names, all scumbags, people who would sell him for a few hundred dollars. I told him so. But he did not listen. He called me before crossing into Syria. I again urged him not to trust his fixer. I am convinced his fixer sold him. As soon as he crossed the border from Turkey, just fifteen minutes after, he was kidnapped. After he crossed into Syria I tried to call his mobile but I got no answer."[190]

Both Steven Sotloff, the aspiring journalist, and Daniel Rye Ottosen, the aspiring photographer, were warned not to cross over into Syria by people who knew how risky their plans were. They did not listen. They were kidnapped and eventually ended up in the hands of the Islamic State.

In the trailer for the HBO documentary about James Foley, *Jim: The James Foley Story*,[191] people like Sotloff, Ottosen, and Foley are presented as journalist-martyrs. The message is that without them we would not know the horrors of the Syrian Civil War. But this is not completely correct. We celebrate them not because they showed us the tragedy of Syria but because they were kidnapped and, in the case of Sotloff and Foley, beheaded by the Islamic State. The proof is that the public did not know who they were before their abduction, as their articles did not appear on the front pages of any distinguished newspapers. Likewise, today the public is still unaware of the names of the free-lancers who are reporting on the Syrian conflict, or even most of the names of abducted journalists who remain in captivity!

The disturbing news that made us aware of the existence of people like Sotloff, Ottosen, and Foley wasn't the news that they reported, but the news of their abductions and their deaths. Professional journalists understand this. Marc Marginedas, also held hostage by ISIS, said that he did not want to discuss his abduction because he is not the news; the news is what is happening in Syria. Nicolas Hénin, another journalist and hostage held captive by the Islamic State, warned readers of his book, *Jihad Academy*, that he did not write about his captivity, of his interaction with "The Beatles"—the British-born jailers of the foreign hostages held by the Islamic State—and his fellow hostages, but about what is happening in Syria and the Middle East, because even while held hostage he did not stop being a journalist.

The mythology that the West constructs around the hostages hides the shocking fact that stories about Syria or the Middle East written by people like Sotloff and Foley never appeared on the front page of the *New York Times* or anyplace else with a substantial readership and thus never stirred any reaction among citizens in Europe or America or Japan or anywhere else in the West. The reason? The public does not care enough about Syria sliding into total anarchy, and the writers were unknown freelancers. People in America were much more interested in the riots in Ferguson, Missouri, than the suffering of the Syrian people. Until the birth of the Caliphate, Western freelancers in Syria only produced very marginal news that was published in very small and peripheral online publications or newspapers.

What kept these freelancers going was the dream of getting a scoop. In her memoir, *A House in the Sky*, Amanda Lindhout describes such a dream. She uses the story of Dan Rather as an example. When in the 1960s Rather was still a young and inexperienced reporter working for a small TV station in Houston, Texas, a huge hurricane reached the Gulf of Mexico, heading for the island of Galveston. Everyone took cover, but Dan Rather drove over the bridge and waited for the hurricane to hit Galveston. When the storm reached the island he delivered his reports in the middle of the hurricane. Lindhout concludes that

that day Dan Rather could have died but instead he survived the storm and got the footage that made his career.[192]

Freelancers wait for that unique opportunity. But the chances are that even when such opportunities materialize today, they don't produce the same results. For a start, today there would be a crowd of reporters and cameramen heading for the hurricane. The report would be a mere blip in the twenty-four-hour news cycle. Finally, with wars a nearly constant reality across the globe, and Western audiences ever more cynical that anything can be done to stop them, the scoop of a lifetime is becoming a thing of the past. Aspiring reporters may spend their lives brushing with death for nothing. Many become so accustomed to the adrenalin of war that they keep going back for more, taking greater and greater risks to get their fix.

Even in the parallel world that they inhabit, however, there are opportunities for true heroism. The James Foley that fellow hostages portray is indeed a hero. He was a pillar of strength for his fellow captives. And this indeed should be news. The man who seconds before being beheaded in front of the camera recites a script condemning his own brother and his country may seem like another unheroic man. But did he agree to recite those sentences to protect his fellow hostages from retaliation by ISIS? It is highly probable.

The media has not even attempted to ask such questions or portray a range of possible perspectives. The wars in Syria, Afghanistan, and Iraq have not been honorable, humanitarian endeavors; they have been dirty wars, wars of continuous embarrassment for politicians, for the army, and for the West. As with the Vietnam War, Western mass media has chosen to avoid the truth of these conflicts to pander to sentiments of Western victims as "supernatural heroes," the better to keep these conflicts at a safe distance from their imagined innocence.

Stereotyping hostages, styling them as heroes as governments do, hides the human complexity of their individual personalities and the complexity also of the situation they are in as hostages. Bowe Bergdahl may have been a bad soldier, but he was also an outstanding POW who survived captivity for five years in abysmal conditions. Not since Vietnam has the US Army had the chance to study and learn from this type of survival: here was a fount of information regarding how an individual copes with harsh captivity, and why such an individual can handle such extremes of stress. The most important contribution made by Sergeant Bergdahl could have been to the science of his very survival, but instead he has been put to only further sensationalist political use.

The narratives of hostages coping with extreme violence and deprivation of freedom tend to be mined for emotional sentiment, shock value, and hero-worship rather than any deeper meaning regarding the causes or effects of their plight. Reducing the lives of hostages to a single news item nearly always hides the truth. Physical pain and emotional trauma trigger complex emotional and psychological responses in anyone who has been a hostage. And the media itself, with its constant craving for each news story to be even more shocking than the last, combined with the current media practice of cutting more and more corners, must also bear some of the responsibility for these kidnappings and deaths. Would the current situation be what it is if the major newspapers of the world still had foreign bureaus in the Middle East as they once did?

IMPRUDENCE, THE SIN OF YOUTH

Hiding the truth also plays into the hands of kidnappers. It prevents the formulation of new strategies by perpetuating a practice (paying ransom), which makes kidnapping a profitable business and improperly alters Westerners' perception of risk. This is particularly true for Italians because they know that their government will always pay the ransom. More than one Italian journalist admitted to me that they take higher risks because of the certainty that Italy will rescue them.

The policy of the Italian government has been to pay a ransom for anyone holding an Italian passport, regardless of who they are: journalists, aid workers, and even tourists who reside abroad, as was the case of Bruno Pelizzari, discussed in Chapter Eight. The Italian government went so far as to pay the ransom for Debbie Calitz, even though she did not have an Italian passport, but rather was sailing with Pelizzari at the time of the abduction. The Italian government also paid the ransom for the Belgian Piccinin abducted together with Quirico, as described by the Al Jazeera documentary *The Hostage Business*.[193]

Naturally, the Italian public is told that no ransom has ever been paid. In the case of Pelizzari, the truth was hidden behind elaborate fabrications. The secrecy surrounding the abduction, negotiation, and ransom payment is fundamental to the construction of any fictitious narrative about the hostages. It becomes an empty box, which the media actively participate in filling with mythological stories about the hostages, as was the case with the Two Simonas.

This web of lies and deceit is at the center of the kidnapping industry. The common narrative—captured heroes saved by payment of a ransom that is never admitted—has the effect of increasing the value of certain hostages and decreasing the bargaining power of those negotiating their release because the kidnappers know that a ransom will eventually always be paid. Finally, as we have seen, profits from the kidnapping industry become seed money for trafficking migrants heading for Europe. Ironically, one of the most popular gates of entry to the Old Continent is southern Italy.

Although the Western public is not aware of these developments, polemics similar to those that erupted about the abduction and ransom paid to liberate Sergeant Bowe Bergdahl are surfacing everywhere, including in Italy. The most recent controversy refers to the payment of a multi-million dollar ransom for Greta Ramelli and Vanessa Marzullo, kidnapped in Aleppo on July 31, 2014, just a few days after their arrival in Turkey and released on January 16, 2015.

As was the case with Sergeant Bergdahl, there are several versions of the kidnapping of Ramelli and Marzullo. Some people said that they were abducted with an Italian journalist, Daniele Raineri, with whom they had crossed the border into Syria. However, Raineri denied this and presented a different account of events. On the night of the kidnapping he was at the house of a rebel leader, a former member of Assad's Special Forces. As he told the Italian newspaper *Il Foglio*, "At five in the morning there were knocks on the door. Two Syrians came in and said, 'They have kidnapped the two Italians [Greta and Vanessa]. They're looking for you, too.'" When Raineri asked whether the men searching for him were guerrillas or just a gang of armed men, they could not tell him. "They told me they wore ski masks, almost all of them, and pointed at my face so I was certain to understand them."[194] According to Raineri, he immediately headed for the Turkish border with an escort that his rebel friends provided. Once in Turkey, he alerted the Italian crisis unit.

After their liberation, Ramelli and Marzullo explained the dynamics of their kidnapping to the Italian magistrates. Hours after they reached their destination, the house of the head of "the Revolutionary Council," a Syrian they had met on Facebook, they were kidnapped. They never met their host. Both women had been in Syria twice between April and May of the same year. After securing donations of €2,400 in Italy, they had brought medicine and food, which they distributed in the region of Idlib, in the north of Syria, and Homs, in the south. According to several sources, in July 2014 Ramelli and Marzullo were bringing camouflaged medical kits, which they showed on the Facebook page of Horryaty, the nonprofit company they had formed in April 2014 to help the Syrian independence cause.

From the reconstruction of the abduction, it appears that their kidnapping had been arranged before their arrival. "Two cars with armed men arrived and we were taken away. We kept our heads down. We tried not to look at them in the eyes. Their faces were covered. The kidnappers spoke very little, only one spoke a few words of English. . . . After being captured we asked 'why are you doing this?' And they replied, 'We do it for the money.'"[195]

During their captivity, the hostages were moved five times. It is likely that they were sold more than once. Possibly the group that contacted Samir Aita, a member of the Syrian Democratic Forum who lives in Paris, was the group that abducted them. Eventually they were purchased by al Nusra, which conducted the negotiations direct with the Italian government.[196] The ransom of €11 millio was filmed and shown by Al Jazeera in the documenta *The Hostage Business*. But according to a new investigatio the Italians paid not €11 million but €13 million of whic €1 or €2 million never reached the kidnappers. The Italia authorities suspect that it was pocketed by an Italian inte mediary who conducted the final negotiations either i Syria or across the border, in Turkey.[197] Part of the ranso about €5 million, was also pocketed by another interm diary, Hussam Atrash, a warlord at the head of the grou Ansar al Islam.

The controversy surrounding the kidnapping of Ramel and Marzullo goes well beyond the amount of the ranso and touches on the very nature of the Italian ONLUS, kind of nonprofit organization with less stringent requir ments than traditional nonprofits. Together with a thir member, Ramelli and Marzullo had founded the ONLU called Horryaty with a few thousand dollars. They wer its only staff. They operated from a Facebook fan pag and raised money using this means. The fact that the tw women were in Syria ostensibly on a charitable missio played a significant role in the discussion surroundin their rescue, despite the fact that their ONLUS was onl just barely legitimate.

Since 1997, when this type of association was introduce by the Italian legislation, ONLUSes have proliferate Today there are about forty thousand of them. This is mor than 10 percent of the total number of Italian nonprof organizations. According to Istat, the national statisti bureau of Italy, at the end of 2013 there were 301,191 nor profit institutions active in Italy, about 28 percent mor

than in 2001. The number of Italians working for these
organizations, either receiving a salary or simply doing
volunteer work, was a staggering 4.7 million.

The popularity of ONLUSes springs from the fiscal
advantages attached to their nonprofit stature and from the
ease and low cost required to establish one, about €2,000.
Once registered, an ONLUS can start raising money for
whichever cause it was created to support: from cultural
events, to sports, to humanitarian aid, as was the case of
Horryaty. Because an ONLUS is essentially a fiscal entity, it
comes under the jurisdiction of the Italian fiscal authorities.

The situation was different before 1997. Humanitarian
NGOs came under the jurisdiction of the Foreign Ministry.[198] Because until about 15 to 20 years ago most of the
funds used by the NGOs were public money, the Ministry
of Foreign Affairs regulated its allocation. During the last
twenty years, however, humanitarian aid organizations
have successfully gathered funds from private donors, a
phenomenon which explains the need for a preferential
fiscal treatment provided by the status of ONLUSes. "Out
of about 40,000 ONLUSes, today about 250 of those organizations formerly recognized by the Ministry of Foreign
Affairs as NGOs qualified according to the legislation of
1987 which regulated international cooperation," says
Marco De Ponte, secretary-general for ActionAid in Italy.
This explains why Horryaty did not appear on this [Min-
istry of Foreign Affairs] list of NGOs, but does not explain
why both Greta Ramelli and Vanessa Marzullo did not
inform the Ministry of Foreign Affairs that they were traveling to Syria.

As with the Two Simonas, the Italian government
denied the payment of the ransom and assumed a soft atti-

tude towards the reckless behavior of Greta and Vanessa. In a TV interview, the Italian foreign minister said that while he recognized that the two women had acted recklessly, they deserved help because they were helping people in difficult circumstances. Once again the narrative woven around the hostages portrayed them as exceptional human beings, even though these women were naïve upstarts. During the interview there is no mention of what in particular Ramelli and Marzullo purported to do in Syria. The reconstruction of their abduction is vague and carefully avoids important details: How did they end up in the house where they were kidnapped? How many times were they moved around? What ever happened to the camouflage medical kits they had brought with them? Answering these questions would have deconstructed the mythology of the two women as modern-day Florence Nightingales.

During the same TV interview, an Italian journalist, Beppe Severgnini, praising the government for having brought home yet another couple of hostages, while admitting that they had been imprudent, added that imprudence is a sin of youth. Naturally, he did not mention that such "youthful" behavior had cost Italian taxpayers €13 million.[199]

NEGOTIATING WITH TERRORISTS

No matter what cover story they use, everybody ultimately negotiates with kidnappers and terrorists. Some countries, like Italy, pay exceptionally high ransoms, while others, like the US, trade hostages for captured enemy combatants. For governments, hostages are political merchandise. They may represent percentage points in opinion polls, or they can be instruments in the implementation of foreign policy strategies. Indeed, this latter role seems to be the one played by Bowe Bergdahl.

From the outstanding reconstruction of his ordeal conducted by the podcast *Serial*,[200] it emerged that Sergeant Bergdahl owes his freedom to a series of exceptional events. As soon as he disappeared, Kim Harrison, listed as the person to contact if something happened to Bowe, began enquiring about the procedures for finding him. Finding few answers and a lot of red tape, she eventually decided to go to the FBI and file a missing persons report. In November 2009 she was contacted by the Taliban, or at least that is what she thought. The FBI translated the Pashto message she received from someone who claimed to know where Bergdahl was being held. In exchange, the sender of the message wanted to move to the US with eight members of his family.

No government agencies wanted to handle the issue, and the US did not have reliable sources in the region to verify the information. By then Bowe was wanted by both the CIA and the military, especially due to questions about why he had left his post. But two women working for the US Army's Personnel Recovery Unit, the one that deals with hostages, began campaigning for his release among top-ranking military officers. They did it quietly, discreetly. At the same time, a military analyst who had worked directly on the case contacted the family and offered his help. All of them felt that no matter why Sergeant Bergdahl had been captured, he was still an American in a hostile country, and he was a hostage. Their primary duty was to bring him home, and then the authorities could deal with his motivations.

In the podcast *Serial*, the military analyst is known by the fictitious name "Nathan." Nathan guided the Bergdahl family in their search for help in recovering Bowe, hoping to reach somebody important in the US government who could authorize negotiations for his safe return. Their objective was to somehow get close to President Obama and get him to back a strategy for bringing Bowe home. Nathan knew that, despite ostensible intransigence, the US indeed negotiates with terrorists and kidnappers to free hostages. As he indicated on *Serial*, if the CIA had gotten contractor Raymond Davis out of Pakistan,[201] despite his arrest for murdering two people, why not negotiate to free Sergeant Bergdahl?

Nathan's coaching of Bowe's parents began to bear some fruit: a couple of generals took the matter to heart, and they, in turn, could advocate among high government officials for Bowe's rescue. But it was only when Bergdahl became part of a major foreign policy project, the reconciliation with the Taliban, that freeing Bowe Bergdahl became a priority. As part of a "trade," he was going to be exchanged for five members of the Taliban held in Guantánamo Bay. Trading these prisoners represented only a small part of the deal; the White House was also anxious to end the war in Afghanistan, to bring the troops back home. To achieve this larger goal, it was imperative to make some appeasements and to end the war with the Taliban.

Naturally, nobody knew about this plan apart from those very close to the president and secretary of state. The full reconciliation project never actually panned out, but the exchange did take place as planned. Had the White House kept a low profile and avoided using the release of Sergeant Bergdahl for publicity purposes at home, it is likely that the public outcry and negative media regarding Bergdahl's desertion and prisoner swap with the Taliban would never have happened. The presentation of Bowe as a hero outraged some of his fellow soldiers in Afghanistan. They publicly denounced Bergdahl's actions and cast aspersions upon the official story of why he had been kidnapped, and the media and politicians like John McCain were quick to join the feeding frenzy.

Hostages can easily become political merchandise, for officials, reporters, businesses—and even for the public.

PART 3

chapter twelve

The End of Truth

In Syria the Islamic State took kidnapping to a new level, transforming it into a very powerful propaganda tool and, ultimately, an instrument of foreign policy. Most likely, its leadership had crafted this strategy years earlier, while Abu Bakr al Baghdadi was imprisoned in Camp Bucca planning the rise to power of the Caliphate with former members of Saddam Hussein's military intelligence. These men, who would become the ruling elite of the new state, had joined al Zarqawi's jihadists in 2003, soon after Paul Bremer launched the de-Baathification program.[202] Among the strategic tasks ISIS would take on was silencing the media in Syria. Indeed, the Baathists had accumulated extensive experience doing this during Saddam Hussein's regime.

Though in the 1960s the Iraqi media was among the most liberal in the Arab world, Saddam Hussein success-fully destroyed it by introducing an institutionalized system of repression and censorship. In Syria, ISIS replicated this violent model using kidnapping, prolonged detention, tor-ture, and even executions of journalists. Milad al Shihabi, a Syrian reporter from the Shahba Press Agency, witnessed this brutality.

"Three masked, heavily armed men came to my office," remembered al Shihabi. "I thought it was a joke, but I was wrong. They took me to the basement of the children's hospital. When I asked what was I accused of, they replied, 'You hate ISIS. This is the charge against you.'"[203] For thirteen days the Syrian journalist was kept in a tiny cell, blindfolded. He was not allowed to wash, not even before praying. "It was very cold and I had to sleep on the floor with a small blanket. The food was insufficient but when I asked for more they hung me from the ceiling and left me there for four hours."

Like all the other prisoners, Milad al Shihabi was tortured and beaten senseless. While in captivity he witnessed the execution of four colleagues from the Shaza al Horya TV channel. Seventeen days after his abduction, he was freed by a group of fighters from the Free Syrian Army when they stormed the hospital. Soon after, he fled to Turkey with no documents or papers, as a refugee.[204]

From as early as the end of 2011, ISIS closely watched Arab journalists who travelled to southern Turkey looking for stories about the Syrian conflict. Replicating Saddam's very efficient censorship bureau, the Islamic State set up an Information Security Team in Turkey, whose task was to collect information about anything or anyone that could harm the Islamic State. Initially, Arab reporters and activists were pursued because they had the power to influence Muslim public opinion. Later on, towards the end of 2012, ISIS spies began targeting foreign media also.

"The media is considered *takfir*," an ISIS informer who asked to be called Abu Hurayrah, explained to Omar al Muqdad in 2015 during the filming of his documentary *We Left Them Behind*. "Reporters are our enemies." Abu Hurayrah had joined ISIS from al Nusra and was working as a spy in Antakya. His task was to identify which journalists, aid workers, or activists represented a threat to ISIS and to file reports about them. Someone else would then make the decision whether they should be kidnapped or eliminated.[205] He even admitted that in 2014, when Omar al Muqdad visited Antakya intending to cross over to Syria, he had targeted him and passed on the information to ISIS. However, at the last minute, al Muqdad decided not to enter Syria.

While ISIS worked at silencing the Arab media, the insurgency targeted foreign journalists, not to silence them but to kidnap them for ransom. Several networks of spies and informants posed as fixers, drivers, or members of the Free Syrian Army in Turkish towns near the Syrian border, from where they could lure foreign reporters into Syria by offering bogus scoops about the civil war and the insurgency. Such was the case with Richard Engel's crew, kidnapped in Syria in December 2012. As soon as they entered Syria the reporters were kidnapped. Though professional journalists like Engel also fell into this trap, most of the victims of the kidnapping racket were freelancers, like Theo Padnos, an American freelance journalist, abducted in the fall of 2012.

Just like Daniel Rye Ottosen, Padnos was not a professional journalist and did not have any experience reporting from war zones. Rather, he was a middle-aged man who had spent a few years learning Arabic in Yemen, and had lived in Damascus for a brief period until the summer of 2012. Back in the US, he had tried to sell essays and articles about Islam to magazines and newspapers, but no publications seemed interested in his writings. In October 2012 he decided to move to Antakya, hoping to collect stories about the Syrian conflict to sell to the US media. Padnos, like Ottosen, had no contacts in Syria nor in Turkey and sought them out when he arrived in Antakya, as all freelancers do, by talking to the local people and other freelancers. When three young men who claimed to be providing supplies to the Free Syrian Army offered to smuggle him into Syria, he did not hesitate to join them. The next day they kidnapped him.

In the account of his capture published in the *New York Times*,[206] Padnos admits to having fallen into a trap because he was very naïve about the jihadists, the insurgency, and the Syrian conflict. Reading the article, one has the feeling that, though he was knowledgeable about the history and culture of Islam and he spoke Arabic fluently, he did not understand the complex politics of the region nor the shifting alliances and loyalties of the Syrian war by proxy.

Unlike many other kidnapped journalists, Theo Padnos was lucky. His kidnappers were from al Nusra and not from the Islamic State: they wanted money, not his head. He was also lucky because Dave Bradley, a Washington, D.C. entrepreneur who owns the media company that publishes *The Atlantic*, got personally involved in the release of the American hostages held in Syria. Unfortunately, Padnos was the only hostage Bradley was able to bring home safely.

Dave Bradley got hold of Ali Soufan, a former FBI agent who knew the jihadist world very well. Soufan suggested contacting the Qataris who had arranged for the exchange of the Taliban prisoners for Bowe Bergdahl, the American soldier kidnapped in Afghanistan, on behalf of the American government. The Qataris agreed to get involved in negotiating Padnos's release.[207]

In August 2014, just days after the barbaric beheading of James Foley, Padnos was released. "The Qataris paid the ransom," says an Arab negotiator. "They had been bank-rolling al Nusra in Syria right from the outset of the civil war, so they had an inside track to its leadership. But it took a long time to convince Abu Mariya al Qahtani, known as the Man of Learning, the commander of the group that kept Padnos hostage, to let him go."

Ironically, it was because the Islamic State had been crushing al Nusra for a while, pushing it out of key areas, that the Man of Learning agreed to the ransom. "He needed money, weapons, and protection to fight back. Padnos was a US citizen; he was worth all of this. I would not be surprised if the ransom also included weapons and training," concluded the Arab negotiator.

HUMAN BOUNTY

The end of 2012 saw the beginning of the season of "jihadist mergers" in Syria as more and more groups decided to join the ranks of the Islamic State. Some of the commanders of al Nusra brought foreign hostages into the negotiations as a sort of human bounty. Among them were John Cantlie and James Foley. By then ISIS was ready to work at silencing the foreign media and at using hostages as an instrument of its foreign policy. In the space of a few months, the Information Security Team targeted several journalists and aid workers. Others were purchased in Syria from the hostage secondary market from smaller groups specializing in kidnapping.

To date, John Cantlie is the sole hostage of that original group of foreigners captured between the end of 2012 and the beginning of 2014 still held by the Islamic State. Interestingly, he has not been beheaded but transformed into a reporter from inside the Caliphate, broadcasting whatever ISIS wants us to believe.

Cantlie is a UK photojournalist with a rather unusual profile. He was a motorcycle aficionado who went from being the editor of a motorcycle magazine to one of the thousand freelance war reporters in the Middle East, a metamorphosis which took place when he, like Padnos, was already middle-aged.

When Cantlie arrived in Syria in 2012, apart from a brief period in Libya he had no experience reporting from war-zones. Hence, his assessment of the risk of his new profession was very poor. "John did not believe in *ad hoc* training or survival courses before going into war zones. He was a bit of a cowboy," remembers an American colleague who in 2012 attended an event on media security at the Frontline Club in London with Cantlie.

John Cantlie, like James Foley, Theo Padnos, and Daniel Rye Ottosen, belongs to a new breed of war reporters: freelancers who appeared for the first time during the war in Kosovo and proliferated during the Arab Spring. In Syria they became ideal human bounty for the kidnappers.

The proliferation of freelancers is the direct consequence of the radical changes that have taken place in the media industry during the last twenty years. Since the end of the 1990s, technological advancements boosted competition among news outlets. Social media coupled with online reporting shrank profits. From online blogs to mainstream newspapers, media outlets became unable to pay for correspondents and professional journalists to cover conflicts. War insurance coupled with the costs of security had become prohibitive when compared to declining sales and profits, so the media relied more and more on freelancers, who often are willing to take risks professional journalists would not. "The idea was to go past where the majority would go. Get better stuff because no one else was there," James Foley explained to *Newsweek* in October 2012, just a month before being kidnapped in Syria. "It's the freelancer's conundrum, taking bigger risks to beat staffers. I think it's just basic laws of competition; you need to have something the staffers don't, but in a conflict zone that means you take bigger risks: go in sooner, stay longer, go closer."[208]

Following this logic, in March 2012, John Cantlie became the first Western journalist to witness an incursion by government ground troops in northwestern Syria. It happened in Saraqeb, where heavily armed tanks rolled in and started shelling indiscriminately.[209] "The tanks opened fire. Fist-sized pieces of shrapnel sliced through the air, decapitating one rebel immediately. His rifle clattered to the ground as his friends dragged his headless torso from the line of fire," Cantlie wrote in the *Sunday Telegraph*.[210] To illustrate what the Syrian rebels were up against, he even took a photograph looking down the barrel of an advancing tank.

High risk, low wages, and no benefits: these are the main characteristics of freelance war reporting in the Middle East. In 2007, in Afghanistan, Jason Howe, a British photojournalist, summarized the tenets of freelancing for Amanda Lindhout, the Canadian freelancer kidnapped in Somalia. "You planned for yourself, paid for yourself, and assumed your own risk. You rode out the bumps, went without insurance and long term plans of any sort, and grew accustomed to being broke. When it comes to assignments you create your own, getting yourself to the most opportune spot."[211] While these tenets sound like a guide to backpacking on a budget, freelance journalism is infinitely more risky.

FREELANCING THE MEDIA

When Amanda Lindhout and Australian freelancer Nigel Brennan arrived in Mogadishu, the fixer they had booked, Ajoos Sanura, told them that someone else would be looking after them. He was busy taking around two journalists from *National Geographic* who were staying at the same hotel. Clearly they were more important than the two freelancers because *National Geographic* has more resources. Lindhout and Brennan had no alternative, as they had invested all their money in reporting from Somalia and could not come back later.

The morning Lindhout and Brennan were abducted, Ajoos had left earlier from the same hotel with the two reporters and two hired SUVs with a security detail to protect them. They were heading in the same direction as Lindhout and Brennan, west on the Afgoye Road. The two freelancers, however, were traveling without any security and they were snatched right outside Mogadishu.

After their abduction, they learned that the intention of their kidnappers was to abduct the two male journalists from *National Geographic* and that they had gotten a tip that that morning they would be traveling on the Afgoye Road, but somehow they abducted the wrong people. What Lindhout and Brennan were not told was that attacking a convoy of three heavily armed SUVs was not as easy as stopping a car with a driver, a fixer, and two freelancers. They were an easy target.

The risk that freelancers take seems disproportion-ately high when compared with the monetary return. Even the big publications pay as little as $200 per article, often less than the cost of a daily fixer and driver, as Nicole Tung, who worked with James Foley in Libya and Syria, explained to *Newsweek*. "We can't afford to pay $200–$300 per day for a fixer or a driver so, logistically, it's really dif-ficult to work when you're on your own, because you're depending on the good will of other people, or cheap ways to get around—which is not often the safest way to get around, but you really don't have any other option because you can't afford it."[212]

As Francesca Borri explained, "James Foley was kid-napped in November 2012 while sharing a fixer and a driver with John Cantlie in an area where just a few months before Cantlie had been kidnapped and subsequently freed. Everybody knew that the word among the jihad-ists in northern Syria was to get Cantlie if he ever set foot back in northern Syria." Cantlie was a wanted man because when he got back to the UK, after his first abduction, his testimony was instrumental in identifying a member of the group that had kidnapped him, a doctor named Shajul Islam, from East London. "This is why nobody in his right mind would have shared a cab ride with him," says Fran-cesca Borri.[213]

Misjudging risks is a common mistake even for veteran journalists. In July 2015 Junpei Yasuda, a freelance Japa-nese journalist who had previously been kidnapped and released in Iraq in 2004, crossed over to Syria through Gaziantep, a crossing located between the Turkish town of Kilis and the Syrian town of Azaz. On the Syrian side, the area is infested with criminal gangs. Yasuda was traveling under the protection of Ahrar ash Sham, a coalition of several Islamist and Salafists groups believed to be close to al Nusra.[214] "Near Azaz they were attacked by a band of criminals, the jihadists did not even fight,"[215] says Francesca Borri, who has spoken with the hostages' Syrian negotiator. The negotiator is a photographer who works for Western media and who, since 2015, has become the *de facto* primary negotiator for foreign hostages held by al Nusra and ISIS.

Junpei Yasuda was held alongside three Spanish journalists, Antonio Pampliega, José Manuel López, and Ángel Sastre, who were kidnapped near Azaz in the summer of 2015 while traveling to Aleppo. The Spanish journalists were freed at the beginning of May 2016 thanks to the mediation of Qatar and Turkey. They were held by a small criminal group, though the negotiations for their release were handled by al Nusra.

According to Borri, "They were all heading for Aleppo from Gaziantep crossing. The road is almost a straight line. Everybody enters Syria through that crossing, even if everybody knows that the road is full of roadblocks held by criminal gangs. People think that they can bribe criminals gangs, pay a few thousands dollars, and carry on, but they are very, very wrong. People like us, Italian, Spanish, or Japanese, we are worth $10 million each. Our governments can pay that kind of money." Borri is right, a few thousands dollars is nothing in comparison to how much a Western hostage from one of these countries will fetch. Even if sold to big organizations such as al Nusra or ISIS rather than directly to a foreign government, the profit yield on hostages is high.

"I always went in through Bab al Hawa, the crossing

between Reyhanlı in Turkey and Atmeh in Syria," continues Borri. "And then to reach Aleppo I crossed the region of Idlib, which is under the control of the Islamic State. I never had any problem at the roadblocks because my driver has good connections with ISIS."

Borri's words confirm that the majority of freelancers wanting to either report on the war in Syria or to carry out any form of humanitarian work, even as recently as 2015, make mistakes and get kidnapped because they have a superficial knowledge of what is happening on the ground and no idea of how quickly things change. According to the Syrian negotiator, the three Spanish journalists kidnapped in 2015 used a fixer, an English teacher, who was no longer reliable, not because he decided to sell them, but because he did not have the right connections. "Ahrar ash Sham cannot guarantee any protection because the power that controls the territory around Azaz is al Nusra, and al Nusra has its own media department and wants people to apply to this department for permission to enter the region they control. It is very difficult to obtain such permission, so people use other Islamist groups to go in, but that is not safe. The only way to enter Syria from that crossing is with al Nusra's permission to do so. Otherwise, it is better not to leave Turkey." The Syrian negotiator confirmed to Borri that the hostages had made a mistake in trusting Ahrar ash Sham. Apparently, the three Spanish journalists were kidnapped while having dinner with people who were paid to protect them, but their protectors did not put up a fight.

Perhaps the most serious consequence of relying upon freelancers to report from the front line, for both readers and journalists, is the manipulation of their work for propaganda purposes. In 2008, Amanda Lindhout was employed by an Iranian TV channel, Press TV, in Afghanistan for a monthly salary of $4,000. As a totally inexperienced freelancer, she believed it was a major breakthrough. She soon realized, however, that she had become part of a propaganda machine that depicted American policy and American soldiers in the worst possible way.[216] But it was not easy to walk away from such a rich salary!

Another negative consequence of not using professional journalists to report about conflicts is the poor quality of the analysis behind the news. This explains why until the end of May 2014, just a month before the birth of the Caliphate, none of the freelancers covering the Syrian conflict had written about ISIS. Few had denounced the shambolic state of the Free Syrian Army, as professional journalists like Robert Fisk had. Nor had anyone denounced the role that the Gulf States were playing in sponsoring a bloody sectarian war.

Part of this failure was due to the fact that freelancers often don't interact with experienced editors or mentors. They do not learn the profession inside a well-oiled news organization; hence, they often have no sense of history. Most of their reporting assumes the form of vignettes, snapshots of tragic events, which shock people without educating them. As a result, their writings can be sensationalist. Indeed, the same superficiality and lack of historical perspective often clouds their own evaluation of the risks they are taking, leading them into trouble.

PERSONAL VENDETTA

On July 19, 2012, Cantlie entered Syria with Dutch photographer Jeroen Oerlemans near the Bab al Hawa crossing. That same morning the Mujahideen Shura Council, the group led by Firas al Absi, the brother of Abu Athir, had taken control of the crossing and raised the black flag of al Qaeda.[217] This was not an irrelevant event in the Syrian conflict. On the contrary, it proved that the jihadists were gaining ground in northern Syria.

The Shura Council of the Islamic State was a small group of foreign jihadists, numbering about one hundred eighty, that Firas al Absi had assembled with the money of his Saudi sponsors. Firas was not less connected than his brother inside the jihadist network. He claimed to have met al Zarqawi in Afghanistan, when the Jordanian ran a camp in Herat. Indeed, he often said that he had been trained there before crossing with al Zarqawi into Iraqi Kurdistan and then into Iraq.

Unlike his brother, Firas al Absi had embraced the jihad in Syria alone, without pledging loyalty to any particular group. He had attempted to use his past connection with al Zarqawi as a sort of calling card. But such a claim had not been enough to convince the Gulf sponsors to continue bankrolling his *katiba* of foreign fighters. So in 2012 he had planned to raise money by kidnapping foreigners entering Syria via the Bab al Hawa crossing. Like Belmokhtar in Mali, he was essentially a jihadist criminal with shifting alliances. Most likely he planned to sell Cantlie and Oerlemans to al Nusra for a few thousand dollars.

Al Absi was playing with fire. Not only did his plan involved kidnapping reporters in a region controlled by the Free Syrian Army, the blockade of Bab al Hawa had enraged the Farouk Brigade because it had prevented Turkish supplies and weapons from reaching them. Cantlie and Oerlemans, who entered Syria near

Bab al-Hawa, had no idea of the power struggle that was taking place on the other side of the border. Nor did they understand the risk that they were running by crossing into Syria in this area.

Just a few miles from Bab al Hawa, the *katiba* of Firas al Absi kidnapped Cantlie and Oerlemans. It seems someone sold them out. In an interview with Channel 4 News, Cantlie actually uses the expression "we [Oerlemans and himself] were handed over to the kidnappers," which implies that someone had alerted the kidnappers to the freelancers' arrival. It is highly unlikely that Cantlie or Oerlemans knew who the al Absi brothers were before being snatched by one of them, indeed a video of the capture of Bab al Hawa was uploaded to YouTube the day they were kidnapped.[218] Cantlie could not have recognized Firas al Absi. Indeed, he had no idea how strong the jihadist movement was in northern Syria. Just like the majority of freelancers, he had contacts only with the Free Syrian Army and had written only about them.

We will never know if Cantlie would have crossed into Syria near Bab al Hawa had he known how strong the ties were between the Iraqi and the Syrian jihadists in that region. But we can comfortably say that he had no idea that they dated back to the 2003 invasion of Iraq, when the jihadist community in northern Syria had facilitated the passage of foreign fighters to Iraq for al Zarqawi's Jama'at al Tawhid wal Jihad, the very organization to which al Baghdadi and former members of Saddam Hussein's intelligence and army belonged. In 2003, rather, Cantlie was busy riding motorcycles.

Cantlie and Oerlemans got caught up in one of the early territorial disputes between secular forces and jihadists inside the Syrian insurgency. Luckily, like Richard Engel, they were rescued. When al Absi refused to comply with the requests of the leaders of the armed groups controlling the region to release the hostages, a commando unit from the Free Syrian Army rescued them. Later on, Firas al Absi was killed by members of the Free Syrian Army, probably the Farouk Brigade, to punish him for invading their turf. His brother, Abu Athir, took over his *katiba* and promised to avenge his death. When in March 2013, Dimitri Bontinck met Abu Athir in a villa in Kafr Hamra, Abu Athir was the *de facto* head of northern Syria for the Islamic State.

The kidnapping of Cantlie and Oerlemans confirms that already in 2012 the Free Syrian Army was struggling to maintain control of northern Syria against the advancing tide of jihadist armed groups. Like all the other journalists taken hostage, Cantlie became a news item and decided to go back to report on his kidnapping. He was a freelancer, so no editor could have stopped him. On the contrary he was sure that he could sell the story of his abduction to the British media.

"Cantlie's kidnapping became instrumental in the death of Firas al Absi," explained a negotiator involved in freeing the European hostages. "After al Absi's death, his brother, Abu Athir, put a warrant out on Cantlie because he thought that had it not been for his kidnapping and rescue, Firas would still be alive. John should never have gone back, and judging by the way he behaved before he was abducted for the second time, completely recklessly, he had no idea of the danger he was in." Nonetheless, the warning signs were clear.

A few days before his second kidnapping, Cantlie had approached a group of European jihadists in Aleppo to chat. His fixer, Mustafa, thought that it was a very bad idea, but Cantlie ignored his advice. "At a certain point they asked him about the British guy who was kidnapped and incriminated their doctor when he got back to the UK," Mustafa said.[219] They knew everything about Cantlie's ordeal, but they did not know his face.

On Thanksgiving Day 2012, just a few days after this incident, John Cantlie and James Foley were on their way back to Turkey from Binnish, less than forty miles from the border. Their fixer realized that he had forgotten his mobile phone in an Internet café, so they stopped to collect it. Inside the café both Cantlie and Foley decided to file their articles, chat with their family online, and read their e-mails. When a foreign jihadist, who looked as if he was from the Gulf, entered the café wearing a beret, Cantlie shouted at him, "Hey, Che Guevara!" The man did not reply but looked at him with clear hostility and left after a few minutes.

"That is exactly the kind of behavior that gets you kidnapped or killed," says the same negotiator. "It is totally foolish; it is juvenile." Though we will never know if the jihadist wearing the Che Guevara beret did recognize Cantlie and alerted his kidnappers, it is likely that this is exactly what happened. Less than an hour later, on the Old Aleppo Road, a large Hyundai overtook the taxi in which Cantlie and Foley were traveling. In the space of a couple of minutes armed masked men snatched the two freelancers, leaving the fixer and the driver speechless on the road.

"I have no doubt that Cantlie and Foley were delivered to Abu Athir," said the negotiator. In the fall of 2012 and winter of 2013 Abu Athir's *katiba* was very close to the fighters of al Nusra. Negotiations about a merger between this organization and the Islamic State of Iraq and Syria were going on at the highest level. Hence, Cantlie and Foley could have been a precious human bounty to satisfy Abu Athir's vendetta. In March 2013 Jejoen Bontinck saw them in the prison in Aleppo run by the *katiba* of Abu Athir.

"Foley was in the wrong place at the wrong time. He was extremely unlucky," concluded the negotiator. "But Cantlie, Cantlie, he should have known better."

SILENCING THE MEDIA

Personal vendettas, not money or political considerations, turned Cantlie and Foley into the first Western hostages of the Islamic State. But once they were in the hands of Abu Athir, ISIS's master plan took off. "They set up a specific group of people in Syria who had the task to handle foreign hostages. Until the end of 2013, they moved them around a lot to avoid rescue missions. Then they brought them to a stretch of safe houses in the north of Syria," says Jean-René Augé-Napoli. It was at that point that the negotiations with the various European governments became serious.

From 2012 to the end of 2013 the hostages were a sort of political investment, and ISIS's leadership considered the pros and cons of exchanging or assassinating each of them. "Eventually, they split them into two groups: those they would execute and those they would exchange," says Jean-René Augé-Napoli.

The tactics used to intimidate foreigners were identical to those applied to Arab journalists. Violence was not only allowed, it was encouraged. This was Saddam Hussein's approach in terrifying his enemies. Hence, the image of the Syrian kidnappers that emerged from the stories of the survivors is one of psychotic individuals with sadistic personalities who enjoyed torturing their prisoners. Indeed this psychological profile fits "The Beatles." Among them there was Jihadi John, the executioner of ISIS.

The narrative that ISIS constructed around the hostage keepers corresponds with the reports of liberated hostages describing their jailers as inhumane and psychotic. The tales of former hostages characterize the kidnappers as evil, pure evil, as do the videos of the beheadings. No rational justification for this behavior can be provided, either politically or religiously. When, at the beginning of September 2013, Marc Marginedas met ISIS's regional commander, the man upon whom his destiny depended, a Russian jihadist told him, "You have come here twice without any problems. Now we are going to kill you."[220] Journalists, aid workers, and foreigners were purposely terrorized in order to silence them, a technique that had worked very well in Saddam Hussein's Iraq.

Fear hid a well-crafted master plan. By September 2013 the elite of the Islamic State had decided that the political value of some of the hostages was far higher if they were executed, whereas for others it was higher if they were exchanged for a ransom. Marginedas belonged to the latter group, and indeed he was the first hostage to be released. Far from being run by a bunch of psychopaths, ISIS is an organization that placed the handling of hostages in the hands of very skillful politicians and negotiators. The hostage jailers, on the other hand, were unskilled labor, low-ranking members of ISIS. For regardless of how cruel "The Beatles" were, they never controlled the destiny of the hostages; they did not decide who was going to be freed and who was going to be beheaded. Jihadi John was little more than a mouthpiece. In front of a camera, he recited a script that he did not write.

"The Beatles" were an example of the banality of evil so well described by Hannah Arendt. They followed orders and their task was to scare the hostages, to make sure they would carry ISIS's terrifying message to the world. Blinded by the inhumanity of such evil, none of the hostages was able to see behind it to glimpse ISIS's powerful political machine. None of them was conscious, while in captivity, of the rationale for their divergent destinies. Even today, reading their memoirs or interviews, what is missing is the description of their role as political bricks in the Caliphate's nation-building project, of how their ordeal was instrumental to silencing international media and hiding the true nature of the Caliphate.

The hostages' beheadings ended the season of freelance journalism in Syria, leaving the reporting of the war to the propaganda of the different forces involved in the conflict. Even veteran war correspondents were banned by their editors from entering Syria. The Caliphate had succeeded in freeing the region of the media, leaving reporting in the hands of its propagandists. In short, it had achieved its goal: the end of truth.

chapter thirteen

Playing Chess with the Hostages' Lives

On December 23, 2013, ISIS's foreign hostages were taken from different locations to a makeshift hideout in the mountains near the border between Syria and Turkey. This was going to be their Guantánamo—they even wore orange jumpsuits—and "The Beatles" were to be their jailers.

To reproduce the conditions of the inmates of Guantánamo, "The Beatles" required the hostages to wear the orange jumpsuits and memorize their identification number in Arabic, which was engraved on their uniform. The numbers replaced their names. The psychological torture included extravagant requests, such as to sing a jihadist version of "Hotel California" by The Eagles on command, when "The Beatles" entered their cell: *"Welcome to Osama's lovely hotel,/ Such a lovely place,/ Such a lovely place./ Welcome to Osama's lovely hotel,/ But you could never leave/ And if you try/ You will die . . . ."*

The physical torture was equally brutal and resembled the way the *katiba* of Abdelhamid Abou Zeid of AQIM treated its hostages. "Nineteen males from nine different countries and cultures, locked for months in claustrophobic spaces that did not exceed 20 square meters, unable to even go out and get some fresh air, permanent hunger and under constant psychological and physical pressure, including the possibility of losing their lives. It is a tough test for the coexistence capabilities for any individual," wrote former hostage Marc Marginedas of his captivity.[221]

But far from being a Guantánamo, a limbo for alleged unlawful combatants, the hideout in the mountains between Syria and Turkey was the warehouse where the leadership of the Islamic State disposed of its human cargo. And it did so following a detailed plan. Hostages were classified according to their nationality and the role that they would play in ISIS's foreign policy and finances, dead or alive. Their destiny, to be exchanged for money or to be beheaded, was decided not by the financial needs of ISIS or by its ideology, but by the politics of the new state, the Caliphate.

First, the leadership disposed of those they would release. While the hostages were brutalized, ISIS negotiators worked at extracting the maximum ransom from European governments, dealing with one country at a time. The first government they negotiated with for the release of hostages was Spain. To intimidate the Spanish government, and all the others, ISIS executed the least valuable human merchandise, Sergei Gorbunov, a Russian engineer of Tatar origins who had been kidnapped by the Muhajireen Brigade. This was a group established in the summer of 2012. Its leader was an ethnic Chechen, Abu Omar al Shishani, an Islamist fighter from Georgia who had fought in the first and second Chechen Wars against Russia. In 2012 and 2013 the Muhajireen Brigade assisted al Nusra in various military raids.

In a video released in October 2013, Gorbunov asked the Syrian authorities to release a Saudi Arabian citizen,

Khalid Mohammed Suleiman, who was in prison in the city of Hama, in exchange for Gorbunov's freedom. No mention of a ransom was made.

ISIS negotiators knew very well that the Russian government would not pay for the release of Gorbunov, nor would anybody else. He apparently had refused to provide a personal e-mail to contact his family, and by the time they stopped torturing him he had lost his mind. ISIS also knew that the Assad regime would never have agreed to the exchange of prisoners. However, the negotiators were sure that his execution would prompt European governments to speed up the negotiations and the payment of ransom for their hostages. It was a tactic used before by other groups, including AQIM, which in June 2009 executed Edwin Dyer, a British hostage.

In March 2014, shortly after the liberation of Marc Marginedas, Gorbunov was taken away and killed. The hostages were shown the photo of his body. He was shot with an explosive bullet, so parts of his brain had landed on top of his beard. "The Beatles" forced Javier Espinosa to describe the picture in detail and told him that this was likely the way he would die too. "All the governments and the secret services of the countries of origin of the foreign hostages were sent pictures and even a video of the execution of Gorbunov. They were told that if they did not pay, the next photo and video would be of their citizens," said one of negotiators of the European hostages. It was an intimidation tactic. "They also showed the picture to the hostages so that once they were debriefed they would confirm it. ISIS negotiators wanted to make sure that their threats were taken seriously."

"The Beatles" also terrorized the hostages for another

reason: to silence them once free. The hostages were told time and time again that if they revealed any information about the hideouts there would be retaliation against those still in captivity. This plan worked very well. Until June 2014 the world had no idea of what was happening in Syria and how strong ISIS had become.

Marc Marginedas was released at the beginning of March 2014. It was mentioned in the press that he had been held by ISIS, a group linked to al Qaeda,[222] information that was only partly correct as al Qaeda (that is, al Nusra) and ISIS were not cooperating. On the contrary, they were enemies. At the end of March, Javier Espinosa and Ricardo García Vilanova were also freed. Again the media failed to produce an accurate picture of their captors. Soon after their release *The Guardian* noted, "Until recently, there had been no communication with the hostage-takers or their proxies, and their demands had been unclear. Even after intensive efforts by European governments to make contact, no key coordinating figure within Isis has emerged. The fate of the captives seems contingent on the whim of local warlords."[223]

Less than a month later, on April 20, 2014 Edouard Elias, Didier François, Nicolas Hénin, and Pierre Torres, the four French hostages, landed safely in France. Again ISIS was only mentioned as the group that had held them, one of many jihadist organizations active in Syria. Between April and May, ISIS also released five Médecins Sans Frontières workers. On May 24, French NGO ACTED posted on its website, "ACTED is pleased to announce the release of its employee, Federico Motka, who was taken hostage in Syria, while working in the framework of ACTED's relief activities in favor of conflict-affected Syrian populations.

[. . .] No further declaration will be made by ACTED on this topic."[224] The Italian government paid the ransom even though Motka was a Swiss Italian. No mention of ISIS was made in the Italian or Swiss media. Finally, in June, ISIS released German hostage Toni Neukirch and Danish hostage Daniel Rye Ottosen.

Overall, the Islamic State netted the highest ransom ever from the release of these hostages, between €60 to €100 million, without anybody noticing it. Even the fact that within three months twelve hostages had been freed by the same organization in Syria had gone totally unnoticed, not only by the media, but also by the parliaments of the countries that had paid the ransoms as well as by the taxpayers who had provided the funds.

"It was a very, very clever plan. ISIS negotiators pocketed large sums of money in total secrecy. They silenced the hostages and the media so their negotiators could boost competition among foreign governments to get their people out. How would it have looked in France if the Spanish hostages and the Italian had come home but the French were going to be executed? This is what they instilled in the minds of the European negotiators. They knew how to manipulate Western governments and how to drive a very hard bargain," said a negotiator who got out two hostages.

By June, ISIS had permitted the release of the human cargo it had sold for ransom and was ready to invade northwest Iraq. The remaining hostages would be used in the political game that the Caliphate was about to play with the West.

ISIS DIPLOMACY

The American and British hostages were kept in the wing waiting for the right moment to be used. Though the ki nappings of Cantlie and Foley had been motivated by t personal vendetta of Abu Athir to avenge the assassinatio of his brother, the choice to execute the American a British hostages was not personal. Nor was it dictated the refusal of their governments to pay ransom. As we ha already seen, given the right circumstances, such as wh the hostage is a soldier, even the US and the UK gover ments negotiate with kidnappers.

On the contrary, the decision to behead the Americ and British hostages was both political and symbolic. Bu and Blair had manufactured false evidence to come with the rationale for invading Iraq, and the Islamic Sta was composed largely of various remnants of their stro gest opponents: the radical Salafists of al Zarqawi and t former members of the military and intelligence system Saddam Hussein. The two sides of the Islamic State, t religious and the secular, both sprang from the anti-C alition insurgency in Iraq. What they have in common the desire to build a new nation, the implementation of t Muslim political utopia. Nationalism became the commo denominator that joined together these two insurge forces. So the idea to use American and British hostag to help lay the foundation of the new nation, a nation th would become the launching pad for an even bigger figh was symbolically very appealing.

In June 2014, when the Caliphate was declared, no or understood this strategy, not even the European negoti tors who had spent months dealing with ISIS to free th hostages; nor those still trying to free the remaining British and American hostages. The Islamic State was dismissed as another bunch of ragged jihadists, religious fanatics, and psychopaths. Nobody realized that unlike the previous jihadist groups, including al Qaeda and the Taliban, the Caliphate was not the final goal of the jihad. For the Islamic State, the Caliphate is an instrument of war, a tool to achieve victory. And the beheadings of the hostages was a strategic tactic to lure its enemy into its own territory.

In August 2014, after knocking down the Syria-Iraqi border, declaring the birth of the Caliphate and invading northwest Iraq, ISIS's leadership set its trap: they beheaded James Foley and within hours the video of his death went viral. This was an event that literally shocked international public opinion and forced the world powers to take action in Syria.

"James was the first to be murdered, and that was a trauma, a personal trauma to me, but also a trauma for the world," Nicolas Hénin, one of the French hostages, told Amy Goodman on the radio and television program *Democracy Now!* "And this is why I open my book with him, because the aim of the Islamic State by murdering him was to open a trap wide open and under our feet. They wanted to impose their agenda on us. They wanted to stone us—that we are so much shocked that we stop acting rationally . . . . [T]here is something very specific with a terror action. The success, the completion of a terrorist attack, does not depend on its perpetrators, but it on its victims."[225]

Hénin was right. Towards the end of August 2014, under mounting pressure from the electorate, President Obama abandoned his position of non-intervention vis-à-vis the regime in Damascus and launched an initiative to form a grand coalition. Its task was to launch a relentless bombing campaign against ISIS as well as Assad's forces. The plan included funding, training, and arming the Syrian insurgency, the so-called "moderate" forces. Hence, the Caliphate, still in its infancy, had succeeded in dragging Washington and its allies into another Middle Eastern quagmire.

The bombing was a success for ISIS for many reasons. It forced Syrian moderates to flee while reinforcing in the hardliners the belief that the enemy were the coalition forces while ISIS was fighting to protect them. Even today, the bombing campaign plays into ISIS's propaganda.

As Hénin put it, "That's a fight for propaganda. So, basically, the side that will—the party that will—win this war is not the party that will fight harder or have the most expensive or newest weaponry or the bravest fighters. It will be the party that will manage to have the people on its side. And the problem is that with all these bombings—because everybody at the moment is bombing Syria—all of these bombings have a terrible side effect. And basically, we—Westerners, but not only Westerners, also the Russians, also the regime—are pushing the Syrian people into the hands of ISIS. We are working for them. We are recruiting for them. So, I'm not saying, no, absolutely, for any strike, but strikes should remain minimal, because we should keep in mind what are the consequences and the side effects of them."[226]

Throughout 2014 and part of 2015 hostages became powerful weapons in the hands of the Islamic State to influence the foreign policy of NATO countries as well, as illustrated by the kidnapping of forty-nine employees of the Turkish Consulate in Mosul when the Islamic State conquered that city. The hostages were released after 101 days, after the beheading of James Foley, Steven Sotloff, and Dave Haines. Two months earlier the Islamic State had also freed thirty-two Turkish truck drivers who were seized in Mosul in June.

The Turkish secret service, the National Intelligence Organization (MİT), handled the negotiations alongside the prime minister's office without any foreign involvement. The go-betweens were the leaders of the Sunni tribes of Mosul who had longstanding good relations with Turkey. Turkish sources confirm that the refusal of Erdogan to agree to the US demand for active support of the grand coalition was instrumental to freeing the hostages.

The best example of how ISIS's diplomacy succeeded in influencing major decisions abroad, however, came during the Japanese hostage crisis of January 2015. Until Prime Minister Shinzō Abe's speech in January 2015 at a business and investment conference in Cairo, when he pledged $200 million in non-military aid to countries fighting ISIS, Haruna Yukawa, who had been kidnapped in the summer of 2014, and Kenji Goto, captured in the fall of 2014, belonged to the human cargo to exchange for money.

Prime Minister Abe admitted that the government knew of Mr. Goto's kidnapping in November 2014. According to Goto's wife, in November she started receiving e-mails, apparently from ISIS, about her husband's abduction. In late December, the kidnappers began talking about ransom, eventually demanding about 2 billion yen (or $17 million) to release him, a request in line with the initial ransom demands that the Islamic State had put forward to other Western governments. The negotiations took place in secrecy, out of the reach of the media. However, every-thing changed after Prime Minister Abe's high-profile visit to the Middle East.

Prime Minister Abe's speech offered the Islamic State an unexpected opportunity to challenge the grand anti-ISIS coalition and to punish Japan for pledging economic sup-port to it. Japan had long earned goodwill in the Middle East by discreetly working in the background rather than grandstanding. Since July 2014, however, the prime min-ister had initiated a campaign to change the interpretation of Japan's pacifist constitution to allow the "exercise of the right of collective self-defense" abroad. The controversial reinterpretation of Article 9 of the Constitution had trig-gered strong opposition in Japan. Abe decided to use his visit to the Middle East to turn around public opinion on this matter.

How did the Islamic State know so much about Japa-nese politics? This is an interesting question because, unlike the Somali pirates, the Caliphate cannot rely upon its own diaspora. However, the Islamic State's new citizens are truly cosmopolitan, coming from across the globe. The leadership keeps an eye on its enemies by asking its citizens to maintain ties to their native countries and act as inter-preters to decipher the politics of their nations of origin. It is not surprising, then, that the political elite of the Caliphate knew all too well what was happening in Japan and that it had a pretty good idea of the controversy over the reinterpretation of Article 9.

Against this exceptional background, the Islamic State saw a unique opportunity to use the two Japanese hostages to prevent Japan from entering Obama's coalition while, at the same time, reinforcing its own claim to statehood.

The negotiations for the release of Yukawa and Goto suddenly became public, producing a social media frenzy. To emphasize the weakness of the enemy, the conditions put forward suddenly changed to ones that could not realistically be met: $200 million in seventy-two hours to free both hostages; the exchange of Goto, in little more than forty-eight hours, for the Jordanian prisoner Sajida al Rishawi—an Arab woman who failed to detonate her suicide belt in 2005, in the attack on the Radisson SAS Hotel in Amman. Not only was the time allowed for the negotiations deliberately too short, the ransom was far too high to be accepted and delivered on time.

From hostages, Yukawa and Goto were transformed into political pawns in ISIS's new jihadist diplomacy, a metamorphosis that Prime Minister Abe had triggered by his sudden willingness to join Obama's grand coalition. Hence, the two Japanese hostages joined the likes of James Foley, and Jihadi John used images of their severed heads to broadcast ISIS's message to the world.

The manipulation of the Japanese hostage crisis was a great success for ISIS. It tipped Japanese public opinion toward keeping a low profile in the fight against Islamist terrorism. Indeed, the hostage videos and the demands for their release were all aimed at increasing frustration and instilling fear in the Japanese population so as to convince them not to back the change in interpretation of the Constitution. By its propaganda, then, ISIS created a dialogue directly with the Japanese people, as it had done with the American people with the beheading of Foley, engaging and manipulating the government through its electorate.

Dragging Jordan into the negotiation simply reinforced the Japanese government's impotence in the eyes of the world. The demand to exchange Goto, and not the captured Jordanian pilot Moaz al Kasasbeh, with Sajida al Rishawi, was an open provocation to Jordan. ISIS knew that King Abdullah II would never accept such conditions. Exchanging al Rishawi for Goto, leaving al Kasasbeh in the hands of the Islamic State, would have enraged the Jordanian population. So by skilfully manipulating the Japanese hostage crisis, ISIS also undermined the Jordanian government.

Despite this complicated statesmanship, many analysts overlooked the sophisticated diplomacy of the Caliphate and remained focused on the messages of violence—gruesome, barbarous violence. Similarly, during 2015, analysts failed to notice another "diplomatic" victory of ISIS: the exposure of Europe's vulnerability via the exodus of migrants from the Middle East.

chapter fourteen

A Refugee Love Story

Before they became one of more than a million Syrian refugees seeking asylum in Europe, Mohammad Jamil Hassan and his wife, Teakosheen Joulak, were members of Aleppo's upper-middle class. In the spring of 2013 the world that this Kurdish Syrian couple inhabited began to collapse. The story of how the Free Syrian Army confiscated Hassan's suit factory and his subsequent arrest and imprisonment by the Assad regime until his uncle paid a $12,000 ransom was detailed in Chapter Six. As they fled the Syrian Civil War, the husband and wife made their way separately to increase their chances of surviving, and each became part of the human cargo traded by the merchants of men. Their shocking tale reveals the existence of a new international network of criminality both in the Middle East and in Europe, a multi-billion dollar business network built by armed organizations and criminal gangs with the ransom money raised from the kidnapping of foreigners collected over more than a decade (and paid by countries like Italy) as seed money.

Here is Mohammad Jamil Hassan's story as he told it me in the fall of 2015 in Denmark:

"I crossed over into Turkey from Syria and reached Gaziantep, the first Kurdish town after the border. It was the end of June 2013. I had a bag full of cash that my uncle had given to me for the journey to Europe. Everything went so fast, I could not say goodbye to my wife . . . but I was optimistic about the future. I would reach Sweden, ask for asylum, and then bring her to Sweden.

"From Gaziantep I took a bus to Istanbul. The driver asked for one hundred dollars not to reveal that I was Syrian. I paid him and boarded the bus. When I got to Istanbul I went to Sirkeci, the district between Sultanahmet and Eminönü, near the Galata Bridge and the Golden Horn. I was told to go to the Hotel Scerim, because it is frequented by smugglers: people who would take those like me to Greece. When I got there there were a lot of Syrians and other migrants from Asia and the Gulf. They all sought passage to Europe.

"I stayed in the hotel for two weeks. I befriended a group of Kurdish, Arab, and Syrian men. One day they approached me and told me that they had found someone who could take us to Greece overland for $1,500. I agreed to join them. The smugglers got twelve of us in a car; when we were near the border they told us to get out of the car and to follow them. We were in total about thirty people, twenty from Afghanistan and nine or ten from Syria. After one hour we reached a river. They inflated a few small dinghies and put five of us into each one. We crossed the river and on the other side, on the Greek side, there were two heavily armed men wearing masks waiting for us. We all got scared when we saw them. These men forced us to walk one after the other along a railway line. We walked for three hours with their guns pointed at us. Finally, they told us to stop, to sit down and rest. They also gave us some water. We waited for a while and then the two men told us to walk down from the railway line towards the highway. By then it was night.

"A huge oil truck had just pulled up on the side of the road. The men opened a door on the back of the truck and told us to get in. It was a very small space and we were thirty people, all cramped inside. You could not sit down; you had to stand up. There were small holes in the roof for air, but we were so many and it was so hot inside that it was hard to breathe. The truck was speeding all the time, so we were jostled against each other. We spent five or six hours inside the truck until we reached Athens.

"We stopped inside a garage in Athens. Someone opened the door and we got out. Two Greek men took us to an apartment on the ground floor of a building and they locked us in. To get out we had to pay $1,500. That was the cost that we had agreed to for the journey from Istanbul to Athens. You pay when you reach the destination, not up front. One of the people I was traveling with, a Syrian, had a friend in the area, so we paid and went to his apartment. His friend told us where to go to find smugglers to take us to Italy. They were all hanging out in a local café. We went there and they told us that to go by plane to Belgium was €3,500. I decided to go by plane. A week later they handed me an ID and a ticket, but at the airport the police stopped me. The ID was fake. At the airport, the police took me inside a room and interrogated me. When they realized I was Syrian, they told me that they understood what I was going through and they let me go.

"I went back to the same café and found someone who could take me by boat to Italy for €2,500. He guaranteed me that I would not be caught. The smuggler said that I had to go to Crete and from there I would board a ship full of tourists, a ferry. So we went to Crete by ferry. There were other refugees with us. When we got to the port a man with a Jeep Cherokee was waiting for us. He had a long beard. He was a Syrian Alawite and his name was Abu Isham. He took us to his house. It was a big house, the finest on the street, which was a cul-de-sac. I could read the street name because I spent ten years working in Greece to avoid the military service in Syria, so I can speak the language. It had two floors with two separate apartments. We stayed on the first floor and above us lived a family.

"In the same apartment there were two women, both going to Germany . . . . We remained in the house of Abu Isham for thirteen days. People started to get very upset. They wanted to leave. Two armed men who worked for Abu Isham threatened us. We had to stay quiet and wait. Finally, a small bus came to take us. Inside there was a woman and a man from Albania. They looked more than fifty years old. They told us to lie down in the van and drove for about three hours until we reached a village near the sea. They stopped the van at the edge of pine woods and took us inside the woods. The two Albanians were armed. At a certain point they told us to sit down and to wait until dark.

"In the evening, four men came. One was from Raqqa, one from Aleppo, and one from Iraqi Kurdistan. The fourth one was their leader. He wore Afghan clothes and was from Afghanistan. They led us through the forest in darkness. They spoke Greek to each other. They did not know that I could understand what they were saying. For example, I understood that the Afghani guy lived in the village nearby. They took us into a cave. They searched us and took our phones. I felt I had been kidnapped once again!

"The day after, when I woke up I realized that there were more than one hundred men in that cave and we were all locked inside. The cave had a small door with three armed guards in front of it. There were two ovens also where they made our food. Inside I met Syrians, Lebanese, Afghanis, Bangladeshis. Some people were very well educated, teachers, engineers. One guy said 'I had one hundred workers in my factory and look at me now, locked inside this cave!' Some had been there for months, waiting to continue their journey to Europe. Their beards were very long.

"At a certain point a group of Syrians shouted that they did not want to carry on. They wanted to go back to Syria. The three Syrian guards came and told them that they would kill and bury them right there if they said another word. Then they told all of us that 'maybe' if we reached Italy, 'maybe' they would let us go. I was lucky because I stayed in the cave for only ten days. There was no bathroom in the cave so the guards took ten of us at a time outside in the morning and in the evening. In the cave I got sick, I started bleeding because of hemorrhoids. It was excruciatingly painful.

"One evening, around 10 p.m., three heavily armed Afghani men came. Their boss was Abu Ali, a Syrian from Afrin, a village northwest of Aleppo. They told us to get ready. Before leaving they beat up three Afghani young men and left them inside the cave, I think because there was a feud between the family of these men and the family of the Afghani boss of the three Syrian guards, the man who had guided us through the forest to the cave.

"When we got to the coast we realized that it was rocky and the sea was rough. The Afghani men told us to spread out along the coast. We were more than one hundred people facing the sea, waiting for the ferry. At a certain point the families came. I do not know where they had kept them, possibly in another hideout. The cave was only for men. We were more than one hundred fifty in total. After about one hour, a twenty-meter boat came. It was too small for all of us. Some people started to complain, but the Afghani smugglers pointed their guns at us and started to push us into the boat. Everybody was scared.

"We headed for the open sea. There were big waves. People began to get sick. They screamed, children cried, some people were praying. A guy from Egypt drove the boat. He had an assistant who also was from Egypt. They ignored our cries. Around 5 a.m. we reached an oil tanker; it was about fifty meters long. It was very old and smelled, and inside there were already lots of people. From the ship they threw some ropes and people were pulled up as if they were sacks of rice.

"There were seven crewmembers, all from Egypt. The boat was from Egypt. By the time we boarded, it was completely packed with people, most of whom were ill. Many were dehydrated, as I was. I spent three days on that boat. All I was given was a piece of falafel and some water. I was so sick and cold that I asked for tea. I had to pay €500 for it! I was so ill that at a certain point I fainted. I was so desperate that I even thought to kill myself, to end my agony by jumping into the sea.

"What the Egyptian oil tanker did was to ferry us across the international waters. When we reached the Italian territorial waters they unloaded us into the small boat. The captain of the small boat told us, 'We are going to Italy.'

"We spent an entire day on this boat. In the afternoon people started to faint. It was so hot, it was unbearable. Then by sunset people began to fight for water. Finally at 10 p.m. we saw some lights from the coast; it was Sicily. The captain used a pistol to launch a smoke alert so that the Italian rescue ship could see and rescue us. The captain pretended to be a refugee. Nobody told the police who he really was.

"The Italian police left us on the dock for more than one hour without giving us water or blankets. A doctor came and checked our hearts a bit. I told him that I was sick, but he ignored me. He told me to wait, but nobody came to see me. Finally, the police came back and took all of us inside the yard of a building and left us there until the morning. The day after they told us that if we wanted to get out we had to be fingerprinted. I did not want to do that; I was heading for Sweden and I knew that if I let them take my fingerprints I had to stay in Italy because of the Dublin Treaty.[227] But I was so sick. I needed a doctor. So I decided to give them my fingerprints.

"Next they took us to a school. There were no beds, only mattresses on the floor. I stayed there for three days, waiting for a doctor, but nobody came. Then the police came and told us to leave. 'We do not want to see you again in Italy. Go wherever you are going and do not come back.'

"Six of us got into a taxi to the bus station where we bought tickets for Milan. We had fake IDs that the traffickers had given us in the cave so we used those. But I realized I had left the bag with the ID in a small café where we had had something to eat. The police had found the bag and had come into the bus, looking for us. They dragged us out into the police station. They shouted at us and fingerprinted us again, but eventually they let us go.

"When I reached Milan I stayed at the station. There was a place where we could get food every day. The old woman I had met in the apartment in Crete called her son in Germany. He came to pick her up and they offered to drive me also. So I got to Munich where someone put us up for a few days. I was told to go to a Turkish restaurant where traffickers hung out. There I met a twenty-three-year-old Algerian who arranged for me to reach Sweden by car for $1,200.

"A fat Iraqi man and a Danish woman picked me up. The woman was tall and blonde and did not speak Arabic. The man drove across Germany but before crossing the Danish and Swedish borders he let the woman drive. I hid inside the car. I reached Sweden in August 2013, a few weeks before my wife, Teakosheen, and her sister arrived."

Mohammad's wife, Teakosheen Joulak, tells me her side of their story. She was an English teacher who had gotten involved as a volunteer with the Red Cross and the Red Crescent to help people in need in Aleppo. Several members of her family were doctors, so she became the go-between for them and these organizations, helping to find medicines and money. Because of this humanitarian commitment, she got in trouble.

"In 2013 Aleppo was divided in two sections: one part was still under the regime and another under the insurgency, which was referred to as the Free Syrian Army. Many old people were trapped in one of those sections and could not move, so we brought them medicine and help. I lived in one of the sections controlled by the regime, which considered what I did to be a crime.

"In late July, after my husband had left, the head of our group, a support group composed of friends without any political connotation, was killed by a sniper. Two of our friends were jailed right away, so my sister and I ran away to our parent's town, Afrin, in Kurdish Syria. When we got there the PKK, which ruled the area, started questioning us because we had brought with us the wife of the man who had been killed by the sniper; she was also a teacher in my school. They were all very suspicious about her in particular because she and her husband had been strong anti-regime activists. We knew that the PKK had some relationships with the Assad regime, so we were very afraid. Several people wanted by the regime had been taken by the PKK and disappeared, so we feared that they would do the same to us. One day in July, someone from the PKK came to my mother's house and said that we had to go to their headquarters for questioning that same evening. My mother said, 'You are not going. You must go to Europe.'

"There were only women in our house, my mother, my two sisters, my girlfriend, and I. There was nobody to protect us. My mother said, 'We have the money, so let's use it to go to Europe.' She sold all our gold to get enough money for us to leave. At the time we were already preparing for my girlfriend, the widow, to go to Turkey, so my mother decided that my sister and I would also go and that she and my other sister would join us later.

"My mother called her sister's husband and asked him to help us. That night we went to sleep at their house. We stayed there for one day only. My uncle got us a Kurdish guy who drove us, three women and two men, across the border, Bab al Salam, which at the time was controlled by the Kurds from the Free Syrian Army. It was the 10th of August. We wore the hijab and kept our heads down; we could not look at the police in the eyes, so nobody realized that we had someone else's passport. That crossing cost us €150.

"I spent two months in a village just fifteen kilometres from the border crossing, at a cousin's place. While we were there we got a message that another girl, Rosa, who had been summoned with us to the PKK headquarters for questioning, had gone and never came back. My mother had been right!

"My cousin organized for a smuggler to take us to Istanbul by bus and then by plane to Sweden for €8,000 each, so it was €16,000 that my mother had to pay. A man travelled with us all the way but he pretended not to know us. At the airport he handed us two IDs. I think they were Turkish and they were not fake. We wore a headscarf and kept our heads down, as good Muslim women do, and nobody paid any attention to us. We got on the plane for Stockholm.

"When we got to Stockholm the man gave us a phone and we called our family to let them know that we had reached Stockholm, so our family paid his partner in Turkey. When the exchange was done the man handed us two European passports. We knew what to do. He had explained that if the border police stopped us we had to ask for asylum right away. But if we were let through we had to hand over the passport to another man who was waiting outside and ask for asylum the day after. We went through and gave the two passports to a man who was waiting for us at the arrivals section. He approached us and said 'Give me the passports.'

"We did not ask for asylum at the airport and that was my biggest mistake, but I did not know the rules. I had no idea that because my husband had been fingerprinted in Italy I would be told to go to Italy. If I had asked for asylum at the airport, I would not have had this problem.

"It was October 8th and my husband was already in Sweden with one of our relatives who was living in Helsingborg, near Malmö. The next day I went to the immigration office with my husband and my sister to ask for asylum, where they fingerprinted us. We waited for six months for an interview but in the end they gave the asylum only to my sister. We were rejected because Mohammad had been fingerprinted in Italy. I told them that he was my husband. I told them the truth and they said that under the Dublin rules the wife must go with the husband.

"They interviewed me alone. They asked, 'If we send your husband back to Italy will you go with him?' I said no, I cannot. We do not know anybody there. Where will we live? I have my sister and some other relations in Sweden. But they said that I had to follow my husband because he is older and he is responsible for me, so I had to go to Italy.

"It was March 2014. They gave us one week to go to Italy. At the train station I burst into tears. I was hysterical. I could not stop crying. Mohammad said: 'Go to Denmark where you have two uncles and ask for asylum there. I will go back to Syria and wait until you get your residence and then you can call for me.' He did not want to go back to Italy. He said that he would rather die than go back to Italy because he had seen so much poverty among refugees and migrants and had understood that there were very little opportunities for people like him.

"He went to Turkey and I went to Denmark where the Danish Refugee Council helped me get asylum. When the Danish immigration called the Swedish immigration they said that I had lied, that they had not rejected my application and that they had not said to me that I needed to follow my husband. I showed the Danish group the rejection papers so they believed me. The Danish immigration contacted the Italians and explained what had happened. In the end, both countries rejected me: Italy because I was without my husband and Sweden because I have a husband.

"At a certain point I was so desperate that I asked to be returned to Syria. I was happy in Syria. I had my own apartment. I had a car; I worked at the university. It was a good life. This is what I was saying, but it is true: we had a great life. This is when the Red Cross got involved. I spent two days with a psychiatric nurse who eventually asked for a lawyer to help me. Finally, the Red Cross put me in touch with their lawyer who took the case. The lawyer said that I was one of those refugees stuck inside the system. He helped me. Within a week I got the residence."

Mohammad stayed in Turkey for a year and an half. He could not go back to Syria. All his family had left for Germany. So he worked in Turkey, waiting for Teakosheen to get Danish residency. When she got it, he paid a trafficker to take him to Denmark for $7,000. It was June 9, 2015. He flew to Germany, possibly to Hamburg, from Istanbul. Just as his wife had been, he was handed a European passport just minutes before going through customs. He gave the passport back to a man waiting for him at arrivals, who took him to two Iraqi traffickers, who in turn smuggled him to Denmark by car. In six hours, he reached the apartment where his wife was waiting for him.

When he asked for asylum the Danish immigration office put him in a refugee camp. They did not let him stay with his wife. It was only when she got sick with cancer that they allowed him to nurse her after her operation.

At the time of writing Mohammad and Teakosheen are still waiting for his residence to come through. They cannot work. They are in a limbo but they still dream of having a family one day.

chapter fifteen

The Political Boomerang

In 2015, 1.8 million people crossed into the European Union, a number that is only going to rise in the near future. That summer the connection between the kidnapping of foreigners and the trafficking of migrants became clear. As the director of Europol admitted, "Ninety percent of migrants arriving in Europe have [had] their journey facilitated by a criminal organization."[228] Hence the decision in Spring 2016 to create the European Migrant Smuggling Centre (EMSC) to dismantle these illicit networks.[229]

Europeans are simply overwhelmed by the biggest exodus since World War II, a business that generates over €1 billion per year flowing to a nebula of local criminal gangs. Outside the borders of the European Union, small criminal and criminal-jihadist groups supply European traffickers with their daily human cargo. These gangs pocket sums of money similar to their European counterparts. As we have seen, during the last decade many of these organizations have been bankrolled with seed money secured by the ransom of foreign hostages: that is, with European taxpayer money. Against the backdrop of rising political destabilization at the edges of Europe, in just a decade, investing ransom money has turned trafficking of migrants into a multi-billion dollar international industry, which, in terms of the profits, now rivals drug smuggling. This is a political boomerang fast heading towards Europe!

Just like the kidnapping of foreigners, so too has the trafficking of migrants been profitable for major jihadist groups, such as the Islamic State, which control key border crossings on the migrants' route to Europe. In 2015 and 2016 there were three major migrations flows. Of these, the Eastern Mediterranean route passes from Syria via Turkey, through Greece, and into the Balkans. This route is by far the busiest avenue to the EU. In 2015 close to 1.5 million people traveled though it. While Syrians make up the largest group of immigrants on this exodus, people from Afghanistan, Bangladesh, and East Africa all traverse the same route.

Traffickers of those coming from Syria primarily use the Islamic State-controlled border crossing to reach Turkey. "It is safer to travel inside the Caliphate," said a former Syrian refugee who asked to remain anonymous. "There are no road blocks set up by different armed groups or warlords. The journey is smooth even if there is bombing, because the traffickers travel away from the villages, towns, and oil facilities. Plus, when you cross over into Turkey, you do not risk being shot at by the Turkish border patrol, as happens at Bab al Salam or at the borders near Afrin, in the Idlib province." This route is also cheaper for migrants, because traffickers pay only one tax at the border, instead of paying several times as they cross territories controlled by different armed groups, criminal gangs, or even troops from Assad's army. In the summer of 2015, the tax on human cargo crossing into Turkey generated about half a million dollars a day for the Islamic State, more than the taxation on smuggled oil.

The less crowded routes traverse the Central Mediterranean, via Libya to Italy, and the Western Mediterranean, from Morocco to Spain. According to Frontex, in 2015 about 300,000 migrants reached Europe via these routes. The Islamic State is profiting from the trafficking business, not only in Syria, but also in Libya. ISIS has established regulations, specifying, for example, that boats sailing from the Western shores of the country under its control may carry a maximum of 120 people. Before allowing boats to sail, members of the Islamic State check each one, making sure that the number of migrants does not exceed the imposed capacity. Traffickers pay 50 percent of their profits to ISIS in exchange for the right to sail, so counting the migrants also establishes the amount of tax each boat must pay. In 2015 this tax generated about $20 million for every ten thousand migrants.[230]

Similarly, before granting a permit to use its shores, the Islamic State checks the identity of each trafficker and verifies that they have complied with the fixed price for the crossing. That is, traffickers are not permitted to charge migrants in excess of the rates set by ISIS. Hence, sailing under the supervision of the Islamic State has become a sort of Declaration of Conformity certificate for migrants. At about $1,600 per person, crossing via the ISIS-controlled territory is more expensive than crossing from the eastern shores of Libya, but the journey is safer. ISIS not only commands higher prices for use of its routes, but it also requires migrants to attend a one-week-long Sharia course in order to qualify for safe passage. Hence, ISIS uses the migration flows to proselytize its creed.[231]

MIGRATION: "PAY AS YOU GO"

As the number of migrants fleeing failed states and Islamist controlled territory surged, trafficking migrants grew into a vast, illicit business. While fifteen years ago, just over one hundred thousand people reached Europe every year, today that number is nearly two million. While the migrants previously were largely poor and uneducated people seeking economic opportunity, today, spurred to depart by political instability, they come from every single social class and profession. Well aware of this reality, traffickers have adapted prices and services according to the ability of the migrants to pay. For example, the cost of reaching Europe by plane from Turkey ranges from €8,000 to €10,000, while taking the more risky overland or sea route costs much less.

No matter how rich or how poor a migrant may be, a trafficker is essential to their journey. Even when, in the summer of 2015, the European Union temporarily opened its borders, traffickers were needed to reach one of the member countries. Once inside the EU, migrants proceed on foot and European traffickers are quick to offer rides to those who can afford them. For example, for $1,000 per person, migrants are loaded onto trucks and cars for the trip to Germany from Bulgaria or Hungary. These journeys inside the European Union aren't so different from those across the Libyan desert.

In August 2015, seventy-one migrants died of asphyxiation while crossing Austria in a locked van from Bulgaria. That same day the Austrian police discovered another truck transporting eighty-one migrants on the verge of suffocation. That same evening, police in Germany stopped a third truck close to the Austrian border with eighty-six migrants. The police report shows that traffickers lined the trucks with wood, as sound insulation to prevent police from discovering their human cargo. Migrants are sometimes locked inside these trucks for more than twenty-four hours, without any stops for water or to use a bathroom.[232]

In the summer of 2015, the booming migrant business convinced criminal gangs operating along the Eastern European route to get involved in trafficking. The trafficking was so profitable that they dropped their other illicit activities. Austrian police, for example, reported a sharp decline in theft of copper wire, a crime once widespread near the Hungarian border. Local gangs and petty criminals instead rented vans and cars to ferry migrants across the border. Austrian police stopped many of these vehicles inside Austria. In September, when the Hungarian government decided to bus migrants free of charge, Austrian police caught no smugglers. As soon as the buses stopped, the trafficking started all over again.

Exactly as in the Sahel and in North Africa, small independent criminal groups, operating locally, smuggle migrants across European borders. Inside Europe, the groups are predominantly petty criminals or traffickers who are from the same diaspora as the migrants. These groups do not have a monopoly. In country after country, border after border, migrants to Europe shop around to find the right traffickers and pay them only when they reach the agreed upon destination.

The "pay as you go" model is the by-product of the highly decentralized nature of the trafficking business. Interestingly, while globalization has pulverized the economic and financial borders of entire nations, turning the world into a global village, kidnappers and traffickers have focused on localized business models, working within national and even regional borders. Piracy and criminal jihadism has blossomed inside culturally and historically homogenous areas, once part of colonial and post-colonial nations. Inside these regions, the central political authority has collapsed, and tribal values and tribal leadership have filled this void. Abduction of foreigners in the Sahel, North Africa, and in Syria took place against this backdrop, often with tribal leaders and local politicians mediating between the kidnappers and the families or governments of the hostages.

This new breed of criminality is in sharp contrast with the old, highly integrated Western model of organized crime, such as the Mafia, because kidnapping of foreigners and trafficking of migrants are illicit activities that developed and evolved away from the Western nation state. Indeed, they breed wherever there is political anarchy, and they prey upon the most valuable resource of these areas: people. This has never been the case with organized crime, which instead needs a centralized political government to establish it as an alternative system.

Non-European traffickers have successfully exported the "pay as you go" criminal model to the European Union, partly because it is the most functional and efficient for the migrants, as the terrifying journey of Mohammad Jamil Hassan proves. They have also exploited the European Union's lack of a unified policy in the matter of national borders and immigration. Hence, inside the EU's borders one finds a political void, produced by the lack of a common European foreign policy, into which petty criminal and migrant communities can easily step.

Trafficking migrants is not the first example of cross-pollination between non-European and European criminality.

The prostitution racket of African women has relied on a similar partnership. "Last summer the police asked us to put up two women from Gambia. They had arrived with a group of refugees from Libya," said Ida Pierotti of Aquiloni, a humanitarian organization based in Verona, Italy. "We were told that they needed help because they had been abused and raped during the journey. We rented a room with a small kitchen and supplied them with an Italian teacher. The women were young and very beautiful. One looked like Naomi Campbell. We noticed that they dressed in a very provocative way and always wore a lot of makeup, so we tried to warn them that this was not what they should do, that it was dangerous, but they ignored us. After just over a month, a friend from Senegal, who was living in Brescia, came to visit them. She stayed just for a short time and then she left. That same day the two women vanished. They left behind many receipts for clothes and shoes they had bought. Some purchases were of over €500. We also found Western Union slips for money transfers from Spain and Brescia for €200, €300 each. A week later an aid worker saw one of the women while she was prostituting herself in the streets of Verona. She approached her and asked what was she doing and offered to help her. The woman laughed at her and left. I cannot prove it, but I am sure that these two women were part of an international prostitution racket that had sent them to Europe as refugees to work as prostitutes." Several humanitarian aid workers concur with Pierotti. African and European criminals use the migrant route for drugs and prostitution.

However, it would be wrong to believe that most women migrants are keen to become prostitutes, as the European anti-migrant champions want us to believe. We must remember that migration is a very complex issue and that people leave their country seeking a better life in Europe, in the US, or in any other rich nation because they cannot improve their existence at home.

After the fall of the Gaddafi regime, there was a surge in East and West African women being smuggled into Europe via Libya to supply a growing market in Spain, Switzerland, and northern Italy.

"From 2010 to 2013 migrants were predominantly young African men, maximum thirty, thirty-two years old," explained Pierotti. "In 2014 we started to get also men from Bangladesh and Pakistan. Soon after the minors arrived, the news that it was easier for them to get asylum spread and boys began migrating. Then came the African women, single, young women, all very good looking, mostly from Nigeria, Gambia, Zambia. More recently, in 2015 and 2016, migrants are predominantly families with children, and pregnant women. Many get pregnant in Libya and reach Italy in the early months of pregnancy because they are told it will be easier to get asylum."

While their request for asylum is processed, the migrants are looked after by organizations like Pierotti's Aquiloni, which provides everything from room and board to clothing, and basic support for doctors' appointments, and assistance with more trivial needs, such as how to get a smartphone, or designer sunglasses. These are not unusual requests. "The majority of migrants we deal with consider the West an immense shopping mall. They want the goods they have seen on TV at home and they want to show that they have it to their friends back home," explained Nadia Albini, who also works for Aquiloni. "Their Facebook profiles are full of photos parading such products. They want people at home to see them, to reinforce this absurd concept of the West. Yes, these people are economic migrants, but many of them come to Europe for the wrong reasons, to become part of a shallow, consumer society."

The European taxpayer pays their bills from the moment they reach Europe's shores until they obtain residency and are allowed to work. This process can take several years. Hence, fulfilling the needs of migrants is another huge industry, one that is enriching a new breed of European entrepreneurs.

GETTING RICH EXPLOITING MIGRANTS

The biggest global exodus since World War II is not only a bonanza for European petty criminals. From aid agencies to independent businessmen, the opportunities for growth are huge, as refugees and migrants need to be housed, clothed, fed, and relocated. This, indeed, is a significant "legitimate" industry, bankrolled once again with taxpayer money.

In 2015, Norway, a country of 5 million people, received 31,500 refugees, more than twice the number it had received in the previous year. Migrants came predominantly from Syria, Afghanistan, Iraq, and Eritrea. The Norwegian Directorate of Immigration (UDI) could not handle such an influx and turned to private entrepreneurs for help.

About 90 percent of Norway's refugees are looked after by private, for-profit companies. For the owners of these companies, the refugee crisis is the equivalent of the Gold Rush. To house and feed the refugees, the Norwegian government pays between $31 and $75 per night. It is easy to see how profits can be extracted from these fees. "Just outside Oslo, a savvy entrepreneur named Ola Moe [. . .] rented a vacant hospital for $10,000 a month, did minimal upgrades, and began charging the government $460,000 a month to house and feed 200 refugees."[233]

Among the beneficiaries of this gold rush is Hero Norway, a hospitality company owned by the Norwegian Adolfsen brothers. Hero offers a variety of products: short stay dormitories for those waiting to be screened by the police; places for longer periods of two to three weeks for those waiting to be interviewed by other immigration authorities; and longer terms camps where people live independently in houses as they wait, sometimes for years, to be resettled in Norway.

Hero Norway is not the only for-profit company on this large scale operating in the Old Continent. ORS Service AG, a Swiss company, in 2014 generated $99 million in revenue caring for refugees in Switzerland, Austria, and Germany. It is impossible to obtain the revenues for 2015 of many of these companies, as for-profit enterprises handling refugees have become extremely secretive.

Migrants and refugees are housed in buildings that have either been abandoned or that have been long out of use, such as old boarding schools, defunct rehabilitation centers, hospitals, and mountain hotels. People like the Adolfsen brothers buy them cheaply and turn them into refugee camps.

This is a model that can be found throughout Europe. In the summer of 2015, about five hundred migrants and refugees were housed in a large estate, Centro di Costa-grande, in Veneto. "The owner is a rich entrepreneur from Verona, Pietro Delaini, who bought the estate for this purpose," says Ida Pierotti. The Italian government pays €35 per day per person: €27.50 for room and board, €2.50 for pocket money and €5 to the organization to fulfill their program needs, from providing language classes to doctors' visits. Humanitarian aid organizations, for example Caritas or Aquiloni, where Pierotti works, get only €30 because they supply this latter service for free, but other companies, such as the cooperative Spazio Aperto, which looks after the refugees at Costagrande, receive the additional €5 per migrant per day. "This is not small cash," said Ida Pierotti. "For 500 people it is about €2,500 per day or €75,000 per month. These funds should be used to pay social workers, one for every ten refugees. That is the standard to provide help on a daily basis. However, most of the companies involved in this business do not employ people full time and instead use volunteers."

Sometimes even ONLUSes, which are nonprofit by definition, do not properly pay social workers to support the migrants. People often complain to me about how they are paid. For example, a refugee who has been translating for one Italian nonprofit, a big player in the refugees business in Milan, told me that she was paid with food vouchers for the work of translator that she was doing. Like many people employed in the industry of refugees, she wants to remain anonymous because she fears the reaction of big ONLUSes that have money and lawyers ready to sue. As in all gold rushes, the one produced by the refugee crisis is crowded with profiteers who take advantage of the situation.

Even more shocking is the fact that the authorities do not check the budgets of the companies in charge of this business, companies paid with taxpayer money to provide hospitality to migrants. Big ONLUSes, for example the aforementioned nonprofit in Milan, get large amounts of money from municipalities to look after the migrants who used to camp inside the central stations. Money they can spend as they please, including employing PR. When in October 2015, a volunteer took me to visit the refugee center near the Milan station, an area donated by the railway workers association and run by the Milan nonprofit, I was approached by a group of people from that nonprofit while I was taking a picture of the cafeteria. A rather rude individual told me that I was not allowed to take pictures and that I needed permission to talk to people inside the center. When I asked him who he was, he told me that he was the nonprofit's press officer. Next to him there was a man holding an expensive camera. He was the nonprofit's official photographer! As I explained that I was researching a book on kidnapping and refugees, they escorted me outside the center.

Inside this hub managed by the nonprofit there were other ONLUSes and humanitarian aid organizations, including the Red Cross which offered services to the refugees. Before being escorted out, I managed to talk to a Syrian doctor. While I was talking to him a man from Eritrea arrived. He was wearing worn out plastic sandals, very old clothes, and was very dirty. He looked exhausted and ill. Nobody offered him any help, food, clothes, or the possibility to take a shower. The doctor told him to wait until he had finished talking to me. The man sat on a chair outside the doctor's office holding his head in his hands. He had no idea that he was worth thirty-five euros per day.

While researching this field I had the distinct feeling that refugees are merchandise for everybody, they are a source of income, and revenues. The industry constructed around their tragedy offers employment to hundreds of thousand of people across Europe. Sometimes these are part time jobs, but they are still jobs in an economy plagued by double digit unemployment.

Regulating the way hospitality is provided for migrants is as hard as regulating the 1849 California Gold Rush. The front-runner in this business is always a step ahead of the game. "Even nonprofit companies can profit," said the translator from Milan. "All they need to do is to invoice 'friendly' companies or pay salaries to people they know." Employing a press officer and a photographer? Even easier is to profit from moving the refugees like merchandise. When it became clear that having five hundred people at Costagrande, women and men together, was not a good idea, less than half were moved to another location. Some ended up in Prada, a mountain village near San Zeno di Montagna, in an abandoned and isolated hotel that had been bought by the owner of Costagrande.

NEW BLOOD FOR THE OLD CONTINENT

Traffickers are busy making money off of people escaping the bombing campaign of Obama's grand coalition and Putin's air force. For-profit and not-for-profit companies provide hospitality to these very people, and both activities are paid for by the taxpayer. To justify this surreal scenario, economists and politicians claim that the sudden influx of a new labor force is positive for Europe. In other words, the European Union can profit from this human tragedy.

In January 2016, UBS, the Swiss international bank, produced a report titled "The Future of Europe"[234] that stated, "To match the US labor growth rate, the EU needs 1.8 million additional immigrants (of working age) annually for the next 10 years." In other words, the migrant crisis—while a nightmare for Western Civilization, for towns and cities across Europe, and for European security—is perfect for those who want more cheap labor on the continent. Naturally, this argument would be correct if the majority of migrants were working-aged men, but they are not. Most of the Syrian migrants are families. Even when the refugees are male, once they receive their residency permit, they use the reunification procedures to bring their families. As pointed out by the *Financial Times*,[235] in the coming years, Europe will have to deal with millions of dependents that they "send home for." Hence, the idea of creating a larger labor force out of this migrant crisis suddenly becomes questionable, especially considering the dependents, the capital outlay required to process, police, and house them, and indeed the pension liabilities that will emerge as a result.

Other studies, from the International Monetary Fund and from the Organisation for Economic Co-operation and Development (OECD), claim that in the long run migration will be positive for Europe, a fast-aging continent which in the near future may end up like Japan, with an overwhelming proportion of pensioners and a very small work force that contributes to their pensions. Germany is among the fastest-aging countries in Europe. By the end of 2060 there will be fifty-nine potential pensioners over the age of sixty-five to one hundred working-age persons. If nothing changes by 2060, for each German pensioner there will be less than two people working and paying taxes to provide for his pension. In addition, the cost of national health and pensions will absorb an extra 5 percent of the GDP.

Demographics seem to recommend migration. According to the OECD, to avoid stagnation, the European Union will need to absorb fifty million migrants before 2060, which is more than one million every year. Without this injection of new blood, the German population will decrease from 81.3 million in 2013 to 70.8 million in 2060. By that date the most populous country in Europe will be the United Kingdom, whose population is set to rise over the same period from 64.1 million to 80.1 million. These figures are directly related to the high migration flows into the United Kingdom, which, interestingly, in recent years have been primarily from EU member states.

Today, however, the influx of refugees and migrants is indeed a problem for the Europeans. "In the short term, additional public spending will increase domestic demand and GDP," the IMF concluded in one of its reports on migration. "IMF staff estimate that this effect will be modest for the EU as a whole (raising the level of GDP by some 0.1 percent in 2017), but more pronounced in the main asylum-seeker destination countries."[236] GDP per capita will be lower, reflecting the weaker labor market performance of refugees and restrictions on labor market access to asylum seekers in some countries. "In the long run, the economic impact will depend on the speed of integration of refugees into the labor market." Because shortsighted politicians care little about the long run, the migrants' crisis is fast becoming a very serious political crisis.

Far from being regarded as a human tragedy, for European leaders the biggest exodus since World War II is a political boomerang fast approaching them. Those in its flying path will be knocked down. No easy solution is appearing on the horizon. Ending the bombing campaign in Syria will only give Russia more power to strengthen the Assad regime and will not stop people from fleeing their homes. Opening the borders has proven disastrous because of the huge number of refugees and migrants entering. The only possible solution, according to the EU, is to do what Berlusconi and Prodi did: stop the migrants at the gates of Europe with the help of a friendly nation, Turkey.

Will Erdogan do for the European Union what Gaddafi did for Italy and the EU until a few years ago? Turkey is asking for money and for a privileged working relationship, including a non-visa entry into the European Union, as a prelude to a possible membership.

Migrants will be blocked inside Turkey and locked in refugee camps where the next generation of kidnappers, jihadists, and criminals will rise. The Caliphate will find plenty of warriors among them.

Brexit

It was the longest night. Minutes after the closing of the polls for the UK referendum on the European Union, a YouGov exit poll showed a confortable margin of victory for the pro-European camp and within minutes the pound to dollar exchange rate jumped to 1.50, a clear sign of confidence in the forecast.

I kept checking the Bloomberg page, whose indicators were all green, everything was rising! The markets and the world were sure that it was a done deal, and why not? For weeks politicians, economists, international institutions, scientists, even Hollywood stars had exhorted the British to remain European, to stick with the status quo, even if it wasn't "ideal."

The markets were particularly optimistic and happy because the EU had been one of the strongest supporters of neo-liberalism and one of the driving forces of globalization; after the fall of the Berlin Wall it had de facto handed over the former Soviet Bloc to the financial markets. The European Union had also come to the rescue of the financial markets more than once. In 2010, at the outset of the sovereign debt crisis, and again in 2011 when the Italian and Spanish banking system seemed about to implode, the European Central Bank was instrumental in preventing a global financial meltdown by bailing out banks and financial institutions. Yes, the markets had been among the primary beneficiaries of the "new," "enlarged" European Union, an institution with twenty-eight members still seeking to add new ones. So it was natural that on the night of the counting of the votes on whether or not to leave such a club, the world of finance was awake and cheering for the Remain camp.

For about one hour, brokers across the world were busy trading, going long on the pound and buying stocks, pushing the indexes up. Speculators were anticipating a fantastic night; Brexit, the much-feared exit of the second-largest economy from the EU, seemed a past nightmare; and making money betting on the rising value of the pound appeared as easy as printing money. As usual, bets in favor of the pound were placed by borrowing, a trick far too common in today's market. You put down a percentage of the bet and borrow the rest from someone else. When you get your profit you pay back the interest and pocket the rest. No movement of money takes place, and the bets are very short-term, often lasting just a few hours. But if the bet is wrong, then the losses are huge!

As soon as the first results came in, the Leave camp reported better than expected numbers and everything changed.

In twenty minutes, the pound to dollar exchange rate dropped from 1.50 to 1.43, drawing a cliff on the screens. It kept falling through the night and ended at a thirty-year low, 1.32. What was meant to be a night of celebration for international finance became a night of confusion and dismay. Brokers panicked, politicians panicked, the world panicked. The status quo was crumbling.

As the votes kept being counted, it became apparent not only that the United Kingdom was heading for Brexit but that the UK was a deeply divided country. England and Wales voted overwhelmingly to leave, their motivation being economic and social: to end the economic stagnation, which many attributed to the excessive rules and regulations of an overly bureaucratic European institution, the EU, and to halt the massive migrations from EU member states into the United Kingdom—a steady and rising tide of people seeking jobs and a future in a country that since 2010 had created more jobs than any of the other twenty-seven members of the EU.

By dawn the map of this divided country appeared on TV screens. However, what the news programs did not offer was a snapshot of a continent divided on the same issues, and in particular on migration. Indeed, what had tilted the balance of the votes towards Brexit wasn't the shambolic way Brussels had handled a series of economic crises over the last few years, or its obsession with rules and regulations, but how it had badly managed the refugee exodus from Africa, the Middle East, and Central Asia. It was unfortunate for the Remain camp that the refugee crisis took place in the summer of 2015. It soon became the focus of the criticism of Brussels. The leaders of the Brexit campaign strongly criticized the sudden opening of the borders without a proper strategy on how to absorb the migrants; they even more vehemently opposed the agreement with Turkey, which they claimed would give the Turkish population the right of entry into the UK without a visa.

A year before Brexit, the fortress of Europe had begun crumbling from the inside, under the pressure of millions of displaced people, victims of the foolish foreign policy Europe had pursued since the beginning of the millennium. A policy masterminded across the Atlantic, in Washington, D.C., not in Brussels! The refugee crisis, the largest exodus since World War II, is the direct consequence of the political destabilization of a large section of the world, an irreversible phenomenon triggered first by globalization and second by the rising tide of criminal jihadism. Do the Europeans or the Americans understand this? Their leaders have been projecting a different scenario, depicting a clash between good and evil. The media has avoided connecting the dots in such a way as to offer a more realistic interpretation of this epic human tragedy. The answer is NO, the European and the American leaders seem to be unable to understand that the root cause lies in their answer to 9/11: the war on terror. But the incompetence of a political class that has failed to steady the ship in the stormy waters of globalization has not escaped the judgment of the people.

Brexit is just the tip of the iceberg. The rising popularity of right-wing groups, the return of xenophobia and racism, the rebuilding of borders, the calls for protectionism are all symptoms of a malaise that is spreading across the Western world. In the years to come we may see a new political class take over the running of our lives, a class that appeals to sentiments of closure. We will see more electoral stalemates like the one in Spain, where for the second time no party has the majority to rule. As long as this scenario remains in place, the merchants of men will continue to make money trafficking desperate people to the gates of Western fortresses, a business that will carry on bankrolling jihadism inside and outside our newly built walls.

Abu Bakr al Baghdadi. The leader of ISIS and self-proclaimed caliph of the Islamic State.

Abu Omar Brigade. Jihadist group of foreign fighters known as Katibat al Muhajireen (Emigrants Brigade), also known as the Muhajireen Brigade, lead by Abu Omar al Shishani who was once the leader of the Jaish al Muhajireen wal-Ansar in Syria before joining IS. Shishani is a disenfranchised former Georgian soldier, who was discharged from the army after contracting tuberculosis.

ACTED (formerly Agence d'Aide à la coopération technique et au développement, or "Agency for Technical Cooperation and Development") is a French humanitarian NGO set up in 1993. It is a non-governmental, apolitical, and nonprofit organization committed to supporting vulnerable populations around the world.

Alawites. A religious sect in Syria that follows a mystical brand of Shia Islam. As they have historically kept their beliefs secret from outsiders, not much is known about them; they comprise a significant minority in Syria, some 12 percent of the population.

Al Nusra. A branch of al Qaeda that operates in Syria and Lebanon. It was created in 2012 during the Syrian Civil War. It has had several clashes with ISIS, and was losing badly in open warfare with the Islamic State.

Ansar al Islam was an armed Sunni group active during the Iraq War. It was established in Iraq in 2001 as a Salafist movement that imposed a strict application of Sharia law. The group continued to fight the Iraqi government following the withdrawal of US troops and sent members to Syria to fight in the Syrian civil war.

The *Armed Islamic Group* or *Groupe Islamique Armé (GIA)* was one of the two main armed Islamist groups that fought the Algerian government and army during the Algerian Civil War. It was created from smaller armed groups following the 1992 military coup and arrest and internment of thousands of officials of the FIS party after that party won the first round of parliamentary elections in December 1991.

Caliph. Title of the chief Muslim civil and religious ruler who protects the integrity of the state and the faith. The Caliphs are regarded as the successors of Mohammed. The term derives from the Arabic *khalifa*, meaning "successor." "Caliph" was also the honorary title adopted by the Ottoman sultans in the sixteenth century, after Sultan Mehmed II conquered Syria and Palestine, made Egypt a satellite of the Ottoman Empire, and was recognized as the guardian of the holy cities of Mecca and Medina.

Caliphate. The dominion or rule of the caliph.

Dublin Treaty, known as the *Dublin Regulation*, is an EU law and cornerstone of the Dublin System, which consists of the Dublin Regulation and the EURODAC Regulation, which establishes a Europe-wide fingerprinting database for unauthorized entrants to the EU. The Dublin Regulation aims to "determine rapidly the Member State responsible [for an asylum claim]" and provides for the transfer of an asylum seeker to that Member State. Usually, the responsible Member State will be the state through which the asylum seeker first entered the EU.

European Migrant Smuggling Centre (EMSC) launched in February 2016 by Europol. The goal of the center is to proactively support EU Member States in dismantling criminal networks involved in organized migrant smuggling. The center will focus on geographical criminal hotspots, and will build a better capability across the European Union to fight human trafficking networks.

Euskadi Ta Askatasuna (ETA), which means "Basque Fatherland and Liberty" in the Basque language, is an armed group fighting for the independence of the Basque country from Spain. ETA started out as the EKIN, a nationalist group that changed its name to the Euskadi Ta Askatasuna in 1958. The group's initial activities involved planting explosives in Basque cities such as Bilbao. In 1968 ETA put its first military initiative into action, and in subsequent years it intensified its violence, targeting security forces and politicians. The group is still active in Spain and maintains ties with armed groups all over the world. Its membership is believed to be quite small, perhaps no more than twenty hard-core activists and several hundred supporters, and its headquarters are believed to be in the Basque provinces of Spain and France.

The *Farouk Brigades* is an armed organization formed by a number of the Free Syrian Army units in Homs. The group rapidly expanded in size and prominence in 2012 before suffering internal splits and battlefield reversals in 2013 that greatly reduced its influence. By 2014 the group was largely defunct, with member factions joining other rebel groups.

The *Free Syrian Lawyers* began protesting at the beginning of the Syrian revolution in Qasr al-Adly, Aleppo's main courthouse. They took their protests to the streets when the regime began to imprison other activists. In addition to protesting and delivering humanitarian aid, the Free Syrian Lawyers are also working to build a better justice system that integrates Syrian tradition and is recognized by the people.

Hezbollah. Arabic for "Party of God," Hezbollah is a radical Lebanese Shia group formed in 1982 in response to the Israeli invasion of Lebanon. It advocates the establishment of Islamic rule in Lebanon as happened in Iran, the liberation of all occupied Arab lands, and the expulsion of non-Muslims from Muslim countries. The group is sponsored by Iran and predominantly operates in the Bekaa Valley, south of Beirut. Its membership is estimated at 40,000 in Lebanon and several thousand supporters. It possesses heavy artillery such as multiple BM-21 rockets. A number of its members are known or suspected to have been involved in numerous armed attacks against the US. Hezbollah also goes by the name of Islamic Jihad, but its official armed wing is called the Islamic Resistance. The latter, created in 1983, oversees military operations in south Lebanon. It has 400 well-trained fighters and 5,000 supporters. Besides sporadic attacks (mostly bombings and murders), it leads proper military operations against the Israeli and Lebanese armies. Militarily organized, the Islamic Resistance's activities have become increasingly illegal since 1993. The group has tried especially to establish a popular base in south Lebanon through social aid activities, such as its Jihad al Hoed ("Holy effort for the reconstruction"), which finances the reconstruction of buildings destroyed by the Israeli army. It also gives $25,000 to the families of the "martyrs" who die during its suicide operations.

Human Rights Watch (HRW) is an international NGO that conducts research and advocacy on human rights.

The *International Organization for Migration (IOM)* was initially established in 1951 as the Intergovernmental Committee for European Migration (ICEM) to help resettle people displaced by World War II. As of April 2015, IOM has 162 member states and 9 observer states. It is the principal intergovernmental organization in the field of migration. IOM is dedicated to promoting humane and orderly migration for the benefit of all. It does so by providing services and advice to governments and migrants.

The *Irish Republican Army (IRA)* is any of several Irish armed movements active in the twentieth and twenty-first centuries dedicated to Irish republicanism, seeking the creation of an all-Irish independent republic. It was also characterized by the belief that in order to achieve this goal political violence was needed.

ISIS. Islamic State in Iraq and Syria. Also known as the *Islamic State of Iraq and the Levant (ISIL)* and the *Islamic State (IS),* this terrorist organization was officially created in 2013, though its history stretches back to the early 2000s and al Qaeda. Its territory covers large swaths of both Iraq and Syria, and its forces were attacking the Iraqi city of Mosul as late as early September 2014.

The *Islamic Salvation Front* was a political party in Algeria. In 1990 the FIS received more than half the valid votes cast by Algerians in the local government election. When it appeared to be winning a general election in January 1992, a military coup dismantled the party, interning thousands of its officials in the Sahara. It was officially banned two months later.

Islamism. A political ideology based on the belief that Muslim religious principles should dominate every aspect of public and private life.

Jihad. This term has often been mistranslated as "Holy War," a concept coined in Europe during the Crusades. *Jihad* is Arabic for "striving," and a better translation of its meaning as a religious doctrine would be "striving in the cause of God." There are two aspects of jihad: great jihad, the struggle to overcome carnal desires and evil inclinations, and small jihad, the armed defense of Islam against aggressors. The term has been used by different armed groups in their violent confrontations with the West; famously, Osama bin Laden called for a jihad in his fatwa against Americans, calling for "just war" against the oppressor.

Koran. The holy scripture of Islam.

Movement for Oneness and Jihad in West Africa (MOJWA), also known as the *Mouvement pour l'unicité et le jihad en Afrique de l'Ouest (MUJAO),* or the *Movement for Unity and Jihad in West Africa (MUJWA),* is an active armed organization that broke off from al Qaeda in the Islamic Maghreb. It announced its first armed action on video on December 12, 2011, with the intended goal of spreading jihad across a larger section of West Africa, though operations have been limited to southern Algeria and northern Mali.

Mujahideen. Plural form of the Arabic word *mujahed*, literally meaning "one who makes jihad." The term was applied to Muslims fighting the Soviet occupation of Afghanistan (1979–89), and has been translated as "holy warriors."

The *Mujahideen Shura Council* is a coalition of Islamist rebel groups formed to fight ISIS in Syria. Its affiliated groups are Al Nusra Front, Jaysh al Islam, Ahrar ash-Sham, Army of Ahl al Sunni wal Jamaa, Jaysh Usud al Sharqiya, al Qa'qa', Jabhat al Jihad wal Bina, Bayareq al Shaaitat, Liwa al Qadisiya, Army of Maoata al Islami, Army of al Ikhlas, and Liwa al Muhajireen wal-Ansar.

Nationalism. Term used to describe the sentiment and ideology of attachment to a nation and its interests. The word originates from the theory that a state should be founded in a nation and that a nation should be constituted as a state. Nationalism requires the consciousness of national identity, which may include territorial integrity, common language, shared customs, and other elements of culture.

Operation Restore Hope was a US-led, United Nations-sanctioned multinational force, which operated in Somalia between December 5, 1992 and May 4, 1993, with the task of creating a protected environment for conducting humanitarian operations in the southern half of the country.

Palestine Liberation Organization (PLO). A Palestinian nationalist movement and the central organization of all Palestinian movements, the PLO was created in 1964 by Ahmed Shukeiry under the auspices of Egypt. Its objective, as stated in its charter established in May 1964, is the creation of an independent Palestinian state on the territory today covered by Israel or, at least, in the Occupied Territories (Gaza and the West Bank). Its leader was

Yasser Arafat from 1969 until his death in 2004, when he was succeeded by Mahmoud Abbas, who continues to hold the post.

PKK (Partiya Karkerên Kurdistanê), or the *Kurdistan Workers' Party*, is a militant left-wing organization based in Turkey and Iraqi Kurdistan. Since 1984 the PKK has waged an armed struggle against the Turkish state for the right of self-determination of the Kurdish people in Turkey. The group was founded in 1978 in the village of Fis by a group of Kurdish students led by Abdullah Ocalan. The PKK's ideology was originally a fusion of revolutionary socialism and Kurdish nationalism, seeking the foundation of an independent Marxist-Leninist state to be known as Kurdistan. In August 2015, the PKK announced that they would accept a ceasefire with Turkey under US guarantees. In a joint declaration with nine other organizations in March 2016, the PKK called for the revolutionary overthrow of the Turkish government and capitalism.

Al Qaeda. Literally meaning "the base," al Qaeda was originally formed around 1988 by Osama bin Laden and Abu Ubaydah al Banshiri, bin Laden's top military commander, as a network to connect the Arabs who volunteered to fight in the anti-Soviet jihad. Al Qaeda also helped to finance, recruit, and train Sunni Islamic extremists for the Afghan resistance. Soon, it became a multiethnic Sunni Islamist insurgent organization that remained active well beyond the end of the Afghan war. Its primary aim is the establishment of a pan-Islamist Caliphate throughout the Muslim world, and therefore it seeks the collaboration of other Islamist armed organizations to overthrow existing regimes regarded as "non-Islamic" and to expel Westerners and non-Muslims from Muslim countries. In 1998, it merged with the Egyptian Islamic Jihad ("al Jihad"). Its membership is thought to be anywhere between several hundred and several thousand people.

Al Qaeda in the Islamic Maghreb (AQIM) is an Islamist armed organization active in West Africa and the Sahel that aims to create an Islamic state. The group has declared its intention to attack European (including Spanish and French) and American targets. Membership is mostly drawn from the Algerian and local Saharan communities (such as the Tuaregs and Berabiche tribal clans of Mali), as well as Moroccans from city suburbs of the North African country. The leaders are mainly Algerians.

Red Brigades. The Red Brigades (*Brigate Rosse,* or *BR*) was formed in 1969 in Italy out of the student and workers' movements. Its ideology advocated violence in the service of class warfare and revolution. The group was based in and operated from Italy and mainly targeted symbols of the establishment such as industrialists, politicians, and businessmen.

The *Royal Canadian Mounted Police (RCMP),* or *Gendarmerie royale du Canada (GRC),* is both a federal and national police force of Canada.

Salafism. A sect of Islam that espouses strict, literal adherence to the tenets of Islam. Originating in the nineteenth century in response to European influence in the region, Salafism is sometimes considered puritanical, and often associated with jihad. Salafists are mostly located in Saudi Arabia, Qatar, and the United Arab Emirates, and are considered to be the "dominant minority" in the Middle East.

Al Shabaab is a jihadist armed group based in East Africa. In 2012, it pledged allegiance to al Qaeda and in 2015 to ISIS. Al Shabaab's troop strength was estimated at 7,000 to 9,000 militants in 2014. As of 2015, the group has retreated from the major cities, controlling a few rural areas.

Al Shabaab is an offshoot of the Islamic Court Union, which splintered into several smaller factions after its defeat in 2006 by Somalia's Transitional Federal Government (TFG) and its Ethiopian military allies. The group describes itself as waging jihad against "enemies of Islam."

Sharia. Literally "legislation," a word that refers to the moral and legal code that binds religious Muslims.

Shiites. The lineage of the supporters of Ali, Mohammed's son-in-law, who refused to submit to Caliph Muawiyah in the Great Fitna, thereby creating the greatest schism in Islam.

Sunnism. The largest sect of Islam. After Mohammed's death, those followers who supported a traditional method of election based on community agreement became known as Sunnis; they were opposed by the Shiites, who favored a hereditary transition in leadership.

Takfir. An accusation of apostasy.

Al Tawhid al Jihad. A militant Islamist group founded in Fallujah in 2003 and headed by Abu Musab al Zarqawi. The group arranged false documents for more than one hundred al Qaeda fighters who escaped from Afghanistan during the 2001 war. It also provided them with funds and a safe haven (near Tehran), and then organized their movement out of Iran to other areas in the Middle East and the West. In 2004, the group declared fealty to Osama bin Laden and changed its name to al Qaeda in Iraq. The name means "Monotheism and Jihad."

The *United Self-Defense Forces of Colombia* (*Autodefensas Unidas de Colombia*, or *AUC*), was a paramilitary and drug trafficking group that was active in Colombia from 1997 to 2006. The militia had its roots in the 1980s when militias were established by drugs lords to combat rebel kidnappings and extortion. The AUC had about 20,000 members and was heavily financed through the drug trade and through support from local landowners, cattle ranchers, mining and petroleum companies, and politicians.

The *PATRIOT Act*, also known as *The USA PATRIOT Act* is an act of Congress that was signed into law by President George W. Bush on October 26, 2001. With its ten-letter acronym (USA PATRIOT), the full title is Uniting and Strengthening America by Providing Appropriate Tools Required to Intercept and Obstruct Terrorism Act of 2001. The law is intended to help government agencies detect and prevent possible acts of terrorism, or sponsorship of terrorist groups.

War by proxy. A term denoting third parties fighting in place of larger world powers. A prime example of this type of warfare is the Vietnam conflict in the late 1960s and early 1970s, where North and South were pitted against each other by foreign powers, especially the United States.

Abu Musab al Zarqawi. Islamic militant from Jordan who ran a terrorist training camp in Afghanistan in 2000. He rose to fame after going to Iraq and being responsible for a number of bombings during the Iraq War. Killed in 2006 by US forces.

notes

1   This chapter uses sentences extracted from a collection of interviews conducted with several negotiators by Loretta Napoleoni during the last 10 years.

2   Author interview with Maria Sandra Mariani, August 2015 via Skype and October 2015 in Florence. All quotes of Mariani in the chapter come from these interviews.

3   The Acacus Mountains or Tadrart Acacus (*Tadrart* is the feminine form of "mountain" in the Berber languages) is a mountain range in the western deserts of Libya, part of the Sahara. They are situated east of the Libyan city of Ghat and stretch north from the Algerian border about 60 miles. The Acacus Mountains have a large variation of landscapes, from differently colored sand dunes to arches, gorges, isolated rocks, and deep ravines (*wadis*). Although this area is one of the most arid of the Sahara, there is vegetation, and there are a number of springs and wells in the mountains. The area is known for its rock-art and was designated as a UNESCO World Heritage Site in 1985 because of the importance of these paintings and carvings dating from 12,000 B.C.E. to 100 C.E. *Wikipedia, The Free Encyclopedia*, s.v. "Tadrart Acacus," https://en.wikipedia.org/wiki/Tadrart_Acacus.

4   cf. Loretta Napoleoni, *Terror Incorporated* (New York: Seven Stories Press, 2005), Chapter 18.

5   Author interview with Europol officer, 2003 in Turin.

6   The new common European currency also reduced the cost of money laundering. "In the old days, the *N'drangheta* used tourist exchange outlets to wash dirty profits in various currencies. It was a costly operation, 50 liras per dollar, and it was also time consuming," explains a high-ranking officer of the Italian Guardia di Finanza. cf. Loretta Napoleoni, *Rogue Economics* (New York: Seven Stories Press, 2008), Chapter 3.

7   Gioia Tauro, for example, is the third largest port in Europe and the eighteenth largest in the world. Approximately 3,000 ships and 3 million containers per year pass through it. The port specializes in transshipment: the transfer of cargo from large ships (50,000 tons) to smaller ones.

8   Timothy Kustusch, "AQIM's Funding Sources—Kidnapping, Ransom, and Drug Running by Gangster Jihadists," *361 Security* (November 28, 2012), http://www.361security.com/analysis/aqims-funding-sources-kidnapping-ransom-and-drug-running-by-gangster-jihadists.

9   cf. Richard Luscombe, "Ally of Hugo Chávez Jailed for Links to Colombian Drugs Cartels," *The Guardian*, November 6, 2014, http://www.theguardian.com/world/2014/nov/06/hug-chavez-colombian-drugs-cartels-jude-jail-venezuela.

10   cf. Daniel Ruiz, "Drugs, Destabilisation and UN policy in Guinea-Bissau," University of Oxford podcasts, http://podcasts.ox.ac.uk/

drugs-destabilisation-and-un-policy-guinea-bissau-role-investigative-journal-ism-oxpeace.

11 Kustusch, "AQIM's Funding Sources."

12 cf. Dario Cristiani, "Al-Qaeda in the Islamic Maghreb and the Africa-to-Europe Narco-Trafficking Connection," *Terrorism Monitor* 8, no. 43 (November 24, 2010), http://www.jamestown.org/single/?no_cache=1&tx_ttnews%5Btt_news%5D=37207.#.Vyiu7yguiIl.

13 cf. Colin Freeman, "Revealed: How Saharan Caravans of Cocaine Help to Fund al-Qaeda in Terrorists' North African Domain," *The Telegraph*, January 26, 2013, http://www.telegraph.co.uk/news/worldnews/africaandindianocean/mali/9829099/Revealed-how-Saharan-caravans-of-cocaine-help-to-fund-al-Qaeda-in-terrorists-North-African-domain.html.

14 Ibid., stating, "Goods in Algeria's oil-subsidized socialist economy have been vastly cheaper than in dirt poor, remote Mali, creating a thriving black market in everything from petrol to semolina. 'In northern Mali, everything that is eaten comes from Algeria and comes illegally,' said Andy Morgan, a British-based Sahara expert."

15 The GSPC was formed in 1998 by a breakaway faction of the Armed Islamic Group (GIA) opposed to the targeting of civilian populations. It became one of the various fundamentalist Islamic movements committed to the pursuit and restoration of the original texts of Islam in North Africa. Its logical strategic objective, therefore, was to overthrow national governments and establish an Islamic state.

16 The Salafist Groups for Preaching and Combat (GSPC), which later became the AQIM, kidnapped 32 European tourists in southern Algeria near the border with Mali. The tourists were released after a ransom of €5.5 million was paid.

17 Kustusch, "AQIM's Funding Sources."

18 R. Filippelli, "Cradle of Resistance: Algeria's Kabylia Region," *Parallel Narratives*, http://parallelnarratives.com/cradle-of-resistance-algerias-kabylia-region/.

19 cf. Jean-Pierre Filiu, "Could Al-Qaeda Turn African in the Sahel?" *Carnegie Papers, Middle East Program* 112, June 2010, http://carnegieendowment.org/files/al_qaeda_sahel.pdf.

20 cf. Amado Philip de Andrés, "Organised Crime, Drug Trafficking, Terrorism: The New Achilles' Heel of West Africa," *Fride Comment*, May 2008, http://fride.org/descarga/COM_Achilles_heel_eng_may08.pdf.

21 cf. Rukmini Callimachi, "Paying Ransoms, Europe Bankrolls Qaeda Terror," *New York Times*, July 29, 2014, http://www.nytimes.com/2014/07/30/world/africa/ransoming-citizens-europe-becomes-al-qaedas-patron.html.

22 While no local or Western intelligence agency has yet linked AQIM to the organization of the trans-Atlantic drug trade, there has been considerable evidence that the jihadists are profiting by charging smugglers a fee for safe passage through lands under their control, particularly in northern Mali. A group of Mauritanian traffickers recently detained by Algerian security forces reported that a convoy of hashish—another drug transported through the region—would cost up to $50,000 to pass through AQIM-controlled territory. While such payments constitute much lower profits than those made from KFRs (Kidnappings for Ransom), they represent a more consistent source of

income as the drug trade grows in the region. cf. Kustusch, "AQIM's Funding Sources."

23   Kustusch, "AQIM's Funding Sources."

24   "Saharawi Culture," Organization for Statehood & Freedom, 2010, http://statehoodandfreedom.org/en/western-sahara/saharawi-culture.

25   cf. Henry Samuel, "French Hostages Return Home from Niger after Al-Qaeda Release," *The Telegraph*, October 30, 2013, http://www.telegraph.co.uk/news/worldnews/europe/france/10414038/French-hostages-return-home-from-Niger-after-Al-Qaeda-release.html.

26   cf. "2015 UNHCR country operations profile—Algeria," UNHCR, http://www.unhcr.org/pages/49e485e16.html.

27   Author interviews with a European negotiator, summer 2015, via Skype and October 2015 in Denmark.

28   Author interview with Liban Holm from the Danish Refugee Council, October 2015 in Copenhagen.

29   Jessica Buchanan, Erik Landemalm, and Anthony Flacco, *Impossible Odds: The Kidnapping of Jessica Buchanan and Her Dramatic Rescue by SEAL Team Six* (New York: Simon & Schuster, 2013/2014), Chapter 1.

30   Amanda Lindhout and Sara Corbett, *A House in the Sky* (New York: Simon & Schuster, 2013/2014), 366.

31   INTERSOS Humanitarian Organization home page, http://www.intersos.org/en.

32   The 2003 Nasiriyah bombing was a suicide attack on the Italian military police headquarters in Nasiriyah, Iraq, south of Baghdad, on November 12, 2003.

33   *Time*. Available at http://content.time.com/time/magazine/europe/0,9263,901041011,00.html.

34   Joe Lopez, "Japanese Government Shaken by Iraq Hostage Crisis," World Socialist Web Site, April 16, 2004, https://www.wsws.org/en/articles/2004/04/jap-a16.html.

35   Bruce Hoffman and Fernando Reinares, eds., *The Evolution of the Global Terrorist Threat: From 9/11 to Osama bin Laden's Death* (New York/Chichester, West Sussex: Columbia University Press, 2014).

36   Robert R. Fowler, *A Season in Hell: My 130 Days in the Sahara with Al Qaeda* (New York: HarperCollins, 2011), 264.

37   Paul Gilbert, *Terrorism, Security and Nationality: An Introductory Study in Applied Political Philosophy* (London/New York: Routledge, 1994).

38   In early 2000, the annual GDP per capita was $1,042 in Mauritania; it was $657 in Mali; and it was $390 in Niger. Some regions, for example northern Mali, already constituted failed states.

39   Vincent Cochetel, "I was held hostage for 317 days. Here's what I thought about…" *TED* talk, March 2015, https://www.ted.com/talks/vincent_cochetel_i_was_held_hostage_for_317_days_here_s_what_i_thought_about/transcript?language=en.

40   Adrian Edwards, "Vous devez trouver en vous les ressources nécessaires pour survivre," UNHCR, August 19, 2010, http://www.unhcr.fr/4c6ce2a410.html. (in French)

41   Filiu, "Could Al-Qaeda Turn African in the Sahel?"

42   Fowler, *A Season in Hell*, 294.

43   Ibid., 296.

44 "France 'Paid $17 Million' Ransom for Mali Hostages," *France 24*, February 8, 2013, http://www.france24.com/en/20130208-france-ransom-mali-hostages-huddleston.

45 Fowler, *A Season in Hell*, 302.

46 "People Trafficking Is Biggest Crime Business after Drugs," *Irin*, September 17, 2004, http://www.irinnews.org/report/51407/west-africa-people-trafficking-is-biggest-crime-business-after-drugs.

47 Ibid.

48 Rachel Donadio, "Race Riots Grip Italian Town, and Mafia Is Suspected," *New York Times*, January 10, 2010, http://www.nytimes.com/2010/01/11/world/europe/11italy.html.

49 Author interview with M, 2009 at centro sociale Ex Snia, Roma.

50 Rukmini Callimachi, "Rise of al-Qaida Sahara Terrorist," Associated Press, May 28, 2013, http://www.ap.org/Content/AP-In-The-News/2013/AP-Exclusive-Rise-of-al-Qaida-Sahara-terrorist.

51 Rukmini Callimachi, "Algeria Terror Leader Preferred Money to Death," *USA Today*, January 20, 2013, http://www.usatoday.com/story/news/world/2013/01/20/algeria-terror-leader/1849045/.

52 Kustusch, "AQIM's Funding Sources."

53 Andrea Segre, "Andrea Segre Come un uomo sulla Terra," YouTube video, April 27, 2013, https://www.youtube.com/watch?v=icV7wzHwhNQ. (in Italian)

54 Ibid.

55 Ibid.

56 Ibid.

57 Not only was Libya not a party to the United Nations Refugee Convention, but it also had no system in place for asylum seekers.

58 "Italy/Libya: Gaddafi Visit Celebrates Dirty Deal," Human Rights Watch, June 9, 2009, https://www.hrw.org/news/2009/06/09/italy/libya-gaddafi-visit-celebrates-dirty-deal.

59 Segre, "Andrea Segre Come un uomo sulla Terra."

60 Ibid.

61 Ibid.

62 Judith Tebbutt interview with Dan Damon, "Hostage in Somalia for 6 Months," BBC World Service Radio, July 29, 2013, https://soundcloud.com/bbc-world-service/hostage-in-somalia-for-6.

63 Judith Tebbutt and Richard T. Kelly, *A Long Walk Home: One Woman's Story of Kidnap, Hostage, Loss—and Survival* (London: Faber and Faber, 2013), 328.

64 *Pirate Trails: Tracking the Illicit Financial Flows from Pirate Activities off the Horn of Africa* (Washington, D.C.: The World Bank, 2013), http://siteresources.worldbank.org/EXTFINANCIALSECTOR/Resources/Pirate_Trails_World_Bank_UNODC_Interpol_report.pdf.

65 *Khat* is a leafy shrub containing an amphetamine-like stimulant, classified by the World Health Organization as a drug of abuse. When chewed, it creates a mild buzz somewhere between caffeine and cocaine. The leaves are chewed and stored in the cheek, where they break down in the saliva and eventually enter the bloodstream.

66 The incident is referred to in Karsten Hermansen and Søren Lyngbjørn, *Sørens Somalia: Søren Lyngbjørns beretning om 839 dage som gidsel i Somalia* (Marstal, Denmark: Marstal Søfartsmuseum, 2014), p. 126-127.

67   Mark Bowden, *Black Hawk Down: A Story of Modern War* (New York: Grove Press, 1999/2010).

68   Brian Stewart, "Tales of a Nation of Poets," *CBC Prime Time News* (August 1992), https://www.youtube.com/watch?v=aR2eivEqHZg.

69   Joana Ama Osei-Tutu, "The Root Causes of the Somali Piracy," Kofi Annan International Peacekeeping Training Center (KAIPTC) Occasional Paper No. 31 (March 2011), http://www.kaiptc.org/Publications/Occasional-Papers/Documents/Occasional-Paper-31-Joana.aspx.

70   The Legislative Decree No. 8 of January 15, 1991, converted in Act No. 82, of March 15, 1991, authorizes the freezing of assets at the disposal of seized terrorists or the terrorists' families.

71   Author interview with Giacomo Madia, October 2015 in Milan.

72   *Pirate Trails* (The World Bank).

73   Ibid.

74   Tebbutt and Kelly, *A Long Walk Home*, 329.

75   *Pirate Trails* (The World Bank).

76   Cochetel, "I was held hostage for 317 days."

77   Ibid.

78   Scott Pelley, "The Rescue of Jessica Buchanan," CBS News, May 12, 2013, http://www.cbsnews.com/news/the-rescue-of-jessica-buchanan/.

79   Tebbutt and Kelly, *A Long Walk Home*, 302.

80   "More Sophisticated than You Thought," *The Economist*, November 2, 2013, http://www.economist.com/news/middle-east-and-africa/21588942-new-study-reveals-how-somali-piracy-financed-more-sophisticated-you.

81   Al Shabab, which means "The Youth" in Arabic, emerged as the radical youth wing of Somalia's now-defunct Union of Islamic Courts, which controlled Mogadishu in 2006, before being forced out by Ethiopian forces.

82   Robert Young Pelton and "MJ," "Mystery of Missing MV Leopard Crew Member," *Somalia Report*, August 7, 2011, http://www.somaliareport.com/index.php/post/1315/Mystery_of_Missing_MV_Leopard_Crew_Member.

83   Available at http://www.manw.nato.int/pdf/Press%20Releases%202011/Press%20releases%20Jan-June%202011/SNMG2/NATOWarshipGAZIANTEPAssists%20MVLeopard12Jan11%20(2).pdf.

84   Hermansen and Lyngbjørn, *Søren's Somalia*.

85   Author interview with Karsten Hermansen, October 2015 via Skype.

86   *Pirate Trails* (The World Bank).

87   Ibid.

88   In addition, Lopez began a proceeding against the media for the exploitation of his condition as a hostage.

89   Author interview with Karsten Hermansen, October 2015 via Skype.

90   Mohamed Ahmed, "Somali Sea Gangs Lure Investors at Pirate Lair," Reuters, December 1, 2009, http://www.reuters.com/article/us-somalia-piracy-investors-idUSTRE5B0IZ920091201.

91   Author interview with Karsten Hermansen, October 2015 via Skype.

92   *Pirate Trails* (The World Bank).

93   Ibid.

94   Ibid.

95   *Desperate Choices: Conditions, Risks & Protection Failures Affecting Ethiopian Migrants in Yemen* (Nairobi, Kenya: Danish Refugee Council and the Regional

Mixed Migration Secretariat, October 2012), p. 23, http://www.refworld.org/pdfid/52401aba4.pdf.

96 Ibid.

97 Ibid.

98 Ibid.

99 Ibid.

100 Marianne Riddervold, "Who Needs NATO to Fight Pirates? Why Europe Launched EU Counter-Piracy Mission Atalanta," *Piracy Studies*, October 13, 2014, http://piracy-studies.org/who-needs-nato-to-fight-pirates-why-europe-launched-eu-counter-piracy-mission-atalanta/.

101 Colin Freeman, "Why Fighting Piracy Won't Work as a Model for Fighting People Traffickers," *The Telegraph*, April 23, 2015, http://www.telegraph.co.uk/news/worldnews/africaandindianocean/libya/11557301/Why-fighting-piracy-wont-work-as-a-model-for-fighting-people-traffickers.html.

102 Author interview with Mohammed, October 2015 in Milano.

103 Author interview with a negotiator, November 2015 in Denmark.

104 Author interview with a negotiator, November 2015 in Sweden.

105 Author interview with Joakim Medin, September 2015 in Gothenburg and November 2015 via Skype.

106 In 2014 Piccinin interviewed one of his kidnappers, and the jihadist described the relationship between his *katiba* and the Farouk Brigade:

> Piccinin: To begin, just one thing that I would like to make very clear: you—and your friends—when I was your prisoner, you didn't hide that you were working for the al-Farouk brigades.
>
> Jihadist: Yes! Yes! It is right . . .
>
> Piccinin: I ask you this question, because, after I returned to Belgium, I denounced al-Farouk, but they contested, saying they didn't know you and they never knew anything about the katiba [of] Abou Omar.
>
> Jihadist: I don't know why they told you that, because our group was part of the al-Farouk brigades. Our katiba worked for al-Farouk brigades in al-Qusayr and our leader, Abou Omar, received his orders from al-Farouk.

Pierre Piccinin da Prata, "Interview with the Jihadist Who Held Me Hostage for Five Months . . ." *Maghreb and Orient Courier*, June 2014, http://lecourrierdumaghrebetdelorient.info/exclusive/syria-interview-with-the-jihadist-who-held-me-hostage-for-five-months/.

107 Richard Engel, "The Hostage," *Vanity Fair*, March 20, 2013, http://www.vanityfair.com/news/politics/2013/04/richard-engel-kidnapping-syria.

108 Richard Engel, "New Details on 2012 Kidnapping of NBC News Team in Syria," NBC News, April 15, 2015, http://www.nbcnews.com/news/world/new-details-2012-kidnapping-nbc-news-team-syria-n342356.

109 Ibid.

110 Ibid.

111 Domenico Quirico, "My 150-Day Ordeal as a Hostage of Syria's Rebels," *Guardian*, September 14, 2013, http://www.theguardian.com/world/2013/sep/15/domenico-quirico-my-hostage-ordeal.

112 Ibid.

113 Author interview with Marc Marginedas, December 2015 via Skype.

114 Javier Espinosa, "La libertad, al otro lado de la valla," *El Mundo*, March 18, 2015, http://www.elmundo.es/internacional/2015/03/18/5508695222601d5f078b4570.html. (in Spanish)

115 Davide Giacalone, "Monica Maggioni da Assad: non transformiamo il leader siriano in un gentlemen," *Libero Quotidiano*, November 20, 2015, http://www.liberoquotidiano.it/news/sfoglio/11850858/Monica-Maggioni-da-Assad--non.html. (in Italian)

116 Piccinin da Prata, "Interview with the Jihadist."

117 Ibid.

118 Author interview with Luis Munar, August 2015 via Skype.

119 Piccinin da Prata, "Interview with the Jihadist."

120 Harald Doornbos and Jenan Moussa, "The Italian Job," *Foreign Policy*, January 15, 2014, http://foreignpolicy.com/2014/01/15/the-italian-job/.

121 Omar al Muqdad, "Inside the Islamic State Kidnap Machine," BBC News, September 22, 2015, http://www.bbc.co.uk/news/magazine-34312450.

122 Ibid.

123 Fowler, *A Season in Hell*, 303.

124 *Royal Canadian Mounted Police* home page, http://www.rcmp-grc.gc.ca/en/home.

125 "Algeria: Ban ki-Moon chiede liberazione cooperante italiana e suoi colleghi,"*Adnkronos*, November 3, 2011, http://www1.adnkronos.com/IGN/News/Esteri/Algeria-Ban-ki-Moon-chiede-liberazione-cooperante-italiana-e-suoi-colleghi_312608742782.html. (in Italian)

126 "Fonti arabe: 'Rossella Urru è viva,'" *Mediaset TgCom24*, June 16, 2012, http://www.tgcom24.mediaset.it/mondo/articoli/1049574/fonti-arabe-rossella-urru-e-viva.shtml. (in Italian)

127 *Rosario Fiorello* home page, http://www.rosariofiorello.it. (in Italian)

128 Deborah Dirani, "Rossella Urru, un sequestro che ha commosso gli italiani," *Il Sole 24 ore*, March 3, 2012, http://www.ilsole24ore.com/art/notizie/2012-02-02/stampa-senegalese-rossella-urru-123227.shtml. (in Italian)

129 Adam Entous and Giada Zampano, "U.S. Says Militants Demanded Ransom for Hostage Bodies in Pakistan," *Wall Street Journal*, August 20, 2015, http://www.wsj.com/articles/u-s-says-militants-demanded-ransom-for-hostage-bodies-in-pakistan-144011245.

130 Ibid.

131 Entous and Zampano, "U.S. Says Militants Demanded Ransom."

132 "Giuramento e discorso di insediamento del Presidente Mattarella, I parte," YouTube video, February 3, 2015, https://www.youtube.com/watch?v=4EXFjpOfMuA.

"Desidero rivolgere un pensiero—aveva detto il neo capo dello Stato—ai civili impegnati, in zone spesso rischiose, nella preziosa opera di cooperazione e di aiuto allo sviluppo. Di tre italiani, padre Paolo Dall'Oglio, Giovanni Lo Porto e Ignazio Scaravilli non si hanno notizie in terre difficili e martoriate. A loro e ai loro familiari va la solidarietà e la vicinanza di tutto il popolo italiano, insieme all'augurio di fare presto ritorno nelle loro case." ("I wish to address a thought—said new head of the State—to civilians who often work in risky areas and who undertake the valuable work of cooperation and development aid. We have no news of three Italians, Father Paolo Dall'Oglio, Giovanni Lo Porto, and Ignazio Scaravilli, who are being held in difficult and tortured lands. The solidarity of the Italian people goes to them and their families with the wish that they come back to their homes as soon as possible." Author's translation) (in Itallian)

133 Author interviews with Margherita Romanelli, August 2015 via Skype and October 2015 in Bologna.

134 Author interview with Francesca Borri, April 2016 via Skype.

135 "E' arrivata in Italia la salma di Lo Porto. Molti Punti oscuri da chiarire," *Libero.it*, August, 2015, http://247.libero.it/lfocus/23816243/1/e-arrivata-in-italia-la-salma-di-lo-porto-molti-punti-oscuri-da-chiarire/. (in Italian)

136 Al Jazeera Investigative Unit, *The Hostage Business*, October 2015, http://www.aljazeera.com/investigations/hostagebusiness.html.

137 Ibid.

138 Ewen MacAskill, Seumas Milne, and Clayton Swisher, "Italian Intelligence Lied about Hostage Rescue to Hide Ransom Payment," *Guardian*, October 8, 2015, http://www.theguardian.com/world/2015/oct/08/italian-intelligence-lied-hostage-rescue-bruno-pelizzari-debbie-calitz.

139 Al Jazeera Investigative Unit, *The Hostage Business*.

140 Lindhout and Corbett, *A House in the Sky*, 354.

141 Author interview with Samir Aita, July 2015 via Skype.

142 Author interview with Francesca Borri, July 2015 via Skype.

143 Author interview with a member of the Italian Senate, June 2015 via Whatsapp.

144 Author interview with Michaël Lescroart, August 2015 via Skype.

145 Joanie de Rijke, *In the Hands of Taliban* (Pune, Maharashtra, India: Mehta Publishing House, 2011), 29.

146 Author interview with Michaël Lescroart, August 2015 via Skype.

147 Author interview with Joanie de Rijke, August 2015 via Skype.

148 Author interview with a European negotiator, October 2015 via Skype.

149 Author interview with a negotiator, October 2015 via Skype.

150 Author interview with a European aid worker, November 2015 via Skype.

151 Rebekah L. Sanders and Richard Ruelas, "Final Months of Freedom: Mueller's Time before Her Capture Detailed," *AZ Central*, February 14, 2015, http://www.azcentral.com/story/news/arizona/2015/02/14/muellers-final-months-detailed/23402231/.

152 Ibid.

153 Author interview with Francesca Borri, August 2015 via Skype.

154 Author interview with a hostage negotiator, October 2015 via Skype.

155 Author interview with Francesca Borri, August 2015 via Skype.

156 Abul Taher, "Heartbroken Lover of ISIS Hostage Kayla Mueller Breaks Silence to Reveal His Desperate Bid to Save Her by Pretending They Were Married . . ." *Daily Mail*, February 14, 2015, http://www.dailymail.co.uk/news/article-2953880/Kayla-Mueller-s-lover-reveals-went-Syria-save-her.html.

157 Author interview with hostage negotiator, December 2015 via Skype.

158 Author interview with Carsten Jensen, August 2015 via Skype.

159 Author interview with Omar al Muqdad, January 2015 via Skype.

160 Author interview with a Syrian negotiator, February 2015 via Skype.

161 Author interview with a former ISIS European hostage, December 2015 via Skype.

162 Author interview with hostage negotiator, December 2015 via Skype.

163 Author interview with Carsten Jensen, August 2015 via Skype.

164 Author interview with hostage negotiator, November 2015 via Skype.

165 Author interview with hostage negotiator, June 2015 via Skype.

166 Author interview with Francesca Borri, April 2016 via Skype.

167 Author interview with Joanie de Rijke, August 2015 via Skype.

168 Author interview with a European psychologist, January 2016 in Brussels.
169 Author interview with a European psychologist, January 2016 in Brussels.
170 Author interview with Joanie de Rijke, August 2015 via Skype.
171 Author interview with Joanie de Rijke, August 2015 via Skype.
172 "Absi's family is from Aleppo, but he was born in Saudi Arabia, probably in 1979. His older brother, a dentist named Firas, trained with al Qaeda in Afghanistan. Amr and Firas are thought to have joined al Qaeda in Iraq, which became the Islamic State of Iraq and Syria; the group's aim was to establish an Islamic caliphate that would spread throughout the Middle East and beyond. In 2007, Amr al Absi was arrested in Syria, and held in the al Qaeda wing of Sednaya Prison, with hundreds of other extremists. Four years later, in June 2011, Assad released them. It was a turning point in the Syrian War. Assad had stated that the opposition was full of terrorists, a claim that the mysterious amnesty then fulfilled. It seemed like a calculated move to poison the nascent Syrian revolution.
  "Absi took up the leadership of a jihadi brigade near the Syrian city of Homs. His brother Firas had recently founded a group called the Shura Council of the Islamic State, which gained notoriety after raising the al Qaeda flag at the border gates near Bab al Hawa, a major crossing point between Turkey and Syria, in July 2012. It was the first mention of an Islamic state in the Syrian Civil War." Ben Taub, "Journey to Jihad," *New Yorker*, June 1, 2015, www.newyorker.com/magazine/2015/06/01/journey-to-jihad.
173 Radwan Mortada, "Al-Qaeda Leaks II: Baghdadi Loses His Shadow," *Al-Akhbar*, January 14, 2014, http://english.al-akhbar.com/node/18219.
174 Author interview with Joanie de Rijke, August 2015 via Skype.
175 Author interview with hostage negotiator, August 2015 via Skype.
176 Ben Taub, "Journey to Jihad," *New Yorker*, June 1, 2015, http://www.newyorker.com/magazine/2015/06/01/journey-to-jihad.
177 Author interview with European negotiator, August 2015 via Skype.
178 Marine Olivesi, "American Took Up Arms with Libya's Rebels," NPR, October 24, 2011, http://www.npr.org/2011/10/24/141646227/u-s-aid-worker-took-up-arms-with-libyas-rebels.
179 Eliot Higgins, "Interview with Kevin Dawes on His Time in Libya," *Bellingcat*, April 8, 2016, https://www.bellingcat.com/news/mena/2016/04/08/interview-with-kevin-dawes-on-his-time-in-libya/.
180 Kevin Patrick Dawes, "Aerial Battlefield Photojournalism," Kickstarter campaign, March 30, 2012–May 14, 2012, https://www.kickstarter.com/projects/177238975/aerial-battlefield-photojournalism.
181 Bobby Pollier, "Kevin Patrick Dawes: 5 Fast Facts You Need to Know," *Heavy*, April 8, 2016, http://heavy.com/news/2016/04/kevin-patrick-dawes-american-prisoner-released-from-syria-freelance-photographer-twitter-bashar-al-assad-regime-age/.
182 "President Obama Speaks on the Recovery of Sgt. Bowe Bergdahl," *White House*, May 31, 2014, https://www.whitehouse.gov/photos-and-video/video/2014/05/31/president-obama-speaks-recovery-sgt-bowe-bergdahl#transcript.
183 The Taliban detainees—known as the "Taliban Five"—who were transferred from Guantánamo Bay, Cuba, to custody in Doha, Qatar, are Mohammad Fazl, Khairullah Khairkhwa, Abdul Haq Wasiq, Norullah Noori, and Mohammad Nabi Omari. They were the Taliban army chief of staff, a Taliban deputy min-

270 *Merchants of Men*

ister of intelligence, a former Taliban interior minister, and two other senior Taliban figures.

184 Sarah Koenig, et al., "DUSTWUN," *Serial* Season 2, Episode 1, December 2015, https://serialpodcast.org/season-two/1/dustwun.

185 Ibid.

186 Ibid.

187 Ibid.

188 Ibid.

189 Lawrence Wright, "Five Hostages," *New Yorker*, July 6 & 13, 2015, http://www.newyorker.com/magazine/2015/07/06/five-hostages.

190 Author interview with Omar al Muqdad, January 2015 via Skype.

191 Brian Oakes, director, *Jim: The James Foley Story* promo video, *HBO*, January 2016, http://www.hbo.com/documentaries/jim-the-james-foley-story/index.html.

192 Lindhout and Corbett, *A House in the Sky*, 100.

193 Al Jazeera Investigative Unit, *The Hostage Business*.

194 Daniele Raineri, "Greta e Vanessa raccontate da vicino," *Il Foglio*, January 17, 2015, http://www.ilfoglio.it/articoli/2015/01/17/greta-e-vanessa-raccontate-da-vicino___1-v-124688-rubriche_c392.htm. (in Italian)

195 Fiorenza Sarzanini, "Greta e Vanessa, il racconto ai pm 'Ci hanno detto: rapite per soldi,'" *Corriere della Sera*, January 17, 2015, http://www.corriere.it/esteri/15_gennaio_17/greta-vanessa-racconto-pm-ci-hanno-detto-rapite-soldi-4e39106a-9e15-11e4-a48d-99327d0f9d0e.shtml. (in Italian)

196 Al Jazeera Investigative Unit, "Italy Paying Ransoms in Syria and Somalia," Al Jazeera, October 9, 2015, http://www.aljazeera.com/news/2015/10/exclusive-italy-paying-ransoms-syria-somalia-151007093239241.html.

197 "Ai Servizi segreti è sparito un milione," *Il Tempo*, February 5, 2016, http://www.iltempo.it/esteri/2016/02/05/ai-servizi-segreti-e-sparito-un-milione-1.1505798. (in Italian)

198 All organizations came under the jurisdiction of the MOFA under law 49/87.
    De facto, many organizations of a non-governmental nature were *not* recognized under law 49/87 even if they did very similar work. Fewer and fewer organizations were in fact even interested in getting Italian MOFA funds, so they did not require recognition (*idoneità*) per law 49/87. ActionAid for example was of course an NGO in the wider generic sense, but was only recognized under 49/87 in 2003. And so were many others, including some current major players such as Save the Children, AMREF, etc. ...
    In 1997 'a different type of legal category was created. Law 460/97, which is one of a fiscal nature, was passed to establish the category of ONLUS (Organizzazioni Non Lucrative di Utilità Sociale), so for a time you could be an ONLUS or not (fiscal perspective) or an "NGO" or not ex lege 49/87. All NGOs recognized under 49/87 were automatically recognized as ONLUS after 2003 and until the end of 2014, when a new development cooperation legislation was passed (lex 125/2014), which only recognized the 200+ "NGOs" as a "residual" category, which is still being discussed in terms of the benefits such organisations can enjoy and in what manners they can operate, including fiscally and commercially.

199 "Greta e Vanessa, il prezzo della libertà," episode of *Otto e Mezzo*, January 16, 2015, https://www.youtube.com/watch?v=IL9E13mX3B4. (in Italian)

200 Sarah Koenig, et al., "Listening Guide," *Serial* Season 2, April 2016, https://serialpodcast.org/season-two/listening-guide.
201 Mark Mazzetti, "How a Single Spy Helped Turn Pakistan Against the United States," *New York Times*, April 9, 2013, http://www.nytimes.com/2013/04/14/magazine/raymond-davis-pakistan.html.
202 "In the early months of the U.S.-led occupation, authorities banned the Baath Party and removed all senior Baathists from the government and security forces. But U.S. officials began to shift their strategy in April 2004 and, in a bid to strengthen the officer corps, allowed some senior ex-Baathists to return to the security forces. Interim Prime Minister Ayad Allawi continued this policy." Sharon Otterman, "IRAQ: Debaathification," Council on Foreign Relations, April 7, 2005, http://www.cfr.org/iraq/iraq-debaathification/p7853.
203 Unpublished footage of Omar al Muqdad documentary, *We Left Them Behind*.
204 Ibid.
205 Author interview with Omar al Muqdad, January 2016 via Skype.
206 Theo Padnos, "My Captivity," *New York Times*, October 29, 2014, http://www.nytimes.com/2014/10/28/magazine/theo-padnos-american-journalist-on-being-kidnapped-tortured-and-released-in-syria.html.
207 Wright, "Five Hostages."
208 Sarah A. Topol, "Rookie Freelancers Risking Their Lives to Cover the Arab Spring," *Newsweek*, October 8, 2012, http://europe.newsweek.com/rookie-freelancers-risking-their-lives-cover-arab-spring-65383.
209 Colin Freeman, "The Video that Shows the Real John Cantlie," *Telegraph*, September 26, 2014, http://web.archive.org/web/20140929041743/http://blogs.telegraph.co.uk/news/colinfreeman/100287672/the-video-that-shows-the-real-john-cantlie.
210 John Cantlie, "Syria Eyewitness Dispatch: 'I Watched as Assad's Tanks Rolled in to Destroy a Rebel Town,'" *Telegraph*, March 31, 2012, http://www.telegraph.co.uk/news/worldnews/middleeast/syria/9177910/Syria-eyewitness-dispatch-I-watched-as-Assads-tanks-rolled-in-to-destroy-a-rebel-town.html.
211 Lindhout and Corbett, *A House in the Sky*, 81.
212 Topol, "Rookie Freelancers Risking Their Lives."
213 Author interview with Francesca Borri, September 2015 via Skype.
214 Harakat Ahrar ash Sham al Islamiyya is a coalition of multiple Islamist and Salafist groups that fight against the Bashar al Assad government.
215 Author interview with Francesca Borri, April 2016 via Skype.
216 Lindhout and Corbett, *A House in the Sky*, 93.
217 "(07-09-12) Bab Al-Hawa, Sarmada | Idlib | FSA Frees Syria / Turkey Border from Regime Forces," a video from *Ugarit News*, July 19, 2012, https://www.youtube.com/watch?v=W13i_Nbj3q8. (in Arabic)
218 Ibid.
219 Unpublished footage of Omar al Muqdad documentary, *We Left Them Behind*.
220 Author interview with Marc Marginedas, December 2015 via Skype.
221 Marc Marginedas, "Los que no pueden contarlo," *El Periódico Internacional*, March 19, 2015, http://www.elperiodico.com/es/noticias/internacional/homenaje-los-rehenes-que-fueron-ejecutados-por-estado-islamico-4029456. (in Spanish)
222 "Journalist Marc Marginedas Back in Barcelona after 6 Months of Captivity in Syria," *Catalan News Agency*, March 3, 2014, http://www.catalannewsagency.

com/society-science/item/journalist-marc-marginedas-back-in-barcelona-after-6-months-of-captivity-in-syria.

223 Martin Chulov, "Spanish Journalists Freed in Syria after Six-Month Ordeal," *Guardian*, March 30, 2014, http://www.theguardian.com/world/2014/mar/30/spanish-journalists-javier-espinosa-ricardo-villanova-garcia-freed-syria.

224 "Syria: ACTED Humanitarian Worker Released in Syria," *ACTED*, May 27, 2014, http://www.acted.org/en/27-may-2014-syria-acted-humanitarian-worker-released-syria.

225 Amy Goodman, et al., "Airstrikes Against Syria Are a Trap, Warns Former ISIS Hostage Nicolas Hénin," *Democracy Now!*, December 7, 2015, http://www.democracynow.org/2015/12/7/airstrikes_against_syria_are_a_trap.

226 Ibid.

227 See Glossary.

228 "Europol Launches the European Migrant Smuggling Centre," Europol, February 22, 2016, https://www.europol.europa.eu/content/EMSC_launch.

229 "Today Europol launched the new European Migrant Smuggling Centre (EMSC). The goal of the Centre is to proactively support EU Member States in dismantling criminal networks involved in organised migrant smuggling. The Centre will focus on geographical criminal hotspots, and will build a better capability across the European Union to fight people smuggling networks . . . Rob Wainwright, Director of Europol, said: '. . . The European Migrant Smuggling Centre will provide the necessary platform by which Member States can improve their exchange of information and operational coordination in the fight against organized migrant smuggling.'" Ibid.

230 Adrian Goldberg, "Terror Finance & Emissions," BBC Radio 5 live, May 15, 2015, http://www.bbc.co.uk/programmes/b05vck3r.

231 Ibid.

232 Joe Parkinson, Georgi Kantchev, and Ellen Emmerentze Jervell, "Inside Europe's Migrant-Smuggling Rings," *Wall Street Journal*, October 28, 2015, http://www.wsj.com/articles/inside-europes-migrant-smuggling-rings-1446079791.

233 Bill Donahue, "Meet the Two Brothers Making Millions Off the Refugee Crisis in Scandinavia," *Bloomberg Businessweek*, January 6, 2016, http://www.bloomberg.com/features/2016-norway-refugee-crisis-profiteers/.

234 Ricardo Garcia, editor in chief, *The Future of Europe* (Basel, Switzerland: UBS AG and UBS Switzerland AG, January 13, 2016), https://www.fundresearch.de/sites/default/files/partnercenter/UBS/News/news_2016/European%20economy_en_1217027.pdf.

235 Duncan Robinson, "Women and Children Refugee Numbers Crossing into Europe Surge," *Financial Times*, January 20, 2016, http://www.ft.com/intl/cms/s/0/dff3b5ea-bf99-11e5-9fdb-87b8d15baec2.html.

236 Shekhar Aiyar, et al., *The Refugee Surge in Europe: Economic Challenges* (Washington, D.C.: International Monetary Fund, January 2016), https://www.imf.org/external/pubs/ft/sdn/2016/sdn1602.pdf.

acknowledgments

The idea of writing this book was not mine. My Japanese publisher, Susumu "Shim" Shimoyama of Bungei Shunju, suggested I consider writing a book on the business of kidnapping. My agent, Diana Finch, thought it was a very good idea, and my American publisher, Dan Simon of Seven Stories Press, agreed to commission the book. Without them I would never have embarked upon such a difficult journey.

I confess that I was very nervous about the topic; kidnapping is a very sensitive issue and extremely secretive. I reached out to all my contacts in the countering terrorism industry, but what made this book possible were a few major breakthroughs. The first one came from my Danish publisher, Claus Clausen of Tiderne Skifter. He put me in touch with Nagieb Khaja, a freelance journalist and author who was kidnapped by the Taliban, and with Carsten Jensen, the acclaimed Danish novelist. Through them I was introduced to several people who work in the hostage and kidnapping business. One of them, a negotiator, agreed to talk to me at length about his job. His insight was fundamental to understanding the complexity of negotiating with kidnappers after the advent of ISIS.

Another breakthrough came from the Italian freelance journalist Francesca Borri. She offered a real-time perspective of the kidnapping business in Syria, and valuable information about how people get snatched and how negotiations are conducted. Francesca also put me in touch with former hostages, among them Joanie de Rijke, the Dutch freelance journalist kidnapped in Afghanistan by the Taliban. Joanie's interviews were extremely valuable for me to understand the importance of the golden hour.

Several journalists offered to help contact former hostages, negotiators, or government officials working in the "crisis unit" of their countries. Among them a special thanks goes to Mònica Terribas, who conducts *El Matí de Catalunya Ràdio* in Barcelona.

Finally the women of MAG Verona—Loredana Aldegheri, Nadia Albini, and Ida Pierotti—offered a vision of the refugee crisis that helped me understand the link between this business and the business of kidnapping.

As my research advanced I met people who were willing to share with me their experience with kidnapping: Giacomo Madia, an Italian insurance broker, who took me through the various negotiation stages with Somali pirates; Karin Weber, a former humanitarian aid worker for the UN and other organizations, who unveiled the contradictions of some aid agencies in war zones; and Omar al Muqdad, a freelance journalist, who shared with me his investigation of the fixers and kidnappers in Syria.

A special thanks goes to Teakosheen Joulak, a former English teacher and refugee in Denmark, for sharing with me the shocking story of her and her husband's journey to Europe. A very special thank you goes to my Danish translator, Joachim Wrang, who went well beyond his duties as translator and checked every name, date, and fact in this book, and to Lauren Hooker and Jon Gilbert for double-checking and inserting all the last minute changes.

I must thank all the people I have interviewed for trusting

me with their stories, including those I have not mentioned in the book. Because of security reasons I agreed to respect their wish to be anonymous but I want them to know how grateful I am to them for talking to me.

This was a very difficult book to research and write, emotionally draining and with plenty of shocking discoveries, such as governments' practice of ranking hostages. I have also encountered some people, even victims of kidnapping, who have refused to talk to me and showed hostility toward my research. Unveiling the truth can be extremely painful for everybody, including former hostages. The politics of silence are successful also because people do not want to face their own nightmare once again. However, if we want to prevent other people from falling prey to kidnappers, we must lift the curtain of silence.

I know that many will attack me for having unveiled yet another corner of the dark side of globalization, for having questioned the celebration of hostages as heroes and for denouncing the manipulation of their image by their own governments. This does not mean that I am insensitive to the human tragedy of hostage taking and killing! On the contrary, as a mother and as an author, I have tried to show enthusiastic young people and their families the danger of "doing good" in some parts of the world, not to discourage them from this honorable task but to encourage them to do it professionally and safely. "Do good without any harm," that should be the motto. We must never forget that ransoms are one of the main sources of financing for many armed groups—money that keeps them in business.

index